The European Union at the Crossroads

The EU's Institutional Evolution from the Schuman Plan to the European Convention

Second edition entirely revised
and updated 2003

P.I.E.-Peter Lang

Bruxelles · Bern · Berlin · Frankfurt/M · New York · Oxford · Wien

Youri DEVUYST

The European Union at the Crossroads

The EU's Institutional Evolution from the Schuman Plan to the European Convention

Second edition entirely revised
and updated 2003

"European Policy"
No.27

"The views expressed in this book are purely those of the author and may not be regarded as stating an official position of the institutions for which the author is or has been working."

© P.I.E.-Peter Lang S.A.
PRESSES INTERUNIVERSITAIRES EUROPÉENNES
Brussels, 2003 (first edition 2002)
1 avenue Maurice, 1050 Brussels, Belgium
info@peterlang.com; www.peterlang.com

ISSN 1376-0890
ISBN 90-5201-183-4
D/2003/5678/10
Printed in Belgium

Bibliographic information published by "Die Deutsche Bibliothek"

"Die Deutsche Bibliothek" lists this publication in the "Deutsche Nationalbibliografie"; detailed bibliographic data is avalaible in the Internet at <http://dnb.ddb.de>.

CIP available from the British Library, GB and the Library of Congress, USA.

ISBN   0-8204-6600-X

Table of Contents

List of Abbreviations

ACP	African, Caribbean and Pacific countries
ALA	Asia and Latin America (financial and technical assistance to and economic co-operation with)
ASEAN	Association of South-East Asian Nations
BSE	Bovine spongiform encephalitis (mad cow disease)
Bull. EC/EU	Bulletin of the European Communities/European Union (published on a monthly basis by the European Commission)
CARDS	Assistance programme to the western Balkans
CESDP	Common European Security and Defence Policy
CFSP	Common Foreign and Security Policy
CJTF	Combined Joint Task Forces
CMLR	Common Market Law Reports
COREPER	Committee of Permanent Representatives
COSAC	Conférence des Organes Spécialisés dans les Affairs Communautaires
EC	European Community
ECB	European Central Bank
Ecofin	(Council of) Economic and Finance Ministers
ECR	European Court Reports (Reports of Cases before the Court of Justice and the Court of First Instance)
ECSC	European Coal and Steel Community
EDC	European Defence Community
EDF	European Development Fund
EEA	European Economic Area
EEC	European Economic Community
EFTA	European Free Trade Association
ELDR	European Liberal, Democratic and Reform Party
EMU	Economic and Monetary Union
EP	European Parliament
EPC	European Political Co-operation
EPP	European People's Party
ERTA	European Road Transport Agreement (European Agreement concerning the work of crews of vehicles engaged in international road transport)
ESCB	European System of Central Banks
ESDI	European Security and Defence Identity

ESDP	European Security and Defence Policy
Euratom	European Atomic Energy Community
EU	European Union
FAO	Food and Agriculture Organisation
FPÖ	Austrian Freedom Party
GATT	General Agreement on Tariffs and Trade
GATS	General Agreement on Trade in Services
GDP	Gross Domestic Product
Gen. Rep.	General Report on the Activities of the European Communities/ European Union (published on an annual basis by the European Commission)
G7	Group of seven major industrialised countries
G8	Group of seven major industrialised countries and Russia
IGC	Intergovernmental Conference
IMF	International Monetary Fund
JHA	Justice and Home Affairs
MEDA	Financial and technical measures to accompany the reform of economic and social structures in the framework of the Euro-Mediterranean partnership
MEP	Member of the European Parliament
NATO	North Atlantic Treaty Organisation
OECD	Organisation for Economic Co-operation and Development
OEEC	Organisation for European Economic Co-operation
OJ	Official Journal of the European Communities
ÖVP	Austrian People's Party
PHARE	Poland-Hungary Assistance to the Reconstruction of the Economies (financial support for partner countries in Central Europe)
PES	Party of European Socialists
PSC	Political and Security Committee
SCA	Special Committee on Agriculture
SEA	Single European Act
TACIS	Technical Assistance for the New Independent States and Mongolia
TEC	Treaty establishing the European Community
TEU	Treaty on European Union
TRIPs	Trade-Related Intellectual Property measures
UK	United Kingdom
WEU	Western European Union
WTC	World Trade Centre
WTO	World Trade Organisation

Introduction

The Union stands at a crossroads, a defining moment in its existence.[1]

The European Union (EU) forms one of the world's largest Internal Markets, now accompanied by the Euro as the single currency for twelve of the fifteen Member States.[2]

In October 1999, the Tampere European Council approved an ambitious action plan for co-operation in the fields of justice and home affairs that should lead to the creation of a European Area of Freedom, Security and Justice. Following the Helsinki European Council of December 1999, the development of a European Security and Defence Policy is gradually taking shape. In March 2000, the Lisbon European Council set itself the strategic goal to ensure that the EU would "become the most competitive and dynamic knowledge-based economy in the world capable of sustainable economic growth with more and better jobs and greater social cohesion".[3] While increasing the level of ambition at each European Council session, the EU is simultaneously pursuing the most challenging enlargement with new Member States yet.[4] Still, in institutional terms, the EU's future is unclear.

Via the Treaties of Paris (1951) and Rome (1957), the Member States established a new polity capable of producing and enforcing binding European Community law through its own institutions and decision-making mechanisms. As such, the European Communities went well beyond international or regional organisations like the United Nations and the Council of Europe. What set the Communities apart from these intergovernmental organisations is the so-called Community method[5]

---

[1] Laeken European Council, "Presidency Conclusions", December 15-16, 2001, *Annex I: Laeken Declaration on the Future of the European Union*, section I.

[2] For the basic structure of the European Union see Box 1, page 16.

[3] Lisbon European Council, "Presidency Conclusions", March 23-24, 2000, para. 5.

[4] For the basic facts on EU's enlargement with new Member States, see Box 2, page 18.

[5] On the Community method, see Philippe de Schoutheete, *Une Europe pour Tous. Dix Essais sur la Construction Européenne* (Paris, Odile Jacob, 1997); Youri Devuyst, "The European Union's Constitutional Order? Between Community Method and *Ad Hoc* Compromise", *Berkeley Journal of International Law*, 18 (2000) 1; J. H. H. Weiler, "The Transformation of Europe", *Yale Law Journal*, 100 (1991) 2403.

which succeeded in combining traditional elements of intergovernmental co-operation with a strong supranational dynamic.[6]

The Communities' supranational powers were largely confined, however, to what was deemed necessary to create a well-functioning common market. Since the early 1990s, the scope of European integration and co-operation has been expanded well beyond the boundaries of the common market. In an attempt to equip the EU with the instruments and decision-making mechanisms necessary to tackle these new ambitions, the Member States launched an institutional adaptation process leading to the Treaties of Maastricht (1992), Amsterdam (1997) and Nice (2001).[7]

During this Treaty reform sequence, the negotiators opted to move forward just one day at the time, through a series of *ad hoc* compromises. As a result, the EU's institutional structure has become a patchwork[8] composed of what European Commission President Romano Prodi has called "constructive ambiguities" in the form of "subtle protocols and increasingly complex formulae".[9] Rather than building on the Community method's supranational ('integration') dynamic, the *ad hoc* compromise formulae of Maastricht, Amsterdam and Nice have tended to reinforce the EU's intergovernmental ('co-operation') dimension.[10] In particular, to the degree the EU's Heads of State or Government have decided to push European integration beyond purely common

---

[6]   See Alberta Sbragia, "The European Community: A Balancing Act", *Publius*, 23 (1993) 23 for the interpretation of the Community as a "balancing act" between a territorial Member State dimension and a non-territorial supranational dimension. According to Commission President Romano Prodi, the Community method is "the recipe for a form of integration which is both supranational and also respectful of the nations and States that it is composed of, however large or small". Romano Prodi, "An Enlarged and More United Europe, A Global Player", Speech at the College of Europe, November 12, 2001, 2.

[7]   For the basic facts on the EU's Treaty reform process, see Box 3, page 17.

[8]   Deirdre Curtin correctly referred to this patchwork as "a Europe of bits and pieces". See Deirdre Curtin, "The Constitutional Structure of the Union: A Europe of Bits and Pieces", *Common Market Law Review*, 30 (1993) 17.

[9]   Romano Prodi, "The State of the Union in 2001", Speech before the European Parliament, Strasbourg, February 13, 2001, 8.

[10] Some authors have interpreted this as the creation of a "new European model" that is neither supranational, nor intergovernmental, but combines both elements in a novel manner. See Paul Magnette and Eric Remacle, "La grande transformation de l'Europe", in Paul Magnette and Eric Remacle (eds.), *Le Nouveau Modèle Européen* (Brussels, Ed. de l'Université de Bruxelles, 2000), 7. Helen Wallace has invented the term "intensive transgovernmentalism" to describe the new form of strengthened co-operation in the EU framework that goes beyond traditional intergovernmentalism but stays below supranationalism. See Helen Wallace, "The Institutional Setting: Five Variations on a Theme", in Helen Wallace and William Wallace (eds.), *Policy-Making in the European Union* (Oxford, Oxford University Press, 2000, 4th ed.), 33.

market questions, they also felt it necessary to reinforce their own direct involvement in the details of EU decision-making. However, European Council summits between the Heads of State or Government work largely as traditional intergovernmental conferences, operating under the constant threat of national veto-rights. In an EU of fifteen Member States, the European Council's intergovernmental working methods have frequently resulted in conclusions reflecting the lowest common denominator.

The EU's institutional set-up is important.[11] When the EU is able to act through the supranational mechanisms of the Community method, the famous "capability-expectations gap" that characterises the EU's inter-governmental activities hardly seems to exist.[12] In competition policy, for instance, the Treaty of Rome has granted the European Commission concrete implementing powers. As a result, the EU is widely recognised as an effective player in this field, both internally and externally.[13] In the more intergovernmental areas, such as the Common Foreign and Security Policy (CFSP) and Co-operation in the fields of Justice and Home Affairs (JHA), where policy must be created on the basis of

---

[11] This book does not review the theoretical approaches developed by political scientists with respect to the EU's institutional evolution. It might be useful to signal, however, that the underlying assumptions of this work are closely related to those put forward by the "historical institutionalist school" to the study of European integration. Institutions are significant because they contribute to the creation of "path dependence". This means that the outcome of political debates is shaped in large measure by earlier institutional choices such as the possibility to adopt decisions in the Council by qualified majority instead of unanimity. The essence of the EU's institutional politics is the constant attempt, by a variety of policy actors, to shift the EU's institutional path in the direction that suits their substantive preferences. For a brief introduction to historical institutionalism in the study of the EU, see John Peterson and Michael Shackleton, "The EU's Institutions: An Overview", in John Peterson and Michael Shackleton (eds.), *The Institutions of the European Union* (Oxford, Oxford University Press, 2001), 6. See also Simon Bulmer, "The Governance of the European Union: A New Institutionalist Approach", *Journal of Public Policy*, 13 (1994) 351; Paul Pierson, "The Path to European Integration: a Historical Institutionalist Analysis", *Comparative Political Studies*, 29 (1996) 123.

[12] Christopher Hill, "The Capability-Expectations Gap, or Conceptualizing Europe's International Role", *Journal of Common Market Studies*, 31 (1993) 305; Christopher Hill, "Closing the Capabilities-Expectations Gap?", in John Peterson and Helene Sjursen (eds.), *A Common Foreign Policy for Europe?* (London, Routledge, 1998), 18.

[13] For an overview of the EC's competition *acquis*, see Christopher Bellamy and Graham Child with Peter M. Roth (ed.), *European Community Law of Competition* (London, Sweet & Maxwell, 2001); Jonathan Faull and Ali Nikpay (eds.), *The EC Law of Competition* (Oxford, Oxford University Press, 1999); Valentine Korah, *Introductory Guide to EC Competition Law and Practice* (Oxford, Hart, 2000); Richard Whish, *Competition Law* (London, Butterworths, 2001).

"fuzzy undertakings",[14] concrete achievements have often remained well below the announced policy intentions. There is a general recognition that the intergovernmental working methods have been an important factor in holding back developments in these areas.[15] As former Commission President Jacques Delors recalls, while underlining the importance of the Community method, "[e]xperience shows that when we stray from this method, Europe goes nowhere".[16]

An analysis of the evolving constitutional structure of the EU is particularly topical in the context of the current enlargement process. At the Copenhagen European Council of December 2002, the EU has been able to conclude the accession negotiations with Cyprus, the Czech Republic, Estonia, Hungary, Latvia, Lithuania, Malta, Poland, the Slovak Republic and Slovenia.[17] It is planned that, after the ratification of the Accession Treaty, these countries become members on May 1, 2004. For Bulgaria and Romania, the EU's objective is to welcome them as members in 2007.[18] A greater number of Member States and an increasing diversity among them will have a profound impact on the EU's integration dynamics. That enlargement requires institutional reform in order to increase the effectiveness of the EU's decision-making process, in particular in those intergovernmental policy domains still functioning by unanimity, has been repeated on numerous occasions. In the words of the European Commission, the challenge is to "ensure that more does not lead to less".[19]

---

[14] Romano Prodi, "The State of the Union in 2001", Speech before the European Parliament, Strasbourg, February 13, 2001, 7; Romano Prodi, "For a Strong Europe, with a Grand Design and the Means of Action", Speech at the Institut d'Etudes Politiques, Paris, May 29, 2001, 6-7.

[15] Particularly interesting in this respect is the report by the Reflection Group that was asked to draft an annotated agenda for the 1996 Amsterdam Treaty negotiations, see *Reflection Group Report and Other References for Documentary Purposes: 1996 Intergovernmental Conference* (Brussels, General Secretariat of the Council, 1995), 49 and 75. According to Finnish Prime Minister Paavo Lipponen, "the intergovernmental method is often inefficient, lacks transparency and leads to the domination of some over others". See Paavo Lipponen, "Address at the College of Europe", Bruges, November 10, 2000, s.p.

[16] Jacques Delors, "Reuniting Europe: Our Historic Mission", *Agence Europe* January 3-4, 2000, 3.

[17] Copenhagen European Council, "Presidency Conclusions" , December 12-13, 2002, para. 3.

[18] Copenhagen European Council, "Presidency Conclusions" , December 12-13, 2002, para. 14.

[19] Commission of the European Communities, "Europe and the Challenge of Enlargement: Report to the Lisbon European Council, June 26-27, 1992", June 24, 1992, para. 19.

It is in this context that the EU truly stands at a crossroads. To deal with the institutional challenge of enlargement, the Heads of State or Government have launched a broad reflection process on the future of the EU. This has taken the form of a constitutional European Convention. In his opening statement, Convention President Valéry Giscard d'Estaing formulated the challenge as follows:

> If we fail, we will add to the current confusion in the European project, which we know will not be able, following the current round of enlargement, to provide a system to manage our continent which is both effective and clear to the public. What has been created over fifty years will reach its limit, and be threatened with dislocation.[20]

It is against this background that the subsequent pages provide an introduction to the EU's institutional evolution. From the Community method of the 1950s to the more recent Treaty reform sequence at Maastricht, Amsterdam and Nice, the following chapters attempt to analyse the institutional tensions characterising today's European integration project in the hope that this will help clarify the constitutional debate on the future of the EU.[21]

---

[20] Valéry Giscard d'Estaing, "Introductory Speech to the Convention on the Future of Europe", February 28, 2002, 2.

[21] In examining the institutional evolution of the EU, this book focuses on the EU's decision-making capacity and efficiency, not on equally interesting questions such as the EU's democratic nature, legitimacy and degree of transparency. On legitimacy and accountability in the EU, see Anthony Arnull and Daniel Wincott (eds.), *Accountability and Legitimacy in the European Union* (Oxford, Oxford University Press, 2002) ; Carol Harlow, *Accountability in the European Union* (Oxford, Oxford University Press, 2002).

Box 1: The Basic Structure of the European Union

The Founding Treaties of the European Communities are:

- the Treaty of Paris establishing the European Coal and Steel Community, April 18, 1951 [hereinafter ECSC Treaty]. It expired in July 2002;
- the Treaty of Rome establishing the European Economic Community, March 25, 1957 [hereinafter EEC Treaty]; and
- another Treaty of Rome establishing the European Atomic Energy Community, March 25, 1957 [hereinafter Euratom Treaty].

The Single European Act, February 17 & 28, 1986, O.J. L 169, 1987, 1 [hereinafter SEA], reinvigorated European integration through the Internal Market initiative.

Since the end of the Cold War, the European Union (EU) has been reshaped by:

- the Treaty of Maastricht on European Union, February 7, 1992, O.J. C 224, 1992, 1 [hereinafter Treaty of Maastricht or TEU]. The TEU established the EU as a three pillar structure. The TEU also changed the name of the EEC Treaty in Treaty establishing the European Community [hereinafter TEC];
- the Treaty of Amsterdam amending the Treaty on European Union, the Treaties establishing the European Communities and certain related Acts, October 2, 1997, O.J. C 340, 1997, 1 [hereinafter Treaty of Amsterdam]. The revision at Amsterdam resulted in a consolidated version of the TEU, see O.J. C 340, 1997, 145 [hereinafter Consolidated TEU]. For the consolidated version of the EC Treaty, see O.J. C 340, 1997, 173 [hereinafter Consolidated TEC];
- the Treaty of Nice amending the Treaty on European Union, the Treaties establishing the European Communities and certain related Acts, February 26, 2001, O.J. C 80, 2001, 1 [hereinafter Treaty of Nice].

The EU serves as the common roof spanning three pillars:

- Pillar I is based on the provisions of the three European Communities. The EC Treaty includes Titles on the free movement of goods; agriculture; the free movement of persons, services and capital; visas, asylum, immigration and other policies related to free movement of persons; transport; common rules on competition, taxation and approximation of laws; economic and monetary policy; employment; common commercial policy; customs co-operation; social policy, education, vocational training and youth; culture; public health; consumer protection; transEuropean networks; industry; economic and social cohesion; research and technological development; environment; and development co-operation. It also contains a Title describing the composition and functions of the EC's institutions (European Parliament, Council, Commission, Court of Justice and Court of Auditors).
- Pillar II deals with the Common Foreign and Security Policy (CFSP).
- Pillar III contains provisions on police and judicial co-operation in criminal matters.

Pillar I functions largely on the basis of the "Community method": the exclusive right of legislative initiative for the Commission; Council voting on legislative matters by either qualified majority or unanimity; co-decision for the European Parliament in a significant number of legislative fields; jurisdiction for the Court of Justice to interpret and verify the legality of Community acts; and primacy of Community law over Member State law.

Pillars II and III, while governed by the same institutions, function according to more traditional intergovernmental practices.

Box 2: The EU Treaty Reform Process

The Treaty reform process in the EU is guided by the provisions of Consolidated TEU, art. 48:

"The government of any Member State or the Commission may submit to the Council proposals for the amendment of the Treaties on which the Union is founded.

If the Council, after consulting the European Parliament and, where appropriate, the Commission, delivers an opinion in favour of calling a conference of representatives of the governments of the Member States, the conference shall be convened by the President of the Council for the purpose of determining by common accord the amendments to be made to those Treaties. The European Central Bank shall also be consulted in the case of institutional changes in the monetary area.

The amendments shall enter into force after being ratified by all the Member States in accordance with their respective constitutional requirements."

In practice, Treaty reform negotiations take place during an Intergovernmental Conference (IGC). Generally, IGCs have been conducted at three levels. Representatives of the governments of the Member States at ambassadorial level have generally held weekly negotiation sessions. Ministers of Foreign Affairs have on a monthly basis exercised political control over the negotiations in the framework of the General Affairs Council. The Heads of State or Government have provided political guidance to the negotiators during European Council sessions. It is also at European Council level that the final decisions are taken. EU Treaty amendments can enter into force only after having been ratified by all Member States.

At the Laeken European Council in December 2001, it was decided to pave the way for the next IGC (2004) through a European Convention. In addition to the Chairman and two Vice-Chairmen, the Convention is composed of 15 representatives of the Heads of State or Government, 30 representatives of the national parliaments, 16 members of the European Parliament and 2 Commissioners. The candidate countries are represented in the same way as the current Member States. Observers to the Convention represent the Economic and Social Committee, the European social partners, the Committee of the Regions and the Ombudsman. The European Convention started its work on February 28, 2002.

Box 3: Evolution in EU Membership

The accession process in the EU is guided by the provisions of Consolidated TEU, art. 49:

"Any European State which respects the principles set out in Article 6(1) may apply to become a member of the Union. It shall address its application to the Council, which shall act unanimously after consulting the Commission and after receiving the assent of the European Parliament, which shall act by an absolute majority of its component members.

The conditions of admission and the adjustments to the Treaties on which the Union is founded which such admission entails shall be subject of an agreement between the Member States and the applicant State. This agreement shall be submitted for ratification by all the contracting States in accordance with their respective constitutional requirements."

ECSC, EEC and Euratom started with six Member States: Belgium, France, Germany, Italy, Luxembourg and the Netherlands.

In 1973, the United Kingdom, Ireland and Denmark joined. The United Kingdom had initially preferred to keep its distance from the Communities and promoted the more intergovernmental European Free Trade Association (EFTA) as an alternative. In 1963, French president Charles De Gaulle had rejected a first application for membership by the United Kingdom as he saw London as the Trojan Horse of the United States.

In 1981 Greece joined, followed in 1986 by Spain and Portugal. Their accession aimed at bringing democratic political stability and economic growth after years of right-authoritarian rule.

In 1995, Austria, Finland and Sweden joined. Their accession was made possible by the end of the Cold War during which these three countries had maintained a neutral attitude.

At the Copenhagen European Council of December 2002, the EU concluded the accession negotiations with Cyprus, the Czech Republic, Estonia, Hungary, Latvia, Lithuania, Malta, Poland, Slovakia and Slovenia. The objective is to welcome these countries as members from May 1, 2004. With Bulgaria and Romania the accession negotiations are continuing. Turkey is recognised as a candidate country, but negotiations have not yet started.

Suggestions for further reading on the EU's historical development and institutional evolution

There are many excellent general introductions to the evolution and functioning of the EU's political system. See:

Desmond Dinan, *Ever Closer Union: An Introduction to European Integration* (Basingstoke, Macmillan, 1999);

Stephen George and Ian Bache, *Politics in the European Union* (Oxford, Oxford University Press, 2001);

Neill Nugent, *The Government and Politics of the European Union* (Basingstoke, Macmillan, 2003);

John Van Oudenaren, *Uniting Europe: European Integration and the Post-Cold War World* (Lanham, Rowman & Littlefield, 2000);

Helen Wallace and William Wallace (eds.), *Policy-Making in the European Union* (Oxford, Oxford University Press, 2000, 4th ed.).

For a specific focus on the institutions, see:

John Peterson and Michael Shackleton (eds.), *The Institutions of the European Union* (Oxford, Oxford University Press, 2001);

Ponzano Paolo, "Le Processus de Décision dans l'Union Européenne", *Revue du Droit de l'Union Européenne* (2002/1) 35.

Among the general introductions to the legal aspects of the European construction, see:

Paul Craig and Grainne de Burca, *EU Law: Texts, Cases and Materials* (Oxford, Oxford University Press, 2002);

Anthony Arnull, Alan Dashwood, Malcolm Ross and Derrick Wyatt, *European Union Law* (London, Sweet & Maxwell, 2000);

K. P. E. Lasok, *Law & Institutions of the European Union* (London, Butterworths, 2001).

For an introduction to the EU's pillar structure, see:

Deirdre Curtin and Ige Dekker, "The EU as a 'Layered' International Organization: Institutional Unity in Disguise", in Paul Craig and Grainne de Burca (eds.), *The Evolution of EU Law* (Oxford, Oxford University Press, 1999), 83;

Bruno de Witte, "The Pillar Structure and the Nature of the European Union: Greek Temple or French Gothic Cathedral?", in Ton Heukels, Niels Blokker and Marcel Brus (eds.), *The European Union after Amsterdam. A Legal Analysis* (The Hague, Kluwer Law International, 1998), 51;

Laurence W. Gormley, "Reflections on the Architecture of the European Union after the Treaty of Amsterdam", in David O'Keeffe and Patrick Twomey (eds.), *Legal Issues of the Amsterdam Treaty* (Oxford, Hart, 1999), 57;

Joseph H. H. Weiler, "Neither Unity nor Three Pillars – The Trinity Structure of the Treaty on European Union", in Jörg Monar, Werner Ungerer and Wolfgang Wessels (eds.), *The Maastricht Treaty on European Union. Legal Complexity and Political Dynamic* (Brussels, European Interuniversity Press, 1993), 49.

For a general overview of the Treaty negotiation process, see:
 Andrew Moravcsik, *The Choice for Europe. Social Purpose & State Power from Messina to Maastricht* (London, University College London Press, 1999);
 Brendan P. G. Smith, *Constitution Building in the European Union. The Process of Treaty Reform* (The Hague, Kluwer Law International, 2002).

On the negotiation of the Treaty of Paris establishing the ECSC, see:
 William Diebold, *The Schuman Plan* (New York, Praeger, 1959);
 John Gillingham, *Coal, Steel and the Rebirth of Europe, 1945-1955: The Germans and French from Ruhr Conflict to Economic Community* (Cambridge, Cambridge University Press, 1991);
 Alan S. Milward, *The Reconstruction of Western Europe 1945-51* (London, Methuen, 1984);
 Klaus Schwabe (ed.), *The Beginnings of the Schuman Plan 1950/51* (Brussels, Bruylant, 1988);
 Pierre Gerbet, "Les Origines du Plan Schuman: le Choix de la Méthode Communautaire par le Gouvernement Français", in Raymond Poidevin (ed.), *Histoire des Débuts de la Construction Européenne (mars 1948-mai 1950)* (Brussels, Bruylant, 1986), 199;
 William I. Hitchcock, "France, the Western Alliance, and the Origins of the Schuman Plan, 1948-1950", *Diplomatic History*, 21 (1997) 603.

On the negotiation of the Treaty of Rome establishing the EEC, see:
 Hanns Jürgen Küsters, *Fondements de la Communauté Economique Européenne* (Luxembourg, EC, 1990);
 Alan S. Milward, *The European Rescue of the Nation-State* (London, Routledge, 1992);
 Enrico Serra (ed.), *The Relaunching of Europe and the Treaties of Rome* (Brussels, Bruylant, 1989);
 Gilbert Trausch (ed.), *The European Integration from the Schuman Plan to the Treaties of Rome* (Brussels, Bruylant, 1993);
 Ennio Di Nolfo (ed.), *Power in Europe? II: Great Britain, France, Germany and Italy and the Origins of the EEC, 1952-1957* (Berlin, Walter de Gruyter, 1992);
 and for the American factor in the negotiations:
 Pascaline Winand, Eisenhower, *Kennedy and the United States of Europe* (New York, St. Martin's Press, 1993).

On the creation of the Single European Act, see:
 Jean de Ruyt, *L'Acte Unique Européen* (Brussels, Ed. de l'Université de Bruxelles, 1989);
 David R. Cameron, "The 1992 Initiative: Causes and Consequences", in Alberta Sbragia (ed.), *Euro-Politics: Institutions and Policymaking in the 'New' European Community* (Washington, D.C., Brookings Institution, 1992) 23;
 Andrew Moravcsik, "Negotiating the Single European Act", in Robert O. Keohane and Stanley Hoffmann (eds.), *The New European Community. Decisionmaking and Institutional Change* (Boulder, Westview Press, 1991) 41;
 Wayne Sandholtz and John Zysman, "1992: Recasting the European Bargain", *World Politics*, 42 (1989) 95;

Maria Green Cowles, "Setting the Agenda for a New Europe: The ERT and EC 1992", *Journal of Common Market Studies*, 33 (1995) 501;
George A. Bermann, "The Single European Act: A New Constitution for the Community? ", *Columbia Journal of Transnational Law*, 27 (1989) 529.

For the negotiation of the Treaty of Maastricht, see:
Michael J. Baun, *An Imperfect Union. The Maastricht Treaty and the New Politics of European Integration* (Boulder, Westview Press, 1996);
Richard Corbett, *The Treaty of Maastricht* (London, Cartermill, 1993);
Jim Cloos, Gaston Reinesch, Daniel Vignes and Joseph Weyland, *Le Traité de Maastricht: Genèse, Analyse, Commentaires* (Brussels, Bruylant, 1994).

For the Treaty of Amsterdam, see:
Bobby MacDonagh, *Original Sin in a Brave New World: An Account of the Negotiation of the Treaty of Amsterdam* (Dublin, Institute of European Affairs, 1998);
Jörg Monar and Wolfgang Wessels (eds.), *The European Union after the Treaty of Amsterdam* (London, Continuum, 2001);
Andrew Duff, *The Treaty of Amsterdam. Text and Commentary* (London, Sweet & Maxwell, 1997);
Finn Laursen (ed.), *The Amsterdam Treaty. National Preference Formation, Interstate Bargaining and Outcome* (Odense, Odense University Press, 2002);
Youri Devuyst, "Treaty Reform in the European Union: the Amsterdam Process", *Journal of European Public Policy*, 5 (1998) 615;
Andrew Moravcsik and Kalypso Nicolaïdes, "Federal Ideals and Constitutional Realities in the Treaty of Amsterdam", *Journal of Common Market Studies* (European Union Annual Review 1997) 13;
Andrew Moravcsik and Kalypso Nicolaïdes, "Explaining the Treaty of Amsterdam: Interests, Influence, Institutions", *Journal of Common Market Studies*, 37 (1999) 59.

On the Treaty of Nice, see:
David Galloway, *The Treaty of Nice and Beyond. Realities and Illusions of Power in the EU* (Sheffield, Sheffield Academic Press, 2001);
Mads Andenas and John Usher (eds.), *The Treaty of Nice. Enlargement and Constitutional Reform* (Oxford, Hart, 2002);
Martin Bond and Kim Feus (eds.), *The Treaty of Nice Explained* (London, Federal Trust, 2001);
Vlad Constantinesco, Yves Gautier and Denys Simon (eds.), *Le Traité de Nice. Premières Analyses* (Strasbourg, Presses Universitaires de Strasbourg, 2001);
Karlheinz Neunreither, "The European Union in Nice: A Minimalist Approach to a Historic Challenge", *Government and Opposition*, 36 (2001) 184;
Wolfgang Wessels, "Nice Results: The Millennium IGC in the EU's Evolution", *Journal of Common Market Studies*, 39 (2001) 197.

For the background of the current enlargemement process, see:
Michael J. Baun, *A Wider Europe. Process and Politics of European Union Enlargement* (Lanham, Rowman & Littlefield, 2000);
Marise Cremona (ed.), *The Enlargement of the European Union* (Oxford, Oxford University Press, 2003);

Alan Mayhew, *Recreating Europe. The European Union's Policy towards Central and Eastern Europe* (Cambridge, Cambridge University Press, 1998);

Karen E. Smith, *The Making of EU Foreign Policy. The Case of Eastern Europe 1988-95* (Basingstoke, Macmillan, 1998).

CHAPTER I

The Creation of the Community Method:
The Primacy of Institution-building

I. The Origins of the Community Method

The institutional order established by the Treaties of Paris and Rome is best summarised by the term Community method. It was developed largely in reaction to the Council of Europe's inefficient intergovernmental decision-making techniques. The Council of Europe, based in Strasbourg, had been established in 1949 as the organisation that was to promote European unity after World War II. Attempts to give the Council of Europe an effective decision-making capacity failed because the United Kingdom (UK) and the Scandinavian countries refused to go beyond traditional diplomatic working methods.[1] The Organisation for European Economic Co-operation (OEEC), created in 1948 in response to the Marshall Plan, suffered from the same intergovernmental paralysis.[2] The need to depart from the exclusively intergovernmental working methods was most eloquently formulated by disillusioned Paul-Henri Spaak following his resignation as President of the Council of Europe's Parliamentary Assembly:

> Do you really want to build Europe without creating a supranational European authority and do you really want to build Europe while maintaining your national sovereignty? If that is your goal, we are no longer in agreement, because I believe you will be blocked by an insurmountable

---

[1] On the creation of the Council of Europe and its institutional system, see A. H. Robertson, *The Council of Europe* (London, Stevens, 1956); Peter M. R. Stirk, *A History of European Integration since 1914* (London, Pinter, 1996), 103; Derek W. Urwin, *The Community of Europe: A History of European Integration since 1945* (London, Longman, 1995), 27.

[2] On the creation of the OEEC and its institutional system, see Richard T. Griffiths (ed.), *Explorations in OEEC History* (Paris, OECD, 1997); Robert Marjolin, *Architect of European Unity: Memoirs, 1911-1986* (London, Weidenfeld and Nicolson, 1989), 191; Alan S. Milward, *The Reconstruction of Western Europe 1945-51* (London, Methuen, 1984), 168; Stirk, *A History of European Integration*, 83; Urwin, *The Community of Europe*, 19.

obstacle; wanting to create a new Europe while keeping national sovereignty intact is like trying to square the circle.[3]

The project for a European Coal and Steel Community (ECSC) met the call for a change of method. Only those countries that accepted the supranational principle of bringing their coal and steel industry under the governance of an independent High Authority were asked to participate in its elaboration. In the words of French Foreign Minister Robert Schuman,

> the participating nations will *in advance* accept the notion of submission to the Authority ... They are convinced that ... the moment has come for us to attempt for the first time the experiment of a supranational authority which shall not be simply a combination or conciliation of national powers.[4]

Of course, institution-building as such was not the ultimate goal of the Community's founders. By pushing Community integration, they were trying to advance their own governments' economic and political objectives. As historian Alan Milward has emphasised, the Schuman Plan was intimately linked to Jean Monnet's ambitious plan for French industrial recovery which, in turn, relied heavily upon continued French access to German coal that could be obtained via the ECSC.[5] The EEC served the economic objectives of Germany's neighbours too. The main purpose was to secure the fast growing West German economy firmly as the pivot of Western Europe's trade expansion.[6] To Germany, who was looking for rehabilitation as a sovereign nation, the Treaties of Paris and Rome offered the status of an equal partner.[7] In addition, the ECSC and

---

[3] Paul-Henri Spaak, "Document 54: Il n'y a qu'un seul partenaire concevable pour les Etats-Unis d'Amérique: ce sont les Etats-Unis d'Europe (7 février 1952)", in Paul-F. Smets (ed.), *La Pensée Européenne et Atlantique de Paul-Henri Spaak* (Brussels, Goemaere, 1980), 297 (translated by the author). On Spaak's disappointment with the functioning of the Council of Europe and the OEEC, see Paul-Henri Spaak, *Combats Inachevés. Vol. II: De l'Espoir aux Déceptions* (Paris, Fayart, 1969), 46; Michel Dumoulin, *Spaak* (Brussels, Ed. Racine, 1999), 433.

[4] Robert Schuman before the Consultative Assembly of the Council of Europe, Records of the Fourth Sitting, 10 August 1950, cited in Michael O'Neill (ed.), *The Politics of European Integration. A Reader* (London, Routledge, 1996), 36 (italics were added by the author). On Schuman's viewpoint regarding European integration, see Raymond Poidevin, *Robert Schuman, Homme d'Etat, 1886-1963* (Paris, Imprimerie Nationale, 1986).

[5] Alan S. Milward, *The Reconstruction of Western Europe,* 395.

[6] Alan S. Milward, *The European Rescue of the Nation-State* (London, Routledge, 1992), 120-121. See also Andrew Moravcsik, *The Choice for Europe. Social Purpose & State Power from Messina to Maastricht* (London, University College London Press, 1999), 86.

[7] Hanns Jürgen Küsters, "The Federal Republic of Germany and the EEC Treaty", in Enrico Serra (ed.), *The Relaunching of Europe and the Treaties of Rome* (Brussels, Bruylant, 1989), 495; Sabine Lee, "German Decision-Making Elites and European Integration: German 'Europolitik' during the Years of the EEC and Free Trade Area

EEC were instruments to restore Paris as a major player in shaping Europe's future. For France, the Communities had the additional advantage of pushing Britain to the margins of Europe's post-war diplomacy.[8]

While trying to achieve their economic and political objectives, Schuman and Monnet repeatedly emphasised that the success of the entire integration effort would depend to a large extent on getting the institutional framework right. In this light, it is not surprising that as Chairman of the Intergovernmental Conference convened in 1950 to negotiate the Treaty of Paris establishing ECSC, Monnet urged the delegates from the start not to saddle the embryonic Community with the shortcomings of traditional intergovernmental institutions.[9] Monnet had a strong belief in the cumulative sagacity of institutions. He was fond of quoting Swiss philosopher Henri Frédéric Amiel:

> Each man begins the world afresh. Only institutions grow wiser; they store up their collective experience; and, from this experience and wisdom, men subject to the same laws will gradually find, not that their natures change but that their behaviour does.[10]

Since the founders of the Communities were well aware that Treaty of Paris and the Treaties of Rome merely constituted "the foundations" of their attempt to build "an ever closer union", they counted on the cumulative wisdom of the institutional framework to give the Community a dynamic of its own. The pragmatic institutional framework created by the Community Treaties build on co-operation between States, but simultaneously went well beyond the traditional intergovernmental set-up.[11] The European Commission obtained the exclusive right to take the legislative initiative. It was also to act as the independent guardian of the Treaties with the power to bring Member States before the Court of Justice for failure to fulfil their Treaty obligations. Furthermore, the Commission was to serve as the Community's voice in international

Negotiations", in Anne Deighton (ed.), *Building Postwar Europe. National Decision-Makers and European Institutions, 1948-63* (Basingstoke, Macmillan, 1995), 38.

[8]   Gérard Bossuat, "Le Choix de la Petite Europe par la France (1957-1963): Une Ambition pour la France et pour l'Europe", *Relations Internationales* (1995-82) 213; Gérard Bossuat, "The French Administrative Elite and the Unification of Western Europe, 1947-58", in Deighton (ed.), *Building Postwar Europe*, 21; William I. Hitchcock, *France Restored: Cold War Diplomacy & the Quest for Leadership in Europe, 1944-1954* (Chapel Hill, University of North Carolina Press, 1998); Stirk, *A History of European Integration*, 119.

[9]   Jean Monnet, *Mémoires* (Paris, Fayard, 1976), 373. See also François Duchêne, *Jean Monnet. The First Statesman of Interdependence* (New York, Norton, 1994), 205.

[10] Cited in Duchêne, *Jean Monnet*, 401.

[11] See in particular Pierre Pescatore, "L'Exécutif Communautaire: Justification du Quadripartisme Institué par les Traités de Paris et de Rome", *Cahiers de Droit Européen*, 4 (1978) 387.

trade negotiations and as the body implementing common policies. The Council of Ministers was the main decision-maker. The Treaty of Rome stipulated that it could, in certain areas and after a transitional period, exercise that function by qualified majority voting instead of unanimity. The Common Assembly, composed of delegates from the national parliaments, was originally set up as a body that had to control the Commission. From the start, the Assembly could vote a motion of censure obliging the Commission to resign. Finally, the European Court of Justice was given jurisdiction to issue binding rulings on the validity and interpretation of Community acts.

Obviously, the Community method also incorporated a number of intergovernmental traits.[12] The most important intergovernmental aspect of the Community Treaties concerned the procedures for reform of the Treaty framework. To change the Treaties, an Intergovernmental Conference (IGC) composed of representatives of the governments of the Member States must be convened to determine by common accord the amendments to be made. Amendments can enter into force only after having being ratified by all the Member States in accordance with their respective constitutional requirements.[13]

The supranational dimension of the Community method faced problems from the start. French President Charles De Gaulle, who returned to power in 1958, was a notorious opponent of supranational integration. While successfully resisting the start of qualified majority voting in the Council,[14] De Gaulle also saw the need to convene summits of Heads of State or Government to give direction to Europe's future. As will become clear in the following chapters, the summits – now institutionalised as European Council meetings – have in practice become the intergovernmental engine of European integration, determining in large measure the speed and content of the EU's adaptation process.

---

[12] As Pascaline Winand has emphasised, even on institutional questions, the founders of the Community method were pragmatic rather than dogmatic. See Pascaline Winand, "Le Comité d'Action pour les Etats-Unis d'Europe de Jean Monnet", in *20 Ans d'Action du Comité Jean Monnet (1955-1975)* (Paris, Notre Europe, Problématiques Européennes No. 8, May 2001), 9-10.

[13] EEC Treaty, art. 236. Currently Consolidated TEU, art. 48.

[14] For a more detailed treatment of the evolution of qualified majority voting, see Chapter III. II..

II. The Community Method and the Process of Political Change in the EU

Already in his famous declaration of May 9, 1950, Schuman underlined that "Europe w[ould] not be made all at once or according to a single plan. It will be built through concrete achievements".[15] The Treaties of Paris and Rome merely constituted a point of departure for a step-by-step integration process. The essence of EU politics is the constant attempt by Member States and other political actors to fix "policy paths" at the European level in directions that suit their preferences. By turning their political compromise formulae into formal, often legally binding, texts, the architects of political adaptation try to ensure the persistence of their preferred policy course. Still, "policy paths" do not form strait-jackets that cannot be changed. Member States and other policy actors are constantly trying to adjust the EU's path to follow the direction which they prefer. This is the essence of EU politics.

According to the Treaty of Rome, four broad levels of political change can be distinguished in the Community.[16] The first level of adaptation is largely in the hands of the governments and parliaments of the Member States. It concerns, in particular, Treaty reform and enlargement with new Member States. According to the Treaty of Rome, the formalisation of agreements at this level requires two stages. First, a consensus must be found between the governments.[17] Second, the results must be ratified by all Member States in accordance with their respective constitutional requirements. It is clear that the Treaty left the Member States in charge as the "Masters of the Treaties" at this first level of political change.

The creation of secondary law in the form of Community regulations and directives is the second level of political adaptation in the EU to be found in the Treaty of Rome. The inter-play between Community institutions is the determining factor at this level. As stated above, the

---

[15]   Robert Schuman, "Declaration of 9 May 1950", in Peter M. R. Stirk and David Weigall (eds.), *The Origins and Development of European Integration: A Reader and Commentary* (London, Pinter, 1999), 76. For the original French version of the Schuman Declaration, see Poidevin, *Robert Schuman*, 261.

[16]   For an alternative use of the level of analysis technique to EU decision-making, see the enlightening analysis by John Peterson, "Decision-Making in the European Union: towards a Framework of Analysis", *Journal of European Public Policy*, 2 (1995) 69.

[17]   This does not imply that the influence of the European Parliament and the European Commission can be completely neglected in the decision-making process at this level. The European Parliament, for instance, must give its assent before an enlargement can take place. European Commission opinions on both enlargement and Treaty reform have often helped to set the tone for European Council debates.

Commission has the exclusive right to take the legislative initiative, the Council of Ministers adopts the legislative texts either by unanimity or by qualified majority voting, and the European Parliament is increasingly involved via the co-decision procedure. In 2001, Parliament and Council together adopted 15 legislative regulations and 23 legislative directives.[18] The fact that the Council may vote by qualified majority on certain legislative issues implies that Member States may find themselves in the minority but are nevertheless obliged to implement the legislative texts adopted by the majority. This has, at times, given rise to high-level protests. [19]

The application of EU policies forms the third level of political change. Its impact is often under-estimated. In 2001, the European Commission enacted 600 implementing regulations, 18 implementing directives and 651 decisions in application of the Community Treaties or of the EU's secondary legislation.[20] Commission decisions are taken after consultation of the Member States.[21] Under its own regulatory implementing powers, the Commission has a certain margin to push for political change. The expanded application of competition policy in such sectors as multimedia or sports, for instance, did not require any change in Treaty law or secondary legislation.

The judicial interpretation of existing primary and secondary law, including the settlement of conflicts on both procedural and substantive matters, forms the fourth level of change. Final decisions at this level are taken by the European Court of Justice. Political disputes often find their way to the Court in the hope that the judges would fix a "legal path" in accordance with the plaintiff's preferences. Obviously, this outcome is not guaranteed. Through its rulings, the Court has gradually defined the boundaries of Community and Member State powers. Most importantly, it is the Court that – during the early 1960s – has promulgated such fundamental principles as the direct effect and primacy of Community law.[22]

---

[18]   General Report on the Activities of the European Union 2001 [hereinafter Gen. Rep. EU], para. 1239.

[19]   See, for instance, the UK's protests against the adoption by qualified majority voting of the so-called Working Time Directive of 1993. John Major, "Statement on the Working Time Directive", November 12, 1996. See also Margaret Gray, "A Recalcitrant Partner: the UK Reaction to the Working Time Directive", *Yearbook of European Law*, 17, 1997, 323.

[20]   Gen. Rep. EU 2001, para. 1239.

[21]   For an explanation of the so-called comitology procedure, see Chapter III. I.

[22]   For an explanation of the terms primacy and direct effect of EC law, see Chapter IV. I.

That the Treaty of Rome's supranational decision-making processes at levels two, three and four can bring about institutional and societal change in the EU, even if some governments object, implies that the Member States have to a certain degree lost direct control over their creation. It also explains why certain governments have been less than eager to continue with European integration through the supranational dimension of the Community method since it implies giving up direct control and veto powers. Instead the Member States have – at Maastricht, Amsterdam and Nice – tended to invent new techniques of political adaptation that allow them to remain in charge, at least in formal terms. As already stated above, the Heads of State or Government have systematically pushed their own direct involvement in European decision-making, although this had not been foreseen by the Community Treaties. Since 1975, the European Council has gradually become the intergovernmental *forum* which steers all politically important processes of change in the EU by consensus.[23] In addition, European co-ordination in new policy fields is, in general, no longer achieved through legislative harmonisation, but rather via the so-called open co-ordination method. Open co-ordination means that the Member States decide by consensus to define a number of policy objectives. Through a process of regular reporting, measuring performance and peer review, the Member States are pushed to conform to the set "policy path". In formal terms, however, open co-ordination does not involve legal obligations with the risk of infringement procedures.[24]

---

[23] For more details, see Chapter III. I.

[24] For more details, see Chapter III. VI.

CHAPTER II

The Legal Foundations
of the EU Polity

I. Between Treaty Framework and Constitution

According to the European Court of Justice "the EEC Treaty, albeit concluded in the form of an international agreement, none the less constitutes the Constitutional Charter of the Community based on the rule of law".[1] The Court has consistently held that the EU Treaties have established a new legal order with its own institutions, decision-making mechanisms and enforcement powers "for the benefit of which the [Member] States have limited their sovereign rights, in ever wider fields, and the subjects of which comprise not only the Member States but also their nationals".[2] Still, in the EU's institutional reality, constitutionalisation remains a controversial topic.[3]

---

[1] Case 294/83, Les Verts v. Parliament, E.C.R. 1986, 1365, para. 23; Opinion 1/91, E.C.R. 1991, I-6079, para. 21.

[2] Opinion 1/91, E.C.R. 1991, 6102.

[3] For the academic debate regarding the constitutional nature of the EU's Treaty framework, see Jörg Gerkrath, *L'Emergence d'un Droit Constitutionnel pour l'Europe: Modes de Formation et Sources d'Inspiration de la Constitution des Communautés et de l'Union Européenne* (Brussels, Ed. de l'Université de Bruxelles, 1997); Christian Joerges, Yves Mény and J. H. H. Weiler (eds.), *What Kind of Constitution for What Kind of Polity?* (Florence, European University Institute, 2000); Paul Magnette (ed.), *La Constitution de l'Europe* (Brussels, Ed. de l'Université de Bruxelles, 2000); J. H. H. Weiler, *The Constitution of Europe. "Do the New Clothes have an Emperor?"* (Cambridge, Cambridge University Press, 1999); Birgit Lafflan (ed.), *Constitution-Building in the European Union* (Dublin, Institute of European Affairs, 1996); Philip Allcott, "The Crisis of European Constitutionalism: Reflections on the Revolution in Europe", *Common Market Law Review*, 34 (1997) 439; Grainne de Burca, "The Institutional Development of the EU: A Constitutional Analysis", in Craig and de Burca (eds.), *The Evolution of EU Law*, 55; Ingolf Pernice, "Multilevel Constitutionalism and the Treaty of Amsterdam: European Constitution-Making Revisited?", *Common Market Law Review*, 36 (1999) 703; Jean-Claude Piris, "Does the European Union have a Constitution? Does it Need One?", *European Law Review*, 24 (1999) 557; Jo Shaw, "Postnational Constitutionalism in the European Union", *Journal of European Public Policy*, 6 (1999) 579.

In the preparatory phase of the IGC of 2000, ultimately leading to the Treaty of Nice, the idea had been launched to reorganise the EU's Treaty framework and give it a more constitutional character. In their report on *The Institutional Implications of Enlargement* (the so-called Wise Men report) former Belgian Prime Minister Jean-Luc Dehaene, former German President Richard von Weiszäcker and former UK Minister David Simon had suggested a division of the EU Treaties in two separate parts: [4]

> The Basic Treaty would only include the aims, principles and general policy orientations, citizens' rights and the institutional framework. These clauses ... could only be modified unanimously, through an IGC, with ratification by each Member State. Presumably such modifications would be infrequent.

> A separate text (or texts) would include the other clauses of the present treaties, including those which concern specific policies. These could be modified by a decision of the Council ... and the assent of the European Parliament.[5]

The main reason for this suggestion was the need for a simplification of the EU Treaty framework. As the fruit of fifty years of European integration, the EU's primary law is made up of a large number of Treaties and Protocols. Over 700 articles form a complex and not very coherent whole, including both fundamental principles and institutional and more technical provisions.[6] According to the European Commission, this construction is "not understandable to the European citizens". It therefore saw considerable merit in the Wise Men's proposal and asked the European University Institute in Florence to study it.[7] To foster a "simplification and rationalisation of the Treaties with a view to making them transparent and intelligible to citizens, ... entrench the rights of the Member States and citizens of the European Union and clarify the competences of the common institutions", the European Parliament also gave

---

[4]   European Parliament, "Resolution on the Preparation of the Reform of the Treaties and the next Intergovernmental Conference", Minutes of the Plenary Session of November 26, 1999, para. 57. See also Giorgios Dimitrakopoulos and Jo Leinen, "Report on the Preparation of the Reform of the Treaties and the next Intergovernmental Conference", European Parliament Session Document, November 10, 1999.

[5]   Jean-Luc Dehaene, Richard von Weiszäcker and David Simon, "The Institutional Implications of Enlargement. Report to the European Commission", October 18, 1999, 12.

[6]   Commission of the European Communities, "A Basic Treaty for the European Union", COM(2000) 434 final, July 12, 2000, 2-3.

[7]   Commission, "Adapting the Institutions to Make a Success of Enlargement", 5. The European University Institute (EUI) presented its study on the reorganisation of the Treaties to the Commission on May 15, 2000. See <http://europa.eu.int/igc2000/offdoc/repoflo_en.pdf>. See also Kim Feus (ed.), *A Simplified Treaty for the European Union?* (London, Federal Trust, Constitution for Europe Series 2, 2001).

its enthusiastic support to the constitutionalisation of the Treaties.[8] When launching the IGC 2000 in December 1999, however, the Helsinki European Council avoided opening the constitutional debate. The simplification of the EU Treaty framework was not included in the IGC's agenda.[9] This was not entirely surprising. A genuine constitutional debate, implying clear choices on the goals, character and institutional conception of European integration was precisely what some Member States had been trying to avoid since the disruptive and inconclusive discussion on the Union's "federal" nature during the Maastricht negotiations.[10]

During the negotiations leading to the Treaty of Nice, the proposal for a constitutionalisation of the EU's Treaty framework nevertheless resurfaced following a stimulating presentation by German Minister of Foreign Affairs Joschka Fischer.[11] Several leading national politicians, including French President Jacques Chirac, British Prime Minister Tony Blair, Belgian Prime Minister Guy Verhofstadt, Finnish Prime Minister Paavo Lipponen, German Chancellor Gerhard Schröder, German President Johannes Rau and French Prime Minister Lionel Jospin replied with their own constitutional proposals for the Union.[12] At Nice, the Heads of State or Government decided to pursue this debate by launching a wide-

---

[8] European Parliament, "Resolution on the Convening of the Intergovernmental Conference", Minutes of the Plenary Session of February 3, 2000, para. B. The European Parliament elaborated its opinion in European Parliament, "Resolution on the Constitutionalisation of the Treaties", Minutes of the Plenary Session of October 25, 2000. See also Olivier Duhamel, "Report on the Constitutionalisation of the Treaties", European Parliament Session Document, October 12, 2000.

[9] Helsinki European Council, "Presidency Conclusions", December 10-11, 1999, para. 16.

[10] Corbett, *The Treaty of Maastricht*, 38; Cloos, Reinesch, Vignes and Weyland, *Le Traité de Maastricht*, 115.

[11] Joschka Fischer, "From Confederacy to Federation – Thoughts on the Finality of European Integration", Speech at the Humbold University, Berlin, May 12, 2000. Former Commission President Jacques Delors, former French President Valéry Giscard d'Estaing and former German Chancellor Helmut Schmidt had been trying to launch the debate on the EU's future since the start of the IGC 2000. See Jacques Delors, "Reuniting Europe: Our Historic Mission", *Agence Europe*, January 3-4, 2000, 3; Valéry Giscard d'Estaing and Helmut Schmidt, "Europe's Lessons", *Agence Europe*, April 17, 2000, 3.

[12] Jacques Chirac, "Notre Europe", Speech at the Bundestag, Berlin, June 27, 2000; Tony Blair, "Prime Minister's Speech to the Polish Stock Exchange", Warsaw, October 6, 2000; Guy Verhofstadt, "A Vision of Europe", Speech at the European Policy Center, Brussels, September 21, 2000; Paavo Lipponen, "Speech at the College of Europe", Bruges, November 10, 2000; Gerhard Schröder, "Nach der Reform: Zukunftsstrategien für Gesamteuropa", Speech at the International Bertelsmann-Forum 2001, January 19, 2001; Johannes Rau, "Plea for a European Constitution", Speech to the European Parliament, Strasbourg, April 4, 2001; Lionel Jospin, "L'Avenir de l'Europe Elargie", Paris, May 28, 2001; Tony Blair, "The Challenge of Reform in Europe", Birmingham, November 23, 2001.

ranging discussion on the EU's future development, in co-operation with
the European Commission and involving the European Parliament, national parliaments and representatives of civil society.[13] It was intended
that this process would lead to new Treaty changes in 2004.[14]

The modalities for the preparation of the new round of Treaty reform
were clarified by the Laeken European Council in December 2001.[15] In
order to pave the way for the next IGC as broadly and openly as possible,
the Heads of State or Government decided to convene a Convention on
the future of Europe.[16] The Convention, which started its work in
February 2002, is composed of 15 representatives of the Heads of State
or Government of the Member States (one from each Member State),
30 representatives of national parliaments (two from each Member State),
16 members of the European Parliament and two members of the European Commission. The candidate countries are represented in the same
way as the current Member States. In addition, the Convention is attend-
ed by three observers of the Economic and Social Committee, two observers of the European social partners, six observers from the Committee of the Regions and the European Ombudsman. Former French President Valéry Giscard d'Estaing was appointed as Chairman of the Convention and former Italian and Belgian Prime Ministers Giuliano Amato
and Jean-Luc Dehaene as Vice-Chairmen. The Convention has to draw
up a final document which may comprise different options for the EU's
future or recommendations if consensus is achieved. The representatives
from the candidate countries will be able to take part in the proceedings
without being able to prevent any consensus which may emerge among
the Member States. The Convention method was inspired by the successful experience with the drafting of the Charter of Fundamental Rights of
the European Union in 2001. The Charter too had been prepared by a
Convention.[17] The Convention on the EU's future will prepare, but not

---

[13]   Nice Declaration 23 on the Future of the Union, para. 4. The choice for an open
       reflection process, with the participation of the national parliaments, as part of the
       new round of Treaty reform was a response to the general feeling at Nice that the old
       IGC method had passed its expiry date. See Michel Petite, "Nice, Traité Existentiel,
       Non Essentiel", *Revue du Droit de l'Union Européenne* (2000/4) 887.

[14]   European Commission President Romano Prodi has suggested that the date of the
       next IGC would have to be brought forward in case of a failure to ratify the Treaty of
       Nice. Romano Prodi, "On the Road to Laeken", Speech at the European Parliament,
       Strasbourg, July 4, 2001, 6.

[15]   Laeken European Council, "Presidency Conclusions", December 14-15, 2001,
       Annex I. On the significance of the Laeken European Council, see Peter Ludlow, *The
       Laeken Council* (Brussels, EuroComment, 2002).

[16]   The work of the Convention can be followed via its website: http://european-conven-
       tion.eu.int. See also http://www.europa.eu.int/futurum/index .

[17]   Grainne de Burca, "The Drafting of the EU Charter of Fundamental Rights", *Euro-
       pean Law Review*, 26 (2001) 126; Florence Deloche-Gaudez, *La Convention pour*

replace the traditional IGC. Amendments to the Treaties will still require a conference of representatives of the governments of the Member States. Furthermore, such amendments would only enter into force after being ratified by all the Member States.[18]

While launching the Convention, the Laeken European Council also adopted a Declaration on the future of the European Union which incorporates around 60 questions to be tackled in preparation for the next Treaty reform. In contrast with previous European Council conclusions, the Laeken Declaration did explicitly mention, as the "ultimate" question, "whether th[e] simplification and reorganisation [of the Treaties] might not lead in the long run to the adoption of a constitutional text in the Union".[19] To avoid any disagreement over semantics, Convention President Giscard d'Estaing proposed to work towards a "Constitutional Treaty for Europe".[20] On October 28, 2002 Giscard presented his preliminary draft Constitutional Treaty.[21] The preliminary draft has three parts. Part one contains the definition and objectives of the Union, the Union's citizenship and fundamental rights, competences, institutions, legislative and implementing procedures and finances as well as provisions on the democratic life of the Union, Union action in the world, relations with the neighbouring States and Union membership. Part two defines the legal bases for Union policies and their implementation. For each policy area, it specifies the type of Union competence and the acts and procedures to be applied. Part three contains a number of general and final provisions, for instance on the adoption, ratification and entry into force of the Constitutional Treaty.

Two general constitutional problems figure high on the Convention's current agenda. The first concerns the link between the future Constitutional Treaty and the current Treaties.[22] The Convention could choose to incorporate the new constitutional provisions in the current legal framework by the classic route of amending the existing Treaties. This would add another layer of texts to the existing Treaties to the detriment of

---

l'Elaboration de la Charte des Droits Fondamentaux: une Méthode d'Avenir? (Paris, Notre Europe, Etudes et Recherches No. 15, November 2001). See also Chapter IV. III. B.

[18] Consolidated TEU, art. 48.

[19] Laeken European Council, "Presidency Conclusions", December 14-15, 2001, Annex I, 6.

[20] Valéry Giscard d'Estaing, "Introductory Speech to the Convention on the Future of Europe", February 28, 2002, 11.

[21] The European Convention, "Preliminary Draft Constitutional Treaty", CONV 369/02, October 28, 2002.

[22] Commission of the European Communities, "Communication on the Institutional Architecture for the European Union : Peace, Freedom, Solidarity", COM (2002) 728 Final, December 4, 2002, 22.

simplicity and clarity. Another route would be to replace the existing Treaties with a new Constitutional Treaty. This approach would have the advantage of simplicity and clarity. However, replacing the current Treaties could create a risk to the continuity of the *acquis communautaire*. A second important item for discussion at the Convention concerns the entry into force of the future Constitutional Treaty. This discussion focuses on the possibility that the Constitutional Treaty might enter into force while it has not been ratified by every Member State. In a working document outlining a draft Constitution of the European Union, the European Commission underlines that under current Treaty rules, one Member State could block the entry into force of the new Constitutional Treaty. To avoid such a situation, the Commission working document proposes that Member States failing to ratify the Constitutional Treaty would be deemed to withdraw from the Union.[23] While Convention President Giscard has spoken in a similar vein, the proposal was immediately rejected by the representative of the UK government who argued that Member States could not be held "at gunpoint" like that.[24]

II. Between a Union of States and a Union of Regions

The EU constitutes a Union of Member States that have signed and ratified the founding Treaties. As the European Court of Justice has repeatedly stated, the Member States remain responsible for a failure to fulfil Treaty obligations, even if the breach is actually committed by a region or agency that is independent according to national constitutional law.[25]

While a Union of Member States, the EU has in recent years made room for the participation of the regions in the decision-making process.[26] Since the Maastricht Treaty, Member States may be represented in the Council by any representative at Ministerial level, whether from the national or regional government, as long as the representative is

---

[23] Commission of the European Communities, "Working Document : Contribution to a Preliminary Draft Constitution of the European Union", December 4, 2002, XI-XII.

[24] Ferdinando Riccardi, "A Look Behind the News", *Agence Europe*, December 13, 2002, 2.

[25] Case 77/69, Commission v. Belgium, E.C.R. 1970, 237, 243. See also Kurt Riechenberg, "Local Administration and the Binding Nature of Community Directives: A Lesser Known Side of European Legal Integration", *Fordham International Law Journal*, 22 (1999) 696. Member States may not rely on national provisions or practices to justify their failure to fulfil their Treaty obligations, see Case 30/72, Commission v. Italy, E.C.R. 1973, 667, 671-672; Case 215/85, Commission v. Belgium, E.C.R. 1985, 1039, 1054.

[26] Jan Kottmann, "Europe and the Regions: Sub-National Entity Representation at Community Level", *European Law Review*, 26 (2001) 159.

authorised to commit the government of that Member State.[27] Thus, Ministers from the regions can directly participate in Council deliberations. In Belgium, for instance, there is no national Minister for culture or education. Representation in the Council is therefore assured on a rotating basis by a Minister from Belgium's Flemish, French-speaking or German-speaking language communities.[28] A co-ordination mechanism between the regions, language communities and the federal government ensures that a single Belgian position is determined before each Council meeting.[29]

The Maastricht Treaty also created the Committee of the Regions.[30] The Committee consists of representatives of regional and local bodies.[31] It has an advisory status and must be consulted by the Council or by the Commission where the Treaty so provides. It may also be consulted by the European Parliament. The Committee may issue opinions on its own initiative when it considers that specific regional interests are at stake. During 2001, the Committee adopted 72 opinions; 14 were on matters where consultation was mandatory and 35 where it was optional; 23 were own-initiative opinions.[32] In practice, the Committee's opinions have not seemed to carry much weight in the EU's decision-making process.[33] The Regions themselves, however, seem to be exerting an ever greater influence on the EU's future.[34] As will be discussed in greater detail

---

[27]   Consolidated TEU, art. 203.

[28]   See "Accord de Coopération entre l'Etat Fédéral, les Communautés et les Régions Relatif à la Représentation du Royaume de Belgique au sein du Conseil des Ministres de l'Union Européenne", *Supplément à la Revue de la Presse* (Brussels, Ministrère des Affaires Etrangères, du Commerce Extérieur et de la Coopération au Développement), March 9, 1994, Annexe II.

[29]   When representing their Member States in the Council, the Regions of a single Member State have to come up with a unified position since Consolidated TEC, art. 205 does not allow splitting the vote of a Member State.

[30]   Consolidated TEC, arts. 263-265. See Jacques Bourrinet (ed.), *Le Comité des Régions de l'Union Européenne* (Paris, Economica, 1997).

[31]   There are currently 222 members. The Treaty of Nice, art. 2(42) set an upper limit of 350 members. The Treaty of Nice added that the members of the Committee of the Regions should either hold an electoral mandate in a regional or local authority, or be politically accountable to an elected assembly.

[32]   Gen. Rep. EU 2001, para. 1235.

[33]   Rosarie E. McCarthy, "The Committee of the Regions: An Advisory Body's Torturous Path to Influence", *Journal of European Public Policy*, 4 (1997) 439.

[34]   Michael J. Baun, "The Länder and German European Policy: The 1996 IGC and Amsterdam Treaty", *German Studies Review*, 21 (1998) 329; Richard E. Deeg, "Germany's Länder and the Federalization of the European Union", in Carolyn Rhodes and Sonia Mazey (eds.), *The State of the European Union. Vol. III: Building a European Polity?* (Boulder, Lynne Rienner, 1995), 197; Rudolf Hrbek, "The German Länder and EC Integration", *Journal of European Integration*, 15 (1992) 180; Eiko R. Thielemann, "Institutional Limits of a Europe with Regions: EC State

below, the German Länder, in particular, have repeatedly been pushing for a more restrictive delimitation of EU competences in an attempt to preserve their own powers.

III. Between an Expansive and a Restrictive Delimitation of EU Powers

Both during the Amsterdam and Nice negotiations, the German Bundesrat adopted resolutions calling for a clearer division of responsibilities between the EU, its Member States and the regions, in light of the subsidiarity principle.[35] The Bundesrat is the chamber of the German Parliament in which the Länder are represented. Its opinion is important as its approval is required as part of the German ratification procedure of the new Treaty.

What has been cause for concern at the level of the Länder is the so-called expansive nature of Community powers. The signatories of the EEC Treaty – while announcing that they were merely laying "the foundations of an ever closer union" – intended to set in motion an evolutive process. This explains why the EEC Treaty foresaw, from the start, the possibility of gradually adapting the integration process to new societal needs without Treaty revision. According to EEC Treaty Article 235, the Council was granted the right to take "the appropriate measures [by unanimity] ... if action by the Community should prove necessary to attain ... one of the objectives of the Community [while the] Treaty has not provided the necessary powers".[36] Between 1958 and 1972, Article 235 was used infrequently and under rather restrictive conditions.[37] It was not until the Paris Summit in October 1972 that the Heads of State or Government took the explicit decision to start making full and expansive use of Article 235 for the development of regional, social, environmental, science and energy policies, as well as economic

---

Aid Control Meets German Federalism", *Journal of European Public Policy*, 6 (1999), 399; and the country studies in Charlie Jeffery (ed.), *The Regional Dimension of the European Union. Towards a Third Level in Europe?* (London, Frank Cass, 1997).

[35]   Bundesrat, "Entschliessung des Bundesrates zur Eröffnung der Regierungskonferenz zu Institutionellen Fragen", Drucksache 61/00, February 4, 2000. See also Bundesrat, "Entschliessung des Bundesrates zu institutionellen Reformen under der Weiterentwicklung der EU", Drucksache 680/00, November 10, 2000. See also Marc Bungenberg, "Dynamische Integration, Art. 308 und die Forderung nach dem Kompetenzkatalog", *Europarecht*, 35 (2000) 879.

[36]   EEC Treaty, art. 235.

[37]   Guiliano Marenco, "Les Conditions d'Application de l'Article 235 du Traité CEE", *Revue du Marché Commun*, 12 (1970) 147.

and monetary integration.[38] In the succeeding years, it effectively served as a basis for action in such areas as consumer or environmental protection before these subjects were explicitly listed in the Treaty as a Community competences.[39]

The expansive nature of the Community's competences was reinforced in the external relations field through the implied powers doctrine developed by the Court of Justice. The doctrine took the form of a parallelism between internal and external Community competences. This restricted the Member States' powers to act on their own in the international field.[40] The two main principles governing the Community's implied external powers can be summarised as follows:

- whenever Community law has conferred upon the Community institutions internal powers for the purpose of attaining a specific objective, the Community is authorised to enter into the international commitments necessary for the attainment of that objective (this is the so-called Opinion 1/76 doctrine);[41]
- where Community rules have been promulgated, the Member States cannot, outside the framework of the Community institutions, assume obligations which might affect those rules or alter their scope (this is the so-called ERTA doctrine).[42]

---

[38] Bull. EC, 10-1972, 24. See also Weiler, *The Constitution of Europe*, 53; Mark A. Pollack, "Creeping Competence: The Expanding Agenda of the European Community", *Journal of Public Policy*, 14 (1994) 95; John A. Usher, "The Gradual Widening of European Community Policy on the Basis of Article 100 and 235 of the EEC Treaty", in Jürgen Schwarze and Henry G. Schermers (eds.), *Structure and Dimensions of European Community Policy* (Baden-Baden, Nomos, 1988) 30.

[39] The need to rely on EC Treaty, art. 235 decreased following the explicit inclusion of new fields of EC competence in the SEA and the Treaty of Maastricht. Nevertheless, Member States often tried to add art. 235 to the legal base of Community acts because it requires decision-taking in the Council by unanimity.

[40] For the classic case-law, see Alan Dashwood and Joni Heliskoski, "The Classic Authorities Revisited", in Alan Dashwood and Christophe Hillion (eds.), *The General Law of EC External Relations* (London, Sweet & Maxwell, 2000, 3); Jean Groux, "Le Parallélisme des Compétences Internes et Externes de la Communauté Economique Européenne", *Cahiers de Droit Européen*, 14 (1978) 3; Pierre Pescatore, "External Relations in the Case-Law of the Court of Justice of the European Communities", *Common Market Law Review*, 16 (1979) 615. For the evolution of the case-law since the 1970s, see Marise Cremona, "External Relations and External Competence: The Emergence of an Integrated Policy", in Craig and de Burca (eds.), *The Evolution of EU Law*, 137; David O'Keeffe, "Community and Member State Competence in External Relations Agreements of the EU", *European Foreign Affairs Review*, 4 (1999) 7; Takis Tridimas and Piet Eeckhout, "The External Competence of the Community in the Case-Law of the Court of Justice: Principle versus Pragmatism", *Yearbook of European Law*, 14 (1994) 143.

[41] Opinion 1/76, E.C.R. 1977, 741.

[42] Case 22/70, Commission v. Council (ERTA), E.C.R. 1971, 263. Since the beginning of the 1990s, the Court has restricted the implied powers doctrine in ERTA terms.

Via the Single European Act and the Treaties of Maastricht and Amsterdam, the Community was granted new explicit powers in such areas as the environment, research and technological development, education, culture, public health, consumer protection, industry and employment. However, in most of these new fields of competence, Community powers were not exclusive, but either shared or complementary. *Exclusive Community competences* are those where the Member States can no longer act on their own. This is, for instance, the case with respect to customs duties levied on products imported in the Community from third countries. The common customs tariff (CCT) is established by the Council and the Member States have lost the competence to establish their own customs duties. *Shared* or *mixed competences* fall partly under the authority of the Community and partly under that of the Member States. Antitrust policy constitutes an example. Community antitrust rules determine what constitutes anti-competive behaviour affecting the common market and trade between the Member States. In addition, the Member States each have their own competition rules governing national anti-competitive practices. Finally, there are the *complementary competences* or *supporting measures*. In case of complementary competence, the Member States retain full powers which does, however, not prevent the introduction of assisting and coordinating measures on the European level.[43] The Community is entitled to take supporting measures in such areas as employment, education, culture, industry, research and technological development, public health and development cooperation.

In the policy areas that are not covered by the Community's exclusive competences, the use of Community powers is guided by the subsidiarity principle. Through the subsidiarity provisions of the Treaty of Maastricht, the Member States underlined the need for respect of their national (and regional) identities.[44] The subsidiarity principle was put

---

The Court has notably held that the Member States maintain an external competence where the internal EC provisions determine only minimum standards. This is often the case with harmonisation directives. See Opinion 2/91, E.C.R. 1993, I-1061. As a result, the Community and its Member States often exercise shared or mixed external competences. See David O'Keeffe and Henry G. Schermers (eds.), *Mixed Agreements* (Dordrecht, Kluwer, 1983); Jacques H. J. Bourgeois, Jean-Louis Dewost and Marie-Ange Gaiffe (eds.), *La Communauté Européenne et les Accords Mixtes: Quelles Perspectives?* (Brussels, Presses Interuniversitaires Européennes [P.I.E.], 1997); Allan Rosas, "Mixed Union – Mixed Agreements", in Martti Koskenniemi (ed.), *International Law Aspects of the European Union* (The Hague, Kluwer Law International, 1998), 125.

[43]   The European Convention, "Final Report of Working Group V on Complementary Competencies", CONV 375/1/02, November 4, 2002.

[44]   On the subsidiarity principle, see George A. Bermann, "Taking Subsidiarity Seriously: Federalism in the European Community and the United States", *Columbia Law Review*, 94 (1994) 331; Grainne de Burca, "Proportionality and Subsidiarity as

forward by federal Member States such as Germany and Belgium whose regional entities refused to see their regionalised competences escape to the European level.[45] But the subsidiarity principle was also pushed for very different reasons by the UK's Conservative government. In line with its successful resistance to the explicitly "federal" aspirations of the draft Maastricht Treaty, Prime Ministers Margaret Thatcher and John Major saw subsidiarity as a means to limit the EU's scope of action, in particular in the field of legislative harmonisation of social, consumer and environmental protection. For the UK Conservative governments, the EU's legislative approximation proposals in these areas were an indication of the federalists' desire to create a "European Superstate" that would drive up the cost of doing business, thus decreasing the UK's competitiveness.[46]

As clarified by the Edinburgh European Council of December 1992, the subsidiarity principle covers three distinct legal concepts with strong historical antecedents in the treaties and the case-law of the Court of Justice.[47] Firstly, the principle of attribution of powers means that the EU can only act where given the power to do so, implying that national powers are the rule and that of the EU the exception. Secondly, the principle of subsidiarity in the strict legal sense stipulates that, in areas that do not fall within its exclusive competences, the EU shall take action only if and in so far as the objectives of the proposed action can by reason of scale or effects not be sufficiently achieved by the Member States. Thirdly, the principle of proportionality means that action by the EU shall not go beyond what is necessary to achieve the objectives of the Treaty.[48] Commission President Jacques Santer interpreted the introduc-

---

General Principles of Law", in Ulf Bernitz and Joakim Nergelius (eds.), *General Principles of European Community Law* (The Hague, Kluwer Law International, 2000), 95; Koen Lenaerts and Patrick van Ypersele, "Le Principe de Subsidiarité et son Contexte: Etude de l'Article 3b du Traité CE", *Cahiers de Droit Européen*, 30 (1994) 3; David Millar, John Peterson and Andrew Scott, "Subsidiarity: a "Europe of the Regions" v. the British Constitution", 32 *Journal of Common Market Studies*, 32 (1994) 47; John Peterson, "Subsidiarity: A Definition to Suit Any Vision?", *Parliamentary Affairs*, 47 (1994) 116.

[45] Juliane Kokott, "Federal States in Federal Europe: German Länder and Problems of European Integration", in Antero Jyränki (ed.), *National Constitutions in the Era of Integration* (The Hague, Kluwer Law International, 1999) 175.

[46] United Kingdom, "Growth, Competitiveness and Employment in the European Community", in Commission of the European Communities, *Growth, Competitiveness, Employment. The Challenges and Ways into the 21st Century* (Luxembourg, EC, 1993), Part C, 271.

[47] Edinburgh European Council, "Presidency Conclusions", December 11-12, 1992, paras. 4 and 15.

[48] The Amsterdam Protocol on the application of the principles of subsidiarity and proportionality includes broad guidelines that further clarify the use of both principles. See also The European Convention, "Report of Working Group I on the Principle of

tion of the subsidiarity principle as the signal that his institution needed to slow down the activism that had characterised the term in office of his predecessor Jacques Delors. At the informal meeting of Heads of State or Government at Pörtschach in October 1998, Santer – whose Commission worked under the slogan "legislate less to act better" – underlined that the number of Commission proposals had gone down from 787 in 1990 to 491 in 1998, the number of consultations with both Member States and interested parties before launching new initiatives had been drastically increased, and in 1998 alone the Commission was withdrawing 70 legislative proposals that were deemed no longer necessary.[49]

As stated above, in preparation for the Amsterdam Treaty negotiations, the German Bundesrat and the major political parties in Denmark tried to go further. They pushed a proposal for a better demarcation between EU and national competences through the inclusion of a limitative list of EU powers in the Treaty.[50] The idea was quickly abandoned. For most Member States, a detailed list of EU powers seemed contrary to the changing, ongoing nature of European integration. Not surprisingly, those proposing a limitative list of EU powers also attempted to repeal EC Treaty Article 235. The issue was not pursued at Amsterdam. Already in the preparatory phase, the Reflection Group that had been asked to draft an annotated agenda for the Amsterdam negotiations had stated it was "not in favour of incorporating a catalogue of the Union's powers in the Treaty and would prefer to maintain the present system, which establishes the legal basis for the Union's actions and policies in each individual case". At the same time, the Reflection Group showed itself "in favour of maintaining Article 235 as the instrument for dealing with the changing nature of interpretation of the Union's objectives".[51]

Subsidiarity", CONV 286/02, September 23, 2002. For an analysis of subsidiarity following Amsterdam, see Christian Calliess, *Subsidiaritäts- und Solidaritätsprinzip in der Europäischen Union: Vorgaben für die Anwendung von Art. 5 (ex-Art. 3b) EGV Nach dem Vertrag von Amsterdam* (Baden-Baden, Nomos, 1999); Grainne de Burca, "Reappraising Subsidiarity's Significance after Amsterdam", Harvard Jean Monnet Chair Working Paper Series (1999/07) available in <http://www.law.harvard.edu/Programs/JeanMonnet/papers/99/990701.html>. Compliance with the subsidiarity principle may be subject to scrutiny by the Court of Justice. But this is after-the-event scrutiny. See Grainne de Burca, "The Principle of Subsidiarity and the Court of Justice as an Institutional Actor", *Journal of Common Market Studies*, 36 (1998) 217; A. G. Toth, "Is Subsidiarity Justiciable?", *European Law Review*, 19 (1994) 268.

49 Commission of the European Communities, "Note for the Press: President Santer's Brief for the Informal Meeting of Heads of State and Government at Pörtschach", October, 24-25, 1998.

50 European Parliament Intergovernmental Conference Task Force, "Briefings on the 1996 Intergovernmental Conference", 1996, Volume III, 335.

51 *Reflection Group Report*, para. 125.

One year after the conclusion of the Amsterdam Treaty, under the heavy influence of the German election climate of September 1998, Chancellor Helmut Kohl insisted on putting the competence and subsidiarity debate back on the agenda.[52] In their joint letter to the Cardiff European Council in June 1998, Kohl and French President Jacques Chirac underlined that their objective had "never been ... to build a central European State" and urged their colleagues "to clarify the limits of the competences of the [EU]".[53] Kohl and his Austrian colleague Victor Klima argued explicitly that "[t]he restitution by Brussels of certain powers in the area of national or regional responsibilities should not be a taboo subject".[54]

In light of the Bundesrat's call for a clearer division of responsibilities at the start of the Nice IGC, the Heads of State or Government decided that the question of "how to establish and monitor a more precise delimitation of competences between the European Union and the Member States, reflecting the principle of subsidiarity" would be tackled by the new round of Treaty reform foreseen for 2004.[55] Not surprisingly, "a better division and definition of competence in the European Union" was one of the main themes running through the Laeken Declaration on the future of the European Union.[56]

No matter how the EU will settle the issue of competence allocation, it will be difficult to avoid mixed or shared competences. It is indeed likely there will remain a significant number of policy domains where various levels of government have a role to play.[57] On the one hand, certain policy challenges will continue to require co-ordinated actions to be taken at different levels, for instance the European employment strategy. On the other hand, the increasing interdependence between policy sectors also fosters shared competences. For instance, the need to integrate environmental concerns in other policies brings authorities with responsibility for the environment at various levels of government into spheres related to agriculture, transport and energy.

---

[52] Youri Devuyst, "The Community Method after Amsterdam", *Journal of Common Market Studies*, 37 (1999) 111.

[53] *Agence Europe*, June 9, 1998, 5.

[54] *Agence Europe*, July 1, 1998, 4.

[55] Nice Declaration 23 on the Future of the Union, para. 5.

[56] Laeken European Council, "Presidency Conclusions", December 14-15, 2001, Annex I, 4-5.

[57] Commission of the European Communities, "On 16 March the Commission Organises a Public Hearing on European Governance: Moving Toward a Better Use of Subsidiarity and Proportionality", Press and Communication Service, Memo/01/88, March 15, 2001, 4.

CHAPTER III

Decision-making
in the European Union

I. Between a Supranational Integration Engine and a Co-operation Process driven by the Member States[1]

A. The Origins of the European Commission

To avoid falling back into an intergovernmental deadlock, the ECSC's founders emphasised the need to establish an independent High Authority that would function as the real engine of the integration process.[2] In Jean Monnet's own words:

> The independence of the Authority *vis-à-vis* governments and the sectional interests concerned is the precondition for the emergence of a common point of view which could be taken neither by governments nor by private interests. It is clear that to entrust the Authority to a Committee of governmental delegates or to a Council made up of representatives of governments, employers and workers, would amount to returning to our present methods, those very methods which do not enable us to settle our problems.[3]

The High Authority, consisting of nine independent members appointed by the six Member State Governments, was the ECSC's central supranational decision-making institution. It was the duty of the High Authority to ensure that the objectives set out in the ECSC Treaty were attained. From the very start, however, some Member States insisted on the creation of a Council of Ministers to exercise political control over the High Authority. Belgium and the Netherlands, in particular, feared that the High Authority would be biased towards France and Germany and

---

[1] Christian Lequesne, "La Commission Européenne entre Autonomie et Dépendance", *Revue Française de Science Politique*, 46 (1996) 389.

[2] Dirk Spierenburg and Raymond Poidevin, *The History of the High Authority of the European Coal and Steel Community: Supranationality in Operation* (London, Weidenfeld and Nicholson, 1994).

[3] "Letter from Jean Monnet to Edwin Plowden, 25 May 1950", cited in Peter M. R. Stirk and David Weigall (eds.), *The Origins and Development of European Integration: A Reader and Commentary* (London, Pinter, 1999), 77.

would prevent the Belgian and Dutch governments from reacting appropriately to the specific problems in their coal and steel sectors.[4] The main task of the ECSC Council was to harmonise the action of the High Authority and that of the Governments, which remained responsible for the general economic policies of their countries. After the failure of the supranational European Defence Community (EDC) – which had been designed along the lines of the ECSC – the negotiators of the Rome Treaties establishing the EEC and Euratom obtained an early consensus not to extend the ECSC High Authority's impressive decision-making powers to the EEC and Euratom Commissions.[5] Instead, decision-making was left in the hands of Member State representatives, in the framework of the Council.[6] The Council's decision-making powers were counterbalanced, however, by the Commission's exclusive right of legislative initiative, its implementing powers and its duty to act as the guardian of the Treaties.[7] The basic principle underlying the EEC and Euratom Commissions remained the duty to act in the Community's general interest, in full independence from the governments of the Member States. Defending this duty remains the Commissions main mission in the European Convention. In the Commission's own words: "we must maintain the European Commission in the form intended by the founding fathers of Europe, as an independent institution working for equal treatment between the Member States and embodying the principles of coherence, synthesis and concern for the general interest."[8]

---

[4]   See Hanns Jürgen Kusters, "Die Verhandlungen über das institutionelle System zur Gründung der Europäischen Gemeinschaft für Kohle und Stahl", in Schwabe, *The Beginnings of the Schuman Plan*, 73; Albert Kersten, "A Welcome Surprise? The Netherlands and the Schuman Plan Negotiations", in Schwabe, *The Beginnings of the Schuman Plan,* 285; Milward, *The European Rescue of the Nation State*, 65 and 94. The best general introduction to the balance between the ECSC institutions remains Paul Reuter, *La Communauté du Charbon et de l'Acier* (Paris, LGDJ, 1953).

[5]   Originally, the ECSC High Authority, the EEC Commission and the EAEC Commission coexisted. The Treaty establishing a Single Council and a Single Commission of the European Communities, April 8, 1965, O.J. 152, 1967, 2 [hereinafter Merger Treaty] created one Commission of the European Communities, exercising competences under the three Treaties. On the Commission and its evolution, see Neill Nugent, *The European Commission* (Basingstoke, Palgrave, 2001); Anne Stevens and Handley Stevens, *Brussels Bureaucrats? The Administration of the European Union* (Basingstoke, Palgrave, 2001); Neill Nugent (ed.), *At the Heart of the Union: Studies of the European Commission* (Basingstoke, Macmillan, 1997); Geoffrey Edwards and David Spence (eds.), *The European Commission* (Harlow, Cartermill, 1997).

[6]   Milward, *The European Rescue of the Nation State*, 210 and 216-218.

[7]   Pierre Pescatore, "Les Travaux du Groupe Juridique dans la Négotiation des Traités de Rome", *Studia Diplomatica*, 34 (1981) 168.

[8]   Commission, "Communication on the Institutional Architecture", 4.

B. The Composition and Functioning of the European Commission

Walter Hallstein, the first President of the EEC Commission, described the relationship between the members of his Commission and their home countries as follows:

> no Commissioner could regard himself as the guardian of the interests of his own country, although his colleagues on the Commission naturally looked to him as the most competent and best qualified interpreter of the situation and political circumstances prevailing in his country. The necessity to think and act as "European" Commissioners undoubtedly makes the highest demands on the moral integrity of the members of the Commission. But it is on this point that the survival of a true European Community depends.[9]

Currently, the Commission includes at least one national from each Member State, with a second Commissioner from Germany, France, Italy, Spain and the United Kingdom.[10] During the negotiations of the Treaty of Amsterdam, the Heads of State or Government had – in view of enlargement – agreed on a Protocol whereby the large Member States would renounce to their right to a second Commissioner on condition that a new weighting of the votes in the Council would be agreed to in favour of those large Member States.[11]

At Nice, proposals to reduce the number of Commissioners even further were viewed with suspicion, both by the smaller Member States and the candidate countries.[12] The Finnish Prime Minister feared that by eliminating the link between the college of Commissioners and each Member State, the Commission's legitimacy would be undermined. In his opinion, "one Commissioner per Member State is the only feasible solution at this juncture of EU development. A smaller Commission without a German or a French Commissioner would in effect weaken the Commission, not make it more effective".[13] The Portuguese State Secretary for European Affairs argued that by reducing the number of Commissioners, the Commission would *de facto* be directed at the level of the senior officials where the large Member States are better "represented" than the smaller Member States.[14] For the Austrian Minister for

---

[9] Walter Hallstein, *Europe in the Making* (London, Allan & Unwin, 1972), 59.

[10] Consolidated TEC, art. 213(1).

[11] Amsterdam Protocol on the Institutions with the Prospect of Enlargement of the European Union, art. 1.

[12] See Conference of the Representatives of the Governments of the Member States, Contributions from the governments of the candidate countries, CONFER/VAR 3951/00 ff.

[13] Paavo Lipponen, "Address at the College of Europe", Bruges, November 10, 2000, s.p.

[14] *Agence Europe*, November 11, 2000, 6; *European Report*, October 18, 2000, I-7.

Foreign Affairs, it was crucial to keep the information flows between the Commission and each Member State through their direct representation in the college:

> What matters for us, is to have complete information on the ideas of the Commission, on its action and its plans. What is important is that there is somebody within it that understands the situation, the problems and sensitivities at home. This is all the more important with regards to public opinion when the Commission takes unpopular decisions.[15]

In the end, the Treaty of Nice provided that from 2005, the Commission will be composed of one national for each Member State.[16] Once the Union consists of 27 Member States, the number of members of the Commission must be reduced to less than the number of Member States.[17] At that moment, the members of the Commission would be chosen according to a rotation system based on the principle of equality.[18]

With respect to the appointment of the Commission, the Treaty of Nice stipulated that the Commission President shall henceforth be nominated by the Council acting by qualified majority instead of unanimity.[19] In the past, potential Commission Presidents have been blocked by a veto of one Member State.[20] As had already been agreed at Amsterdam, the nomination of the Commission President must be approved by the European Parliament.[21] With regard to the other members of the College of Commissioners, it is up to each Member State to draw up a proposal.[22] In accordance with these proposals, the Council will, by common accord with the nominee for President, adopt the list of persons whom it intends to appoint as members of the Commission.[23] Finally, the entire College of Commissioners will continue to be subjected to a vote of approval by the European Parliament.[24]

---

[15]   *Agence Europe*, January 18, 2001, 3.
[16]   Nice Protocol on the Enlargement of the European Union, art. 4(1).
[17]   *Ibid.*, art. 4(2).
[18]   *Ibid.*
[19]   Treaty of Nice, art. 2(22) amending Consolidated TEC, art. 214(2).
[20]   At the Corfu European Council, June 24-25, 1994, the nomination of Belgian Prime Minister Jean-Luc Dehaene to become Commission President was vetoed by UK Prime Minister John Major.
[21]   Treaty of Nice, art. 2(22) amending Consolidated TEC, art. 214(2).
[22]   *Ibid.*
[23]   *Ibid.* Here too, the Treaty of Nice shifted Council decision-making from unanimity to qualified majority voting.
[24]   *Ibid.*

In order to increase the Commission's political legitimacy, proposals have been made to have the Commission President appointed by the European Council, by the European Parliament or directly elected by the citizens. The Laeken Declaration has put this issue on the agenda for reflection on the future of the EU.[25]

To maintain efficiency in the absence of a significant reduction in the number of its members, the Commission had, in preparation for the Nice negotiations, suggested a reorganisation of its functioning.[26] The Commission proposed in particular a strengthening of the Commission President's powers.[27] The Treaty of Nice confirmed that the Commission works under the political guidance of its President.[28] In addition, the Treaty specified that it is the President who decides on the Commission's internal organisation,[29] allocates responsibilities to the members of the College[30] and appoints Vice-Presidents.[31] The Treaty of Nice also stipulated that Members of the Commission should resign if the President so requests, but only after obtaining the collective approval of the College.[32] When taking office, President Romano Prodi had already insisted that the members of his College would promise to resign on his demand. He wanted to avoid a scenario whereby an entire Commission would have to resign because of the misbehaviour of one of its members. This was the lesson learned following the resignation of the Commission presided by Jacques Santer (1995-1999), triggered by accusations of fraud and nepotism against one Commissioner, former French Prime Minister Edith Cresson.[33] At the same time, the Prodi Commission launched a more

---

[25]   Laeken European Council, "Presidency Conclusions", December 14-15, 2001, Annex I, 6.

[26]   Commission of the European Communities, "Communication from the Commission to the Intergovernmental Conference on the Reform on the Institutions: The Commission's Internal Organisation", COM(2000) 771 final, November 22, 2000, 2.

[27]   *Ibid.*, 5-6.

[28]   Treaty of Nice, art. 2(24) amending Consolidated TEC, art. 217(1). This principle had already been included in the Treaty of Amsterdam.

[29]   Treaty of Nice, art. 2(24) amending Consolidated TEC, art. 217(1).

[30]   *Ibid.*, art. 217(2).

[31]   *Ibid.*, art. 217(3).

[32]   *Ibid.*, art. 217(4).

[33]   On the end of the Santer Commission and its consequences, see Paul Craig, "The Fall and Renewal of the Commission: Accountability, Contract and Administrative Organisation", *European Law Journal*, 6 (2000) 98; Laura Cram, "The Commission", in Laura Cram, Desmond Dinan and Neill Nugent (eds.), *Developments in the European Union* (Basingstoke, Macmillan, 1999), 44; John Peterson, "The Santer Era: the European Commission in Normative, Historical and Theoretical Perspective", *Journal of European Public Policy*, 6 (1999) 46; John Peterson, "The College of Commissioners", in Peterson and Shackleton (eds.), *The Institutions of the European Union*, 71; David Spence, "Plus ça Change, Plus c'est la Même Chose?

comprehensive internal reform, notably designed to improve the Commission's capacity to deal with its growing financial management tasks.[34]

C. The European Commission's Independent Powers under Siege

The Commission's role as the engine of the European integration process is most clearly defined in the Community's legislative process. The Commission alone can propose Community legislation. The Commission's exclusive right to take the legislative initiative serves two purposes. First, it ensures that the starting point for legislative discussions is the general interest of the Community, not that of individual Member States. Second, it helps to protect the smaller Member States against the dominance of the larger Member States which is typical for intergovernmental decision-taking. Whenever the Council wants to deviate from the Commission's proposal it needs unanimity. As Michel Petite has indicated, this last element is still essential to the EU's institutional balance.[35] The exclusive right of initiative would be a mere illusion if Commission proposals could be easily amended without its agreement and participation. In practice, the Commission generally tries to facilitate Council decision-making by qualified majority. At the end of a Council negotiation among the Member States, the Commission often adopts the amended compromise text as its own, thus allowing the Council to vote by qualified majority.[36]

Some Member States have never been enthusiastic about the Commission's independent right of initiative. During the 1960s, French President Charles De Gaulle resented the way in which Walter Hallstein operated autonomously as if he was the head of an embryonic European Government.[37] Upon De Gaulle's insistence, the Luxembourg Com-

---

Attempting to Reform the European Commission", *Journal of European Public Policy*, 7 (2000) 1.

[34] David O'Sullivan, "La Réforme de la Commission Européenne", *Revue du Droit de l'Union Européenne* (2000/4) 723.

[35] Michel Petite, "Avis de Temps Calme sur l'Art. 189 A Paragraphe 1: Point d'Equilibre entre le Droit d'Initiative de la Commission et le Pouvoir Décisionnel du Conseil, *Revue du Droit de l'Union Européenne* (1998/3), 197.

[36] In the few cases that the Commission has made qualified majority voting impossible by refusing to accept a compromise in the Council as its own, the Commission's motive was (1) to protect a minorisation of the countries with the heaviest economic interest in a dossier; (2) to avoid the lack of coherence with an already established policy; and (3) to avoid the lack of compatibility with a general Treaty principle. See Petite, "Avis de Temps Calme", 197.

[37] See in particular Charles De Gaulle, *Mémoires d'Espoir. Le Renouveau, 1958-1962* (Paris, Plon, 1970) 195.

promise of 1966 stated that "[b]efore adopting any particularly important proposal, it is desirable that the Commission should take up the appropriate contacts with the Governments of the Member States".[38]

More recently, the Commission's institutional position has been affected by three developments: the creation of the co-decision procedure by the Treaty of Maastricht; the expansion of the comitology process; and the establishment of specialised agencies outside the Commission.

The co-decision procedure – which has now turned the European Parliament into an equal legislative partner of the Council – has perhaps not been helpful to the Commission's central position in EC law-creation. As the Parliament's *Activity Report* on co-decision underlines, "Parliament is now in direct contact with the Council and no longer needs the mediation and filtering role the Commission played in the past to communicate with the Council".[39] While the Commission is still present at all conciliation meetings and is often requested by the other institutions to help reconcile conflicting positions, one privileged observer of conciliation practice has observed that "the Commission sometimes feels in a clear position of inferiority, whereas the other two institutions enjoy an increased sense of solidarity which in turn serves to improve the chances of an agreement being found".[40] It must be added that during the co-decision's conciliation phase between Council and Parliament, the Commission has lost the possibility of preventing a qualified majority vote in the Council even if a compromise text deviates substantially from the Commission's original proposal.[41]

With regard to the Commission's implementing tasks, the Member States have gradually established a strict consultation and control mechanism. The Treaty of Rome specified that the Commission would exercise the powers conferred on it by the Council for the implementation of the

---

[38] Bull. EEC, 3 – 1966, 8. See also Miriam Camps, *European Unification in the Sixties: From the Veto to the Crisis* (New York, McGraw-Hill, 1966); Hans von der Groeben, *The European Community. The Formative Years. The Struggle to Establish the Common Market and the Political Union 1958-66* (Luxembourg, EC, 1987); John Lambert, "The Constitutional Crisis, 1965-66", *Journal of Common Market Studies*, 4 (1966) 205.

[39] Nicole Fontaine, Renzo Imbeni, Joseph Verdi i Aldea, "Codecision Procedure under Article 189b of the Treaty of Maastricht. Activity Report of the Delegations to the Conciliation Committee, November 1, 1993 – April 30, 1999. From Entry into force of the Treaty of Maastricht to Entry into Force of the Treaty of Amsterdam", European Parliament, Delegations to the Conciliation Committee, 1999, 12.

[40] Michael Shackleton, "The Politics of Codecision", *Journal of Common Market Studies*, 38 (2000) 336.

[41] This constitutes a formal Treaty exception to the rule that the Council can only change Commission proposals by unanimity.

rules laid down by the latter.[42] In 1962, when delegating implementing powers to the Commission in the agricultural field, the Council devised the so-called comitology process, i.e. it established committees composed of national officials to be consulted by the Commission before it could take the necessary implementing decisions. By December 2001, the total number of such committees had grown to 244.[43] In 1986, while negotiating the Single European Act, the Member States made a point of strengthening their position in the implementation of Community law. They explicitly stipulated that the Council may impose certain requirements when delegating implementing powers to the Commission or may even reserve the right to exercise directly implementing powers itself.[44] It seemed that the Member States wanted to ensure that the Internal Market project, which involved the adoption of around 280 directives, would not lead to an exponential expansion of the Commission's executive powers.[45] In fact, the first legal measure to be adopted under the Single European Act's provisions was the Council's Comitology Decision of 1987, structuring the exercise of implementing powers conferred on the Commission.[46] In practice, three groups of Member State committees (advisory, management and regulatory) exercise surveillance on the Commission's executive powers.[47] The comitology procedure has been

---

[42] Consolidated TEC, art. 211.

[43] Commission of the European Communities, "Report on the Working of the Committees during 2000", COM (2001) 783 final, December 20, 2001, 8. In 2000, the total number of consultations which the Commission has put on the agenda of one of the 244 committees was 4,323. The largest number of consultations in 2000 concerned agriculture (1,889) followed by customs union questions (512) and health and consumer protection (449).

[44] Consolidated TEC, art 202.

[45] Jean de Ruyt, L'Acte Unique Européen (Brussels, Ed. de l'Université de Bruxelles, 1989), 140; Claude Blumann, "Le Pouvoir Exécutif de la Commission à la lumière de l'Acte Unique Européen", Revue Trimestrielle de Droit Européen, 1 (1988) 23.

[46] "Council Decision 87/373 of 13 July 1987 Laying Down the Procedures for the Exercise of Implementing Powers Conferred on the Commission", O.J. L 197, 1987, 33.

[47] For the currently applicable Comitology rules, see "Council Decision 1999/468/EC of 28 June 1999 laying down the procedures for the exercise of implementing powers conferred on the Commission", O.J. L 184, 1999, 23. On the Comitology process, see Mads Andenas and Alexander Türk (eds.), Delegated Legislation and the Role of Committees in the EC (The Hague, Kluwer Law International, 2000); Thomas Christiansen and Emil J. Kirchner (eds.), Committee Governance in the European Union (Manchester, Manchester University Press, 2000); Christian Joerges and Ellen Vos (eds.), EU Committees. Social Regulation, Law & Politics (Oxford, Hart, 1999); Robin H. Pedler and Günter F. Schaefer (eds.), Shaping European Law and Policy: The Role of Committees and Comitology in the Political Process (Maastricht, European Institute of Public Administration, 1996); Kieran Bradley, "Comitology and the Law: Through a Glass, Darkly", Common Market Law Review, 29 (1992) 693; Michelle Egan and Dieter Wolf, "Regulation and Comitology: The EC Committee

the subject of severe criticism. The Committee of Independent Experts that examined mismanagement in the Santer Commission was particularly clear in this respect:

> [T]he pro-integration perspective of the Commission tends to create tensions with the intergovernmental perspective of the Council. These have led the Council to strengthen its own position ... through the creation of an array of committees allowing ... the representatives of the Member States an opportunity to exercise a high level of monitoring and supervision over the management of programmes by the Commission ... [I]n practice, they tend to be a mechanism through which national interests are represented in the implementation of Community policies, sometimes to the extent that they become a forum for "dividing up the spoils" of Community expenditure and permit the Member States, at times, to use their influence in programme management committees to ensure that contractors from each Member State obtain a "fair share" of the overall funding available.[48]

Another challenge to the Commission's executive powers is the creation of specialised agencies charged with the implementation of particular EU's tasks.[49] Since the mid-1990s, several Member States host one or more of these European agencies.[50] Their institutional set-up generally allows the Member States to keep a direct control over the work per-

---

System in Regulatory Perspective", *Columbia Journal of European Law*, 4 (1998) 499; Koen Lenaerts and Amaryllis Verhoeven, "Towards a Legal Framework for Executive Rule-making in the EU? The Contribution of the New Comitology Decision", *Common Market Law Review*, 37 (2000) 645.

[48] Committee of Independent Experts, "Second Report on Reform of the Commission. Analysis of Current Practice and Proposals for Tackling Mismanagement, Irregularities and Fraud", September 10, 1999, paras. 7.15.3 and 7.15.12.

[49] These Community agencies include the European Centre for the Development of Vocational Training (Thessaloniki), the European Foundation for the Improvement of Living and Working Conditions (Dublin), the European Environment Agency (Copenhagen), the European Agency for the Evaluation of Medicinal Products (London), the Office for Harmonisation of the Internal Market (Alicante), the European Training Foundation (Turin), the European Monitoring Centre for Drugs and Drug Addiction (Lisbon), the Community Plant Variety Office (Angers), the European Agency for Health and Safety at Work (Bilbao), the Translation Centre for the Bodies of the European Union (Luxembourg), the European Monitoring Centre on Racism and Xenophobia (Vienna) and the European Agency for Reconstruction (Thessaloniki). Pending overall agreement on the seats of a number of new agencies, the Laeken European Council, in December 2001, decided that the Food Authority and Eurojust would be able to begin operations in Brussels and The Hague respectively.

[50] See "Decision taken by common agreement between the Representatives of the Governments of the Member States, meeting at Head of State and Government level, on the location of the seats of certain bodies and departments of the European Communities and of Europol", Brussels European Council, "Presidency Conclusions", October 29, 1993, Annex II.

formed.[51] Each agency functions under the authority of an administrative or management board that, in addition to a representative from the Commission, always includes representatives from the administrations of all Member States.[52] Agency boards may also include members appointed by the European Parliament or representatives of industry. In preparation for the Amsterdam negotiations, a German proposal for the creation of a new European Competition Agency was successfully dismissed by the Commission as another attempt to cut its wings.[53]

At the Laeken European Council, the Heads of State or Government failed to reach an agreement on the seats of a whole series of new agencies. Italian Prime Minister Silvio Berlusconi, in particular, insisted without success on imposing Parma as the seat of the Food Agency while the Presidency had proposed Helsinki. Berlusconi emphasised that he considered the seat of the Food Authority as a matter of "national interest". The beauty of the building where the agency would be located and the quality of Parma ham were in themselves two major arguments in favour of Parma, he claimed.[54]

D. The European Council as the Intergovernmental Engine of the Co-operation Process

The discussion on the establishment of the Food Agency is an illustration of the recent functioning of the European Council. The European Council brings together the Heads of State or Government of the Member States and the President of the European Commission.[55] Since the Treaty of Maastricht, the European Council has been institutionalised as the body that "shall provide the Union with the necessary impetus for its development and ... define the general political guidelines thereof".[56] The

---

[51] On the agencies see, Eduardo Chiti, "The Emergence of a Community Administration: The Case of European Agencies", *Common Market Law Review*, 37 (2000) 309; Giandomenico Majone, "Functional Interests: European Agencies", in Peterson and Shackleton (eds.), *The Institutions of the European Union*, 299; Ellen Vos, "Reforming the European Commission: What Role to Play for EU Agencies?", *Common Market Law Review*, 37 (2000) 1113.

[52] The Translation Centre for the Bodies of the European Union forms an exception. Its board includes representatives of the bodies that use the Centre.

[53] Commission of the European Communities, "IGC 1996: Should a European Competition Agency be Created?", Background Paper for the Press, 1996. See also Stephen Wilks and Lee McGowan, "Disarming the Commission: The Debate over a European Cartel Office", *Journal of Common Market Studies*, 33 (1995) 259.

[54] *Agence Europe*, December 16, 2001, 6.

[55] Consolidated TEU, art. 4.

[56] *Ibid.*

European Council was not foreseen by the Treaties of Paris and Rome.[57] In 1961, the first summit of Heads of State or Government took place in Paris at the initiative of French President Charles De Gaulle. As a strong opponent to the Community method, General De Gaulle held the view that only the highest representatives of the Member States possessed the necessary legitimacy to determine the future course of European co-operation. According to his draft Treaty for a Union of States (also known as the Fouchet plan), the Council would meet three times a year at the level of the Heads of State or Government to set the general policy lines of the Union.[58] While the Fouchet plan was formally rejected, the current EU structure nevertheless reflects the plan's main traits.[59] This is particularly true with respect to the role of the Heads of State or Government. In December 1974, the Heads of State or Government, on the initiative of French President Valéry Giscard d'Estaing and German Chancellor Helmut Schmidt, decided to replace their irregular Summits with more formal European Council sessions. The European Council's existence was given legal recognition in the Single European Act of 1986. The European Council's political process has traditionally func-tioned by consensus and could therefore be easily blocked.

During European Council sessions, the Heads of State or Government and the President of the Commission are assisted by the Ministers of Foreign Affairs and by a Member of the Commission.[60] Furthermore, the President of the European Council invites the Finance Ministers to parti-cipate when the European Council is discussing matters relating to eco-nomic and monetary union.[61] In practice, the Ministers of Finance are often present at European Council meetings. Participation of the Mini-sters of Social Affairs and Employment, on the contrary, is not foreseen. This has given rise to critical comments. Whenever socio-economic questions are on the agenda of the European Council, the Finance

---

[57] On the European Council, see Philippe de Schoutheete, "The European Council", in Peterson and Shackleton (eds.), *The Institutions of the European Union*, 21; Horst Reichenbach, Thea Emmerling, Dirk Staudenmayer and Sönke Schmidt, *Integration: Wanderung über Europäische Gipfel* (Baden-Baden, Nomos, 1999); Mary Troy Johnston, *The European Council: Gatekeeper of the European Community* (Boulder, Westview Press, 1994); Jan Werts, *The European Council* (Amsterdam, North-Holland, 1992); Simon Bulmer and Wolfgang Wessels, *The European Council. Decision-Making in European Politics* (Basingstoke, Macmillan, 1987).

[58] On the Fouchet Plan, see Robert Bloes, *Le Plan Fouchet et le Problème de l'Europe Politique* (Bruges, College of Europe, 1970); Edmond Jouve, *Le Général de Gaulle et la Construction de l'Europe (1940-1966)* (Paris, LGDJ, 1967), 316.

[59] See C. W. A. Timmermans, "The Uneasy Relationship between the Communities and the Second Pillar: Back to the 'Plan Fouchet'?", *Legal Issues of European Integra-tion* (1996) 61.

[60] Consolidated TEU, art. 4.

[61] Declaration 4 annexed to the Maastricht Final Act.

Ministers are able to directly influence the EU's course of action, whereas the Ministers of Social Affairs are kept outside the meeting room.

History-making decisions such as Treaty reform and the accession of new Member States start and end in the framework of the European Council. It also defines the principles of the CFSP and decides on the framing of a common defence policy.[62] Furthermore, the European Council discusses annually the broad guidelines of the economic policies of the Member States as well as the employment situation in the Community.[63] The Treaty also foresees the possibility to refer requests for the creation of enhanced co-operation for discussion to the European Council.[64] In addition, the Heads of State or Government are responsible for confirming which Member States fulfil the necessary conditions for the adoption of the single currency. They are also in charge of determining whether there exists a serious and persistent breach by a Member State of the fundamental principles on which the EU is founded.[65] In practice, the European Council's role goes well beyond these tasks assigned to it by the Treaty. The Heads of State or Government have gradually become directly involved in all important questions on the agenda of the EU.

The terrorist attacks of September 11, 2001 in New York and Washington, D.C. have been used by the Heads of State or Government to reinforce their institutional position further. Traditionally, Presidency conclusions of European Council meetings have included "recommendations" and "requests" to the Community institutions. The Extraordinary European Council of September 21, 2001, however, "directs" and "instructs" the Justice and Home Affairs Council to take a number of specific measures in reply to the terrorist attacks.[66] The language of the Extraordinary European Council leaves no doubt that the Heads of State or Government see themselves as the top of the EU's hierarchical decision-making structure, able to give instructions to the other institutions.

The Seville European Council of June 2002 further strengthened the European Council's leadership role. Starting in December 2003, the European Council shall adopt a multiannual strategic programme for the

---

[62] Consolidated TEU, arts. 13 and 17.

[63] Consolidated TEC, arts. 99(2) and 128(1).

[64] Consolidated TEU, arts. 23(2) and 40(2) and Consolidated TEC, art. 11(2). The Treaty of Nice, arts. 1(9) and 2(1) amended respectively Consolidated TEU, art. 40(2) and Consolidated TEC, art. 11(2).

[65] Consolidated TEU, art. 7(1) and Consolidated TEC, art. 121(4).

[66] Extraordinary Brussels European Council, "Conclusions and Plan of Action", September 21, 2001, 2. See also Ferdinando Riccardi, "A Look Behind the News", *Agence Europe*, September 27, 2001, 2.

three years to come.[67] In addition, the Seville European Council decided that the European Council's agenda would henceforth make a distinction between (1) items to be approved or endorsed without debate; (2) items for discussion but not intended to be the subject of conclusions; (3) items for discussion with a view to defining general political guidelines; and (4) items for discussion with a view to adopting a decision.[68] Where an item is placed on the agenda of the European Council with a view to adopting a decision, the political conclusions drawn from the positions emerging during the European Council are to be brought to the attention of the Council of Ministers. The Council of Ministers is to consider the implications of those positions for subsequent proceedings, in accordance with the applicable Treaty provisions. This procedure was established in the context of enlargement and for use in exceptional cases.[69] Its concrete implications remain far from clear. It seems, however, that this part of the Seville conclusions was inspired by a joint letter from British Prime Minister Tony Blair and German Chancellor Gerhard Schröder.[70] Blair and Schröder notably suggested to move away from systematic decision-taking by consensus in the European Council: "unanimity should only be applied in areas where it is provided for in the Treaties. Decisions referred to the European Council under Treaty bases subject to qualified majority voting should be decided by qualified majority voting. Failure to do so can impede progress in key areas". Jack Straw, the UK's Foreign Secretary had earlier referred to the lack of decision on the sites of the Community agencies at the Laeken European Council: "No one needs a repeat of the unedifying and unproductive stalemate we saw at Laeken. It would be absurd to require 25 or more countries to reach consensus on issues like these".[71]

The creation of the European Council, as a forum allowing Heads of State or Government to discuss the future of European policy, constituted a significant moment in the history of European integration. It would, indeed, have been difficult to imagine the creation of the Euro or the definition of a Common European Security and Defence Policy without the direct involvement of the highest political representatives of the Member States. At the same time, the European Council's dominant role,

---

[67] Seville European Council, "Presidency Conclusions", June 21-22, 2002, Annex II, para. 4.

[68] Seville European Council, "Presidency Conclusions", June 21-22, 2002, Annex I, para. 3.

[69] Seville European Council, "Presidency Conclusions", June 21-22, 2002, Annex I, para. 9.

[70] Gerhard Schröder and Tony Blair, "Reform of the European Council. Joint Letter to Prime Minister Aznar", February 25, 2002.

[71] Jack Straw, "Reforming Europe: New Era, New Questions", The Hague, February 21, 2002.

its intergovernmental nature and consensus practice have raised many questions. As observed by Pierre Pescatore in 1978, merely three years after its creation, the European Council "risked introducing a "ferment" of disintegration in the Community".[72] Pescatore feared that "[t]o the degree it would escape from the rules that guide the functioning of the Community" the European Council would

> accentuate the intergovernmental traits of the construction to the detriment of its integrationist character. The consequences would be grave in every respect: from the point of view of the efficiency of the decision-making process, from the point of view of the maintenance of the equilibrium between the interests of all partners, from the point of view also of the democratisation of the Community ...[73]

One of the problems is that the European Council functions without the Community mechanisms designed to protect the smaller Member States, such as the exlusive right of initiative for the Commission. The Nice European Council underlined this point. The French Presidency's initial proposal at Nice on the reweighting of the votes in the Council, consisting of a tripling of the votes of the larger Member States and a doubling for the smaller Member States, immediately put the latter on the defensive.[74] According to Portuguese Prime Minister Antonio Guterres, this amounted to nothing less than "an institutional *coup d'état* in favour of the big Member States".[75] In a comment made after Nice, Luxembourg's former Minister of Foreign Affairs Jacques Poos made an assessment of the European Council resembling that of Pescatore two decades earlier:

> As the European Council has gained in strength and increased its authority, it has also changed the character of procedures and the institutional balance

---

[72] Pescatore, "L'Executif Communautaire", 401 (translation from French by the author). Pierre Pescatore was one of the negotiators of the Treaties of Rome, representing Luxembourg, and later became a judge at the European Court of Justice. Not everyone agrees with his assessment. Jacques Delors (*Agence Europe*, September 16, 1999, 5) believes that the European Council "is well integrated in the Community architecture" and plays a useful role. C. W. A. Timmermans ("The Uneasy Relationship between the Communities and the Second Pillar", 61) points out that "without a European Council it would have even been more difficult for the Community system in the daily struggle against vested national interests preferring to be voiced through the intergovernmental bargaining process and intrinsically allergic to the supranational method". Timmermans also recalls that the creation of the European Council was a concession to the French government in order to obtain its agreement to direct elections for the European Parliament.

[73] Pescatore, "L'Executif Communautaire", 401 (the author's translation).

[74] *European Report*, December 13, 2000, I-5.

[75] *Ibid.*

of power: intergovernmental procedures and secret diplomacy have come back in through the front door.[76]

In a perceptive comment in *Agence Europe*, Ferdinando Riccardi expressed a more nuanced, but not less critical view on the ambivalent nature of the European Council after Nice:

> the increasingly pre-eminent role of the European Council is both salutary and dangerous. Salutary, because the Heads of State and Government have indisputable democratic legitimacy, are "visible" to the public and may provide the EU with the political impetus it needs. Dangerous, because the European Council could slide towards a "G8"-type mechanism, in which some essential elements of a Community are lacking: the largest powers dominate, and no independent institution prepares decisions basing itself on the "general interest", nor manages the follow-up to directions decided upon. To slide along that path would be the end of Community Europe.[77]

II. Between Decision-making Efficiency and the Unanimity Trap

Early attempts to create organisations for European unity after World War II failed to overcome the traditional intergovernmental deadlock caused by unanimous decision-taking. In the framework of the Organisation for European Economic Co-operation and the Council of Europe, the United Kingdom and the Scandinavian countries refused to give up their right to veto decisions of any importance. In the words of a disillusioned Belgian Minister of Foreign Affairs Paul-Henri Spaak, "unanimity formulae [proved to be] the formulae of impotence".[78] For Spaak, who chaired the conference leading to the Treaty of Rome establishing the EEC in 1957, the success of European integration would largely depend on the willingness of the participants to leave ancient notions of sovereignty behind and accept the principle of majority voting in the EEC's Council of Ministers.[79] The Council was devised as the EEC's main decision-making body. It was composed of a representative of each Member State at ministerial level who could commit the government of that Member State.

The EEC Treaty stipulated that from January 1966 the transitional unanimity rule would give way to qualified majority voting in a limited number of policy fields. According to Walter Hallstein, the German

---

[76] Jacques Poos, "Report on Reform of the Council", European Parliament Session Document, September 17, 2001, 12.

[77] Ferdinando Riccardi, "A Look Behind the News", *Agence Europe*, March 7, 2001, 3.

[78] Paul-Henri Spaak, "Document 52: Il n'y a plus un moment à perdre si nous voulons nous sauver (11 décembre 1951)", in Smets (ed.), *La Pensée Européenne*, 283 (the author's translation).

[79] Spaak, *Combats Inachevés,* Vol. II, 97-98.

negotiator of the EEC Treaty and later the first President of the EEC Commission, the introduction of qualified majority voting was "basic to the constitution of the Community".[80] In Hallstein's own wording:

> The Council of Ministers ... seems in some ways to resemble that of a classical international organisation, but in one important respect it represents an advance beyond this stage. The principle of majority voting is employed by the Community for its regular proceedings; the rule of unanimity, which was one of the stumbling blocks of previous experiments, is here reserved for exceptional cases which bear heavily upon national sovereignty ... Moreover, majority voting becomes more and more the norm for Council decisions as the treaty's transition period progresses. This again is natural ... because as time goes by the Community's sense of solidarity becomes that much greater.[81]

In practice, the introduction of qualified majority voting in the Community system turned out to be much more difficult than expected by the founders. To French President Charles De Gaulle, qualified majority voting in such areas as agriculture proved unacceptable. In order to prevent qualified majority voting from entering into force as foreseen in 1966, De Gaulle brought the Community to a halt by practising a seven month empty chair policy starting in June 1965. For De Gaulle it was inconceivable that France would oppose a decision and still be obliged to carry it out. As explained by his Minister of Foreign Affairs Maurice Couve de Murville,

> how could anyone imagine that one would, without our agreement and *a forteriori* against our will, dispose of our sovereignty? It is also a question of good sense: who could imagine that a policy measure would be made acceptable and applicable in a country that has refused it because it believes it goes against its principles or against its political or economic interests.[82]

The crisis was resolved by the so-called Luxembourg compromise of January 1966: where in the case of decisions which could be taken by qualified majority vote, a Member State would invoke its vital interests, the Council would endeavour to reach solutions that could be adopted by all Members. France, however, added that "where very important interests are at stake, the discussions must be continued until unanimous agreement is reached".[83] While noting that there was a divergence of views on what should be done in the event of a failure to reach unani-

---

[80] Hallstein, *Europe in the Making*, 68.

[81] Walter Hallstein, *United Europe. Challenge and Opportunity* (Cambridge: MA: Harvard University Press, 1962), 23.

[82] Maurice Couve de Murville, *Une Politique Etrangère 1958-1969* (Paris, Plon, 1971), 297 (the author's translation).

[83] Bull. EEC (3-1966) 9.

mous agreement, the Council, in practice, refrained from applying qualified majority voting for two decades.

The pressure to create an Internal European Market by the end of 1992 – characterised by the free movement of goods, persons, services and capital – made a return to qualified majority voting a necessity.[84] In order to bring the Internal Market into being, approximately 280 directives had to be approved. It seemed highly unlikely that this could be achieved under the unanimity rule. The Member States, including the UK under Prime Minister Margaret Thatcher, agreed that the development of the Internal Market necessitated a more effective decision-making system.[85] As a result, the Single European Act of 1986, which had the Internal Market goal as its main provision, explicitly allowed qualified majority voting for the adoption of the Internal Market directives.[86] The scope of qualified majority voting was further expanded by the Treaty of Maastricht of 1992, although several important fields of Community action remained under the unanimity rule.[87]

In preparation for the Treaty of Amsterdam of 1997, the extension of qualified majority voting was again an important item on the agenda. In the context of the enlargement process with the countries of Central and Eastern Europe, the European Commission argued that "the difficulty of arriving at unanimous agreement rises exponentially as the number of Members increases". As "adherence to unanimity would often result in stalemate", the Commission proposed "qualified majority voting [as] the general rule".[88] The obstructive behaviour of UK Prime Minister John Major added another reason to extend majority voting. In protest against the Community embargo on the export of British beef and veal during the BSE crisis, he announced to the House of Commons on May 21, 1996 that his government could not continue to co-operate "normally" in the Community's legislative process as long as there was no agreement on a framework allowing a progressive lifting of the export ban. As a result, the UK reserved its position on virtually all questions requiring unanimity in the Council, leading to the temporary blocking of around

---

[84] de Ruyt, *L'Acte Unique*, 149; SEA, art. 13.

[85] It is interesting to note that French President François Mitterrand and German Chancellor Helmut Kohl had already in 1984 agreed on the necessity to return to the qualified majority voting procedures foreseen in the Treaty of Rome as a way to circumvent Margaret Thatcher's negativism towards further European integration. See Jean Lacouture, *Mitterrand: Une Histoire de Français, Vol. 2: Les Vertiges du Sommet* (Paris, Seuil, 1998), 115.

[86] SEA, arts. 14, 16 and 18.

[87] *The New Treaty on European Union. Vol. 2: Legal and Political Analysis* (Brussels, Belmont European Policy Centre, 1992), 57.

[88] Commission, "Opinion to the Intergovernmental Conference 1996", 21.

60 acts at various Council meetings.[89] In spite of this provocation, the Amsterdam result regarding qualified majority voting was extremely meagre.[90] In the run-up to the Nice IGC, the Commission's position remained largely the same:

> qualified majority voting should be the rule and unanimity the exception ... in the knowledge that unanimity in an enlarged Europe will make decision-making extremely difficult and, in the case of some policies, will mean the end of any serious prospect of deepening European integration.[91]

In February 2000, Austrian FPÖ leader Jörg Haider illustrated the Commission's point by threatening to block EU decision-making if Austria remained isolated following the FPÖ's participation in the coalition government: "If no one sits around the table with us, there will be no decisions taken in Europe. Europe needs our vote," he said.[92] Haider's threat failed to shock the negotiators into action. In quantitative terms, the Nice European Council of December 2000 succeeded in moving to qualified majority voting in about 30 Treaty articles of the 70 still subject to unanimity. However, in the most sensitive areas, Member States blocked the move to qualified majority voting in order to safeguard what they considered as their vital national interests.[93]

Spain, Portugal and Greece wanted to make sure at Nice that they would continue to have a decisive say in the division of the Structural Funds, designed to aid poorer areas, even after the accession of the Central and Eastern European countries. For that purpose, they made certain that qualified majority voting would not come into force until after the adoption of the EU's financial perspectives for the years after 2007. On German insistence, the Treaty of Nice specified that the gradual move towards qualified majority voting on immigration and asylum policy would be possible only after common rules and basic principles have been defined by unanimity. France succeeded in safe-

---

[89]   Gen. Rep. 1996, para. 1031. Agreement on a framework for the lifting of the export embargo was finally reached at the Florence European Council of June 1996. See Florence European Council, "Presidency Conclusions", June 21-22, 1996, para. 8.

[90]   Devuyst, "Treaty Reform in the European Union", 626; Heidi Kaila, "Qualified Majority Voting: The Key to Efficient Decision-Making in an Enlarged Union", in Edward Best, Mark Gray and Alexander Stubb (eds.), *Rethinking the European Union. IGC 2000 and Beyond* (Maastricht, European Institute of Public Administration, 2000), 131.

[91]   Commission, "Europe and the Challenge of Enlargement", 22.

[92]   Nigel Glass and Martin Fletcher, "Haider Threatens to Paralyse EU", *The Times*, February 5, 2000; Denis Staunton, "Haider Threatens Anti-EU Revolt", *The Observer*, February 6, 2000.

[93]   For a good overview of the positions of the Member States on qualified majority voting at Nice, see *European Report*, October 18, 2000, I-6; *European Report*, December 6, 2000, I-3; *European Report*, December 2000, I-5.

guarding unanimity with respect to external trade in cultural and audio-visual services, as well as educational services and social and human health services. It thus ensured the possibility to block any international trade agreement that could be seen as a threat to the French "cultural exception". Perhaps most significant at Nice was the lack of movement towards qualified majority voting with respect to taxation and social security. In a statement reflecting the spirit of the negotiators, British Prime Minister Tony Blair declared: "We have maintained our right to veto over taxation and social security. We have renounced nothing to which we did not want to renounce".[94]

III. Between Sovereign Equality, Avoiding Dominance and Demographic Reality

Two basic principles stand at the centre of the Council's original decision-making system: (1) the equality between France and Germany; and (2) the avoidance of dominance of the larger over the smaller Member States. In the 1950s, the founders of the Communities aimed at creating a suitable climate for Franco-German reconciliation in a framework that would also be congenial for the smaller Benelux countries (Belgium, the Netherlands and Luxembourg). To achieve this, the founders set up a delicate institutional system that aimed at preventing a return to the power politics of the inter-war period. The first element of this construction was the principle of equality in Franco-German institutional relations. Historically, the principle goes back to April 4, 1951 when Jean Monnet made the following declaration to German Chancellor Konrad Adenauer

> I have been authorised [by the French government] to propose to you that relations between France and Germany in the European Community be based on the principle of equality in the Council, the Assembly, and all future or existing institutions ... The spirit of discrimination has been the cause of the world's greatest ills, and the Community is an attempt to overcome it.[95]

Chancellor Adenauer, who was looking for ways to rehabilitate his country after World War II, immediately replied positively. The Monnet declaration has remained the cornerstone of Franco-German institutional relations in the European framework ever since. As a result, France and Germany have traditionally received equal numbers of votes in the Council of Ministers and equal numbers of seats in the various Com-

---

[94] *Agence Europe*, December 12, 2000, 8. The UK was backed by Luxembourg, Ireland and Sweden.

[95] Monnet, *Mémoires*, 414. For the translation and the current significance of this declaration, see Pascal Fontaine, *A New Idea for Europe. The Schuman Declaration 1950-2000* (Luxembourg: EC, 2000), 20.

munity institutions and bodies. The first exception to this rule was made at the Edinburgh European Council, in December 1992. Following its reunification in 1990, Germany (with 80 million inhabitants, including 17 million East Germans) was allocated 99 seats in the European Parliament. France, Italy and the United Kingdom (each having approximately 57 million inhabitants at that time) were granted 87 seats.[96] France could accept that Germany's increased population weight would be reflected in the composition of the European Parliament. But during the Amsterdam negotiations, it blocked a proposal that would have given Germany a greater weight in the Council. France continued to reject similar proposals during the negotiations of the Treaty of Nice.

In addition to the equality between France and Germany, the Communities were also built on mechanisms to prevent the dominance by the larger over the smaller Member States. In the words of Christopher Tugendhat, a former Vice-President of the European Commission:

> In the Community, a system of rules, obligations and procedures of a detailed kind was laid down and has since been further developed to guarantee that ... reconciliation between the larger ones will not be at the expense of the smaller.[97]

As far as the Council of Ministers was concerned, this implied the introduction of a weighting of the votes of each Member State whereby the smaller Member States have traditionally been allocated a relatively higher share votes than the larger Member States.[98] Currently, Belgium with ten million inhabitants has five votes. Germany with its 82 million inhabitants has only ten votes. During the Amsterdam negotiations, France in particular argued that, following the accession of several smaller Member States, the original distribution of Council votes had caused an exaggerated over-representation of the smaller countries.[99]

In its opinion for the IGC 2000, the European Commission recommended adopting a straight forward system of double simple majority: a decision would stand adopted after having obtained the support of a

---

[96] Edinburgh European Council, "Presidency Conclusions", December 11-12, 1992, para. 26.

[97] Christopher Tugendhat, *Making Sense of Europe* (Harmondsworth, Viking, 1986), 36.

[98] According to Consolidated TEC, art. 205(2), where the Council is required to act by qualified majority, the votes of its members shall be weighted as follows: Belgium 5; Denmark 3; Germany 10; Greece 5; Spain 8; France 10; Ireland 3; Italy 10; Luxembourg 2; the Netherlands 5; Austria 4; Portugal 5; Finland 3; Sweden 4; the United Kingdom 10.

[99] This resulted in the Amsterdam Protocol on the Institutions with the Prospect of Enlargement of the European Union, art. 1.

simple majority of Member States and a simple majority of the EU's total population.[100] This system would have the advantage of simplicity and transparency. Moreover, it would not have to be modified with each new accession. While a majority of the smaller Member States supported the Commission's proposal, the larger Member States were in favour of a reweighting of the votes.[101] As stated above, for France, it was essential to maintain parity with Germany. Spain insisted that it should continue to represent a significant number of votes, allowing it to block decisions together with two large countries. The Netherlands fought for a larger number of votes than its Benelux partner Belgium, to reflect the six million population difference. Belgium could accept being granted fewer votes than the Netherlands, but only if the logic of a true differentiation according to population was also introduced between Germany, France, Italy and the United Kingdom. Furthermore, Belgium also insisted on an equal treatment of current Member States and the candidate countries. In the original French Presidency proposal at Nice, the future Member States had been allocated less votes than comparable current Member States.

In the end, the Nice European Council arrived at a complex political compromise that failed to follow any particular logic.[102] The new system is designed to enter into force in January 2005. The largest Member States (Germany, United Kingdom, France, Italy) go from 10 to 29 votes. Thus, France succeeded in maintaining parity with Germany. Spain, while totalling 20 million inhabitants less than France, the United Kingdom and Italy, nevertheless received 27 votes. Smaller middle-sized countries (like Greece, Belgium and Portugal) went from 5 to 12 votes. The Netherlands managed to get one vote more: 13. In an EU with 15 Member States, this would bring the total number of votes in the Council to 237. The qualified majority threshold was set at 169.

The Treaty of Nice also added two new requirements to the qualified majority threshold. First, Council decisions based on a Commission proposal require the backing of at least a majority of the members. In other cases, the qualified majority requires the support of at least two thirds of the members. Second, any member of the Council is able to

---

[100] Commission, "Adapting the Institutions", 32.

[101] For an overview of this discussion, see *European Report*, October 18, 2000, I-6-7; *European Report*, December 6, 2000, I-3; *European Report*, December 13, 2000, I-5-6.

[102] Nice Protocol on Enlargement of the European Union, art. 3: Germany 29 votes (82 million inhabitants); United Kingdom 29 (59 million); France 29 (59 million); Italy 29 (58 million); Spain 27 (39 million); Netherlands 13 (16 million); Greece 12 (11 million); Belgium 12 votes (10 million); Portugal 12 (10 million); Sweden 10 (9 million); Austria 10 (8 million); Denmark 7 (5 million); Finland 7 (5 million); Ireland 7 (4 million); Luxembourg 4 (400,000 thousand).

request verification that the qualified majority comprises at least 62% of the total population of the Union. Should that condition not be met, the decision is not adopted. This population criterion aims at making the qualified majority without the support of the larger Member States more difficult than before. In fact, it also grants a greater weight to the German vote than to that of any other Member State.[103]

In a Declaration to the Nice Final Act, the Heads of State or Government also fixed the number of votes for the applicant countries.[104] In addition, they decided that the qualified majority threshold will increase steadily to 73.4% maximum in a Union of 26 Member States (whereas it currently stands at 71.3%).[105] When the number of Member States reaches 27, the qualified majority threshold will further increase to 73.9%.

The amendments made at Nice to the qualified majority requirements have been criticised from the point of view of decision-making efficiency.[106] In the words of Richard Corbett, a member of the European Parliament, this outcome

> represents a step backward and is arguably worse than the *status quo* ... It introduces a triple threshold: number of states, population, and the percentage of the votes set at a higher level than is the case at the moment. At the moment it is 71% of the votes. That is already very high. It was set high to make sure that under any permutation such a qualified majority represented a majority of the population. Now that we have a population criterion in there anyway, it should have been possible to lower the threshold in terms of the number of votes. Instead it seems that it has been raised ... that is a very worrying situation.[107]

---

[103] On the outcome of the Nice negotiations on voting rules in the Council, see Axel Moberg, "The Nice Treaty and Voting Rules in the Council", *Journal of Common Market Studies*, 40 (2002) 259; George Tsebelis and Xenophon Yataganas, "Veto Players and Decision-Making in the EU After Nice", *Journal of Common Market Studies*, 40 (2002) 283.

[104] Nice Declaration 20 on the enlargement of the European Union: Poland 27 votes (39 million inhabitants); Romania 14 (22 million); Czech Republic 12 (10 million); Hungary 12 (10 million); Bulgaria 10 (8 million); Slovakia 7 (5 million); Lithuania 7 (4 million); Latvia 4 (2 million); Slovenia 4 (2 million); Estonia 4 (1.5 million); Cyprus 4 (750,000); Malta 3 (380,000).

[105] Nice Declaration 21 on the qualified majority threshold and the number of votes for blocking minority in an enlarged Union.

[106] Richard Baldwin, Erik Berglöf, Francesco Giavazzi and Mika Widgrén, *Nice Try: Should the Treaty of Nice be Ratified?* (London, Centre for Economic Policy Research, 2001).

[107] European Parliament, Verbatim Report of the Plenary Sitting of December 12, 2000, 52-53.

The representatives of the European Parliament at the IGC 2000, Elmar Brok and Dimitrios Tsatsos, were equally sharp:

> in general terms the cumulative nature of the various hurdles makes blocking minorities easier to achieve, thereby increasing the likelihood of proposals being thwarted in future by destructive minorities. Moreover, the new system is complicated and lacking in transparency ...[108]

IV. Between a Centralist and a Centrifugal Decision-making System in the Council

The EU's core decision-making centre is still the Council. It consists of a representative of each Member State at ministerial level. The Council is a key player in the Community's legislative process, but it also has an executive role, in particular in the EU's more intergovernmental pillars. The Council's working methods have undergone substantial change since the Community's early days.[109] Although the Merger Treaty created only one single Council for the three Communities,[110] a differentiation in specialised Council groupings has taken place from the outset.

In the early years, specialised Council configurations included Foreign Affairs (General Affairs); Agriculture; and Economic and Financial Affairs (Ecofin). Over time, other specialised configurations have been added. At the Seville European Council of June 2002, it was decided to limit the number of Council configurations to nine: General Affairs and External Relations; Economic and Financial Affairs; Justice and Home Affairs; Employment, Social Policy, Health and Consumer Affairs; Competitiveness (Internal Market, Industry and Research); Transport, Telecommunications and Energy; Agriculture and Fisheries; Environment; and Education, Youth and Culture.[111]

The number of actual Council sessions appears to have stabilised at 80 to 90 per year.[112] In spite of the nine configurations, the Council has remained legally one. This implies that there is no hierarchy between the

---

[108] Elmar Brok and Dimitrios Tsatsos, "Overview of the Results of the Intergovernmental Conference", European Parliament, December 19, 2000, 2.

[109] On the functioning of the Council, see Fiona Hayes-Renshaw and Helen Wallace, *The Council of Ministers* (Basingstoke, Macmillan, 1997); Philippa Sherrington, *The Council of Ministers: Political Authority in the European Union* (London, Pinter, 2000); Martin Westlake, *The Council of the European Union* (London, Cartermill, 1999).

[110] Merger Treaty, art. 1.

[111] Seville European Council, "Presidency Conclusions", June 21-22, 2002, Annex II, para. 3.

[112] Report from the Secretary General of the Council to the European Council, "Preparing the Council for Enlargement", June 7, 2001, 10.

Council's different compositions and also that an act on any subject can be adopted by the Council in any composition.

A. The Co-ordination of Council Activities

In order to ensure a minimal level of co-ordination between the different Council groupings, the Ministers of Foreign Affairs have been given a horizontal responsibility to ensure coherence in the integration process. This horizontal function was recognised at the Paris Summit of 1974[113] and in the Stuttgart Solemn Declaration of 1983.[114] The Treaty also provides that the Ministers of Foreign Affairs shall assist the Heads of State or Government at the European Council.[115] While the functional need for a ministerial forum ensuring co-ordination, consistency and arbitration has been repeated several times, there seems to be a general recognition that the General Affairs Council has not adequately fulfilled this role.[116] Several reasons have been advanced.[117] First, Community activities are increasingly related to a variety of domestic policy fields that are not the natural area of competence for Ministers of Foreign Affairs. Second, within their own governments, Ministers of Foreign Affairs do not enjoy political authority over the other Ministers, thus making it difficult for them to co-ordinate and arbitrate in the area of their colleagues at European level. Third, in the external relations field the Ministers of Foreign Affairs have a heavy schedule on their own, leaving little time for general affairs. Fourth, there is the increasing role of the Ecofin Council.

The Ecofin Council is notably responsible for monitoring Member States' economic and budgetary policies and is able to penalise a Member State in the event of an excessive budget deficit. In practice, the Ecofin Council has also been acting as the arbiter in matters with significant implications for the EU's budget. Furthermore, Maastricht's Final Act explicitly foresaw that the Finance Ministers shall be invited to

---

[113] "In order to ensure consistency in Community activities and continuity of work, the Ministers of Foreign Affairs, meeting in the Council of the Community, will act as initiators and coordinators." Bull. EC 12-1974, para. 1104.

[114] "The consistency and continuity of the work needed for the further construction of European Union as well as the preparation of meetings of the European Council are the responsibility of the Council (General Affairs) and its members." Bull. EC 6-1983, para. 2.2.1.

[115] Consolidated TEU, art. 4.

[116] Poos, "Report on Reform of the Council", 12; Jean-Louis Bourlanges, "Report on the Decision-Making Process in the Council in an Enlarged Europe", European Parliament Session Document, January 28, 1999, 15.

[117] Report by the Working Party set up by the Secretary General of the Council, "Operation of the Council with an Enlarged Union in Prospect", March 10, 1999, 40-41.

attend the European Council when it deals with EMU questions.[118] According to Luxembourg's former Minister of Foreign Affairs Jacques Poos, the result is that the "General Affairs Council no longer has an overview and [that] its ability to co-ordinate has been undermined by both the specialist Councils (for example Ecofin) and by the European Council".[119]

Since July 2002, there has been a concrete attempt to restore the General Affairs Council's horizontal co-ordinating role. On the occasion of each General Affairs meeting, the Ministers of Foreign Affairs receive a progress report on the most important issues under discussion in the Council's other configurations.[120]

B. The Preparation of Council Meetings

Co-ordination at Council level is in large measure a problem of pre-paration. The Council's preparatory process has become more important as the number of delegations around the Council table grew from six to fifteen and the number of languages increased from four to eleven. As a result, the time taken for a *"tour de table"* when each delegation expresses its views is now such that Ministers themselves can only discuss a limited number of subjects in detail at each meeting. More and more matters must therefore be resolved in the *fora* which prepare Council meetings.

According to the EC Treaty, the Committee of Permanent Represen-tatives (Coreper) is responsible for preparing the work of the Council.[121] Each Member State maintains a Permanent Representation (an Embassy) to the EU in Brussels. Since 1962, Coreper has been divided into two parts each of which meets weekly. Coreper Part 2 (composed of the Permanent Representatives themselves) prepares the proceedings for the General Affairs and External Relations Council, the Ecofin and the Justice and Home Affairs Council. Coreper Part 1 (composed of the Deputy Permanent Representatives) is in charge of the more technical Council formations such as Environment or Employment, Social Policy, Health and Consumer Affairs.

Coreper prepares in principle all items entered on the agenda of all Council meetings. It does so on the basis of the reports from around 185 specialised Council Working Parties and Committees. These Council Groups are composed of representatives of each Member State (staff

---

[118] Declaration 4 annexed to the Maastricht Final Act.

[119] Poos, "Report on Reform of the Council", 11.

[120] General Affairs Council, "Press Release", July 16, 2001, 5.

[121] Consolidated TEC, art. 207(1). See Jeffrey Lewis, "National Interests: Coreper", in Peterson and Shackleton (eds.), *The Institutions of the European Union*, 277.

from the Permanent Representations and/or from the national capitals) and Commission officials. The number of Working Party meetings has increased from 2,705 in 1997 to 3,537 in 2000.[122] Since it is permanently based in Brussels, meets weekly, devotes itself exclusively to compromise-building to advance European integration and has a horizontal view of what is happening in the EU's various sub-fields, Coreper's role is essential for ensuring the coherence and continuity of Union action. In practice, however, Coreper's role has begun to weaken. This is notably due to the creation of a number of high-level specialised Committees composed of top officials from the capitals.

Some of those Committees such as the 133 Committee for the common commercial policy and the Special Committee on Agriculture (SCA) have already existed for a long time. Others have been added more recently such as the Political and Security Committee, the Committee for JHA, the Economic and Financial Committee and the Employment Committee. In the Treaty of Nice, the Member States decided to add a new Social Protection Committee.[123] These Committees tend to rival with the Coreper for the final influence on the Council's agenda and decision-making process which is not always beneficial for the consistency of the EU's actions.

C. The Council Presidency

The key player in keeping the expanding Council machinery under control is the Council Presidency.[124] The Treaties are not very explicit on the Council Presidency. The EC Treaty simply states that the "office of President shall be held in turn by each Member State in the Council for a term of six months …"[125] and that its role is to convene the Council.[126] With respect to the CFSP and police and judicial co-operation in criminal matters, the EU Treaty conveys more explicit representative functions to the Presidency.[127] The Treaties thus give a very incomplete picture of the central political role of the Council Presidency.

In practice, the rotating Presidency fulfils the following functions: it is the central agenda-setter for all European Council and Council

---

[122] Report from the Secretary General, "Preparing the Council for Enlargement", 15.

[123] Treaty of Nice, art. 2(11) amending Consolidated TEC, art. 144.

[124] For somewhat older perspectives on the role of the Presidency, see Guy de Bassompierre, *Changing the Guard in Brussels: An Insider's View of the EC Presidency* (New York, Praeger, 1988); Emil J. Kirchner, *Decision-Making in the European Community. The Council Presidency and European Integration* (Manchester, Manchester University Press, 1992).

[125] Consolidated TEC, art. 203.

[126] Consolidated TEC, art. 204.

[127] Consolidated TEU, arts. 18, 21, 22, 23, 24, 39.

meetings; prepares and chairs every Council meeting and Council working party or committee[128]; draws the conclusions after each meeting; is expected to lead whenever political compromise formula and new initiatives need to be invented; and represents the Council in contacts with the other institutions, third countries and the press. With the expansion of the EU's activities in more intergovernmental domains and the relatively modest role of the Commission in those areas, the Council Presidency has gradually become the EU's central political function. At the same time, the task of the Presidency is becoming ever more difficult, precisely because of the larger number of subjects to be dealt with and the greater diversity among the expanding number of Member States. Even for the most capable national administration, the Presidency constitutes an exhausting experience.

The organisation of the Council Presidency is an important element in the reflection on the EU's future.[129] British Prime Minister Tony Blair has been one the most outspoken critics of the current Presidency system. In Blair's own words:

> The six-monthly rotating Presidency was devised for a Common Market of 6: it is not efficient nor representative for a Union of 25 and more. How can the Council with constantly shifting leadership be a good partner for the Commission and Parliament? How can Europe be taken seriously at international Summits if the Chair of the Council is here today, gone tomorrow? The old system has reached its limits. It creates for Europe a weakness of continuity in leadership: a fatal handicap in the development of an effective Common Foreign and Security Policy.[130]

Blair therefore proposed a fixed chair(wo)man for the European Council. France and Germany largely shared Blair's viewpoint. In their joint contribution to the European Convention, Chirac and Schröder emphasised the need for a full-time and fixed President of the European Council.[131] The President would be elected by the European Council by a qualified majority and would have a term in office of five years or of two

---

[128] There are a few exceptions to this rule: The chair of the Economic and Financial Committee is elected by the Committee for a renewable two-year period; the chair of the Code of Conduct Group (business taxation) is elected for two years by the members of the Group; the chair of the Military Committee is appointed by the Council for a period of three years, on the recommendation of the Committee; the chair of the Military Committee Working Group is appointed by Coreper for an 18-month period on the recommendation of the Military Committee.

[129] Laeken European Council, "Presidency Conclusions", December 14-15, 2001, Annex I, 6.

[130] Tony Blair, "A Clear Course for Europe", speech delivered in Cardiff, November 28, 2002, 4.

[131] "Contribution Franco-Allemande à la Convention européenne sur l'Architecture Institutionnelle de l'Union", *Agence Europe*, January 17, 2003, 24.

and a half years on a renewable basis. Several of the smaller Member States and the Commission, however, saw the proposals for a permanent President of the European Council as a threat to the Community system. Belgian Prime Minister Guy Verhofstadt and Commission President Romano Prodi both asked what the permanent European Council President would be doing for the other 360 days of the year when the European Council is not meeting and when George Bush is not searching for the mythical single phone number for "Europe".[132] Both feared that a permanent chairperson of the European Council would become a duplicate or rival of the Commission President, create his own staff and open a rift in the EU's institutional system. Instead, the Benelux countries proposed that the President of the Commission would chair the General Affairs Council. A new "Mr. External Relations", combining the functions of the High Representative for the CFSP and the Commissioner for External Relations, would chair the External Relations Council. For the European Council, the Benelux favoured maintaining the rotation system.[133] Verhofstadt had initially proposed that the presidency of the European Council would be occupied by the President of the European Commission.[134]

D. The Council's Future

The discussion on the Council's future goes well beyond the debate on the Presidency. In German Chancellor Gerhard Schröder's federal vision presented in 2001, the Council would be transformed into a second Chamber of States, along the model of the German Bundesrat or the United States Senate. French Minister of Foreign Affairs Hubert Védrine did not agree:

> There is something that we do not accept and that will not be accepted, and that is the fact of transforming the Council of Ministers, which is the heart of executive power and co-ordination in Europe, into a second Chamber. The French, whatever the slight differences between them may be, will defend a scheme in which the executive power remains shared between the Council and the Commission.[135]

---

[132] Guy Verhofstadt, "Montesquieu and the European Union", speech delivered at the College of Europe, Bruges, November 18, 2002, 6 ; Romano Prodi, "The European Union's New Institutional Structure", speech delivered at the European Parliament, December 5, 2002, 4.

[133] "Memordandum of the Belelux : A Balanced Institutional Framework for an Enlarged, more Efficient and more Transparant Union", *Agence Europe*, December 6, 2002, 26.

[134] Verhofstadt, "Montesquieu and the European Union", 8.

[135] *Agence Europe*, May 19, 2001, 3.

V. Between Democratic Deficit and Parliamentary Governance

A. Composition of the European Parliament

To the Community's founders, its democratic nature seemed self-evident since it was based on democratic Member States.[136] Moreover, the ECSC Treaty provided for a Common Assembly composed of delegates from the national parliaments of the Member States.[137] Upon the entry into force of the EEC and Euratom Treaties, the powers of the Assembly were extended to the new Communities.[138] The Assembly changed its name to European Parliament in 1962.[139] The first direct elections of the European Parliament took place in 1979.[140] The voter turnout for the European Parliament elections of June 1999 was the lowest since 1979 (49.8%).[141]

The current representation system in the European Parliament aims to "ensure appropriate representation of the peoples of the States brought together in the Community".[142] The European Parliament that was elected in 1999 counts 626 members.[143] Its composition is based on the decision of the Edinburgh European Council in December 1992.[144] In

---

[136] Kevin Featherstone, "Jean Monnet and the 'Democratic Deficit' in the European Union", *Journal of Common Market Studies*, 32 (1994) 149.

[137] ECSC Treaty, arts. 20-21.

[138] Convention on Certain Institutions Common to the European Communities, March 25, 1957, art. 1.

[139] "Resolution of March 30, 1962", O.J. 1962, 1045. The Assembly's name change to European Parliament was formalised in the SEA, art. 6.

[140] The direct elections are based on the "Act concerning the Election of the Representatives of the Assembly by Direct Universal Suffrage Annexed to the Council Decision of 20 September 1976", O.J. L 278, 1976, 1. On the development of the European Parliament since its direct election, see Richard Corbett, Francis Jacobs and Michael Shackleton (eds.), *The European Parliament* (London, John Harper, 2000); Richard Corbett, *The European Parliament's Role in Closer EU Integration* (Basingstoke, Macmillan, 1998); Olivier Costa, *Le Parlement Européen, Assemblée Délibérante* (Brussels, Ed. de l'Université de Bruxelles, 2000); Julie Smith, *Europe's Elected Parliament* (Sheffield, Sheffield Academic Press, 1999).

[141] Gen. Rep. EU 1999, para. 1012.

[142] Consolidated TEC, art. 190(2).

[143] *Ibid.*

[144] Edinburgh European Council, "Presidency Conclusions", December 11-12, 1992, para. 26: Belgium 25; Denmark 16; Germany 99; Greece 25; Spain 64; France 87; Ireland 15; Italy 87; Luxembourg 6; the Netherlands 31; Austria 21; Portugal 25; Finland 16; Sweden 22; United Kingdom 87.

preparation for the EU's enlargement, the Treaty of Amsterdam placed a limit of 700 on the number of members of the European Parliament.[145]

To make place for representatives of the candidate countries, the negotiators of the Treaty of Nice had to agree on a new distribution of the seats that will enter into force for Parliament's 2004-2009 term.[146] Instead of following a coherent allocation method, a purely political agreement was arrived at without any mathematical logic.[147] In fact, the compromise on the allocation of seats in Parliament has to be seen against the background of the discussion on the weighting of the votes in the Council. Member States that had made concessions during the debate on Council votes received a compensation regarding the number of seats in the European Parliament. Germany, that had accepted parity with the other larger Member States in terms of Council votes, was allowed to keep its 99 parliamentarians. Almost all other Member States had to accept a reduction in the number of Parliament seats. Large Member States such as the United Kingdom, France and Italy saw their number of seats reduced from 87 to 72, representing a 17% reduction. Spain, that had obtained an advantageous deal in number of Council votes, went down from 64 to 50, which represents a 22% reduction. To compensate Belgium, Greece and Portugal for the decoupling of their number of Council votes *vis-à-vis* the Netherlands, they were allowed to keep 22 of their 25 seats (representing a 12% reduction). The Netherlands, however, went down from 31 seats to 25 (representing a 19% reduction). Luxembourg, the smallest Member State, was allowed to keep its six members of the European Parliament. Together with the seats allocated to the candidate countries, the total number of members of the European Parliament will reach 732. The Amsterdam limit of 700 was adapted accordingly.[148] A complicated arrangement was added to help smooth the transition to the new system.[149]

---

[145]   Consolidated TEC, art. 189.

[146]   Nice Protocol on the Enlargement of the European Union, art. 2(1) and (2).

[147]   Nice Declaration 20 on the Enlargement of the European Union: Germany 99 MEPs; United Kingdom 72; France 72; Italy 72; Spain 50; Poland 50; Romania 33; the Netherlands 25; Greece 22; Czech Republic 20; Belgium 22; Hungary 20; Portugal 22; Sweden 18; Bulgaria 17; Austria 17; Slovakia 13; Denmark 13; Finland 13; Ireland 12; Lithuania 12; Latvia 8; Slovenia 7; Estonia 6; Cyprus 6; Luxembourg 6; Malta 5.

[148]   Treaty of Nice, art. 2(17) amending Consolidated TEC, art. 189.

[149]   Nice Protocol on the Enlargement of the European Union, art. 2(3); Brussels European Council, "Presidency Conclusions", October 24-25, 2002, Annex I (c).

B. The Role of Political Parties in the European Parliament

In the hemicycle, the members of the European Parliament (MEPs) do not sit together according to their nationality, but following their membership of one of Parliament's transnational Political Groups.[150] The most numerous Groups, who determine to a large extent Parliament's agenda, are those of the European Peoples Party (EPP),[151] the Party of European Socialists (PES)[152] and the European Liberal, Democrat and Reform Party (ELDR). Since the Treaty of Maastricht, political parties at European level have been explicitly recognised as an important factor for integration.[153] While the Political Groups attempt to co-ordinate positions on a European scale, in the past they have not been marked by strong party discipline. In practice, the political behaviour of the members of the European Parliament is determined largely by national politics. European elections still take place within a national context. National parties remain master over the composition of the electoral lists. They determine which candidates secure a position that might allow them to be (re-)elected. Also, election districts never reach beyond the Member State borders. MEPs who disregard the guidelines of their own national party in an attempt to build genuine European-scale strategies are likely to be punished. The fate of Wilfried Martens, a former Belgian Prime Minister who served as President of both the EPP and its Parliamentary Group (1994-1999), can serve as an example. Martens' successful strategy of turning the EPP into the most powerful group by bringing in the British Conservatives and Berlusconi's *Forza Italia* was disliked by the Flemish Christian Democrats. As a result, Martens got into trouble with his home base and did not return to the European Parliament after the 1999 elections.

During the Nice negotiations, a Commission proposal to strengthen the role of political parties at European level by electing a number of

---

[150] On the EU's transnational political parties in formation, see the innovating study by Amie Kreppel, *The European Parliament and Supranational Party System. A Study in Institutional Development* (Cambridge, Cambridge University Press, 2002). See also David S. Bell and Christopher Lord (eds.), *Transnational Parties in the European Union* (Aldershot, Ashgate, 1998); Simon Hix and Christopher Lord, *Political Parties in the European Union* (Basingstoke, Macmillan, 1997); Tapio Raunio, "Political Interests: The EP's Party Groups", in Peterson and Shackleton (eds.), *The Institutions of the European Union*, 258.

[151] Thomas Jansen, *The European People's Party: Origins and Development* (Basingstoke, Macmillan, 1998).

[152] Robert Ladrech, *Social Democracy and the Challenge of European Union* (Boulder, Lynne Rienner, 2000).

[153] Consolidated TEC, art. 191. See Triantafyllia Papadopoulou, *Politische Parteien auf Europäischer Ebene: Auslegung und Ausgestaltung von Art. 191 (ex 138a) EGV* (Baden-Baden, Nomos, 1999).

MEPs from Union-wide lists was not accepted.[154] The Treaty of Nice did, however, add that the Council would lay down the regulations governing political parties at European level and in particular the rules regarding their funding.[155] Such funding shall apply on the same basis to all political forces represented in the European Parliament.[156] For the Commission, the reinforcement of the European political parties seemed fundamental to organising the European political debate and giving it a solid link to civil society.[157]

C. The Powers of the European Parliament

Since the 1950s, Parliament has been in charge of controlling the Commission. Parliament's ultimate weapon is the possibility of voting a motion of censure.[158] Once such a motion has been adopted, the Commission is obliged to resign as a body. A double majority is required for a motion of censure to succeed: a majority of the component Members of Parliament and two-thirds of the votes cast. Six censure motions have been tabled since Parliament was directly elected in 1979, but so far none have been adopted.[159] The motion of censure weapon has been reinforced

---

[154] Commission, "Adapting the Institutions to Make a Success of Enlargement", 8.

[155] Treaty of Nice, art. 2(19) amending Consolidated TEC, art. 191.

[156] Nice Declaration 11 on Article 191 of the Treaty establishing the European Community.

[157] Romano Prodi, "The time has come for a properly structured debate on the future of Europe", speech before the European Parliament, Strasbourg, January 17, 2001, 5.

[158] Consolidated TEC, art. 201. See Jean-Louis Clergerie, "L'Improbable Censure de la Commission Européenne", *Revue du Droit Public et de la Science Politique*, 111 (1995) 201.

[159] The most significant motion was tabled on December 17, 1998 by Pauline Green, then Chair of the Socialist Group. The same day, Parliament had decided not to grant the Commission the budget discharge for 1996. According to Ms Green, this meant that the Commission was not assured of the Parliament's confidence at a moment when crucial decisions on the EU's future were being prepared in such areas as enlargement, the financial perspectives for 2000-2006 and the related discussion on the reform of the EU's agricultural and cohesion policy. Ms Green proposed a motion of censure – in lieu of a motion of confidence which is not foreseen by the Treaties – as the only way for Parliament to mark its confidence in the Commission. In the mean time, almost daily press stories accusing French Commissioner Edith Cresson of financial mismanagement, fraud and nepotism were quickly undermining the credibility of the entire College. To save itself from a defeat in Parliament, the Commission agreed with the creation of a Committee of Independent Experts that would examine the charges. The creation of this Committee enabled Ms Green to withdraw her motion. A "real" motion of censure tabled by French nationalist Hervé Fabre Aubespy nevertheless succeeded in gathering 232 votes in favour, 293 against and 27 abstentions. When on March 15, 1999 the Committee of Independent Experts surprisingly accused the entire Commission of total absence of responsibility, the College of Commissioners – for the first time in EU history – decided to resign collectively. While the real target of most criticism had been Commissioner Cresson,

since the Treaty of Maastricht granted Parliament the right to establish temporary Committees of Inquiry to investigate alleged contravention or misadministration in the implementation of Community law. [160] The Committee of Inquiry charged with the examination of the Commission's attitude during the BSE crisis, for instance, had a considerable impact on the strengthening of the EU consumer protection policy both in administrative practice and in Treaty law.[161] Parliament had issued a warning that a motion of censure would be tabled if its recommendations were not carried out.[162]

In comparison with the position of national parliaments *vis-à-vis* national governments, the European Parliament is a much more independent and threatening institution. In most West European parliamentary systems, parliaments' ability to sack the government is counterbalanced by the executive's power to dissolve the assembly. In most Western European countries, parliamentarians know that by voting down a government they might provoke early parliamentary elections, thus putting their own seat in danger. This constitutional balance is absent in the EU, giving members of the European Parliament the freedom to criticise and censure the Commission without any fear for personal consequences.[163]

Another area where Parliament's political power has been visible since the 1970s is the budget. The Council has the final say over the compulsory side of the budget, necessarily resulting from the Treaties or

---

she had successfully used the "shield of collegiality" to rebuff attempts at sanctioning her individually. The result was the resignation of the entire College.

[160] Consolidated TEC, art. 193. See also Michael Shackleton, "The European Parliament's New Committees of Inquiry: Tiger or Paper Tiger?", *Journal of Common Market Studies*, 36 (1998) 115; Andreas Mauer, "(Co-)Governing after Maastricht. The European Parliament's Institutional Performance 1994-1998. Lessons for the Implementation of the Treaty of Amsterdam", European Parliament Directorate General for Research, 1999, 33.

[161] See Reimer Böge, "Report on the European Commission's Follow-Up of the Recommendations made by the Committee of Inquiry into BSE", European Parliament Session Documents, November 14, 1997.

[162] Since the Maastricht Treaty, in addition to exercising control on the Commission's activities, the Commission's investiture is preceded by a Parliamentary vote of approval on the Commission as a whole. Before this vote, each of the candidates to become Commissioner is grilled during a Parliamentary hearing. Since the Treaty of Amsterdam, the nomination of the person whom the governments intend to appoint as President of the Commission must also be approved by the European Parliament. Consolidated TEC, art. 214. See Martin Westlake, "The European Parliament's Powers of Appointment", *Journal of Common Market Studies*, 36 (1998) 431.

[163] In the alternative constitutional model, based on a genuine separation between the branches of government, neither parliament, nor the executive have the ability to bring each other down. There is no such complete separation between European Parliament and Commission in the EU system.

from acts adopted in accordance therewith. This is mainly agricultural expenditure. In 1970, Parliament received the final word over the so-called non-compulsory expenditures which currently cover 55% of the budget, including most of the non-agricultural budget lines.[164] Furthermore, in 1975, Parliament was granted the right to reject the budget as a whole.[165] It made use of this possibility in 1979 and 1984. To avoid the annual repetition of budgetary fights, Parliament and Council have since 1988, on the Commission's initiative, started with the adoption of Inter-Institutional Agreements that determine the EU's financial perspectives on a multi-annual basis. Since 1975, Parliament also became the institution with the authority to grant the "discharge" to the Commission in respect of the implementation of the budget. The discharge procedure has become highly political. While based on an examination of the Commission's accounts and annual report by the Court of Auditors, it has turned into a general opportunity for Parliament to criticise the Commission's management policies.[166]

Finally, the expansion of the European Parliament's powers has been most spectacular in the legislative field. The first step was taken with the introduction of the co-operation procedure in the Single European Act.[167] Via the co-operation procedure, Parliament was for the first time fully involved in the legislative process. While the co-operation process granted Parliament the possibility to propose formal amendments during the Community's legislative process, the Council nevertheless remained the final master of the procedure. Today, the co-operation procedure still applies in legislative procedures related to economic and monetary policy. With the creation of the co-decision procedure by the Maastricht Treaty, Parliament has in the mean time become the Council's equal in the legislative process.[168] In those areas where it applies, the co-decision procedure leads to the adoption of Community legislation signed jointly by the Presidents of Parliament and the Council, for which the two

---

[164] Treaty amending Certain Budgetary Provisions of the Treaties establishing the European Communities and of the Treaty establishing a Single Council and a Single Commission of the European Communities, April 22, 1970, O.J. L 2, 1971, 1.

[165] Treaty amending Certain Financial Provisions of the Treaties establishing a Single Council and a Single Commission of the European Communities, July 22, O.J. L 359, 1975, 1.

[166] On the EU's budgetary process, see Iain Begg and Nigel Grimwade, *Paying for Europe* (Sheffield, Sheffield Academic Press, 1998); Brigid Laffan, *The Finances of the European Union* (Basingstoke, Macmillan, 1997); Brigid Laffan and Michael Shackleton, "The Budget", in Wallace and Wallace (eds.), *Policy-Making in the European Union* (2000, 4th ed.), 211.

[167] Consolidated TEC, art. 252. See David Earnshaw and David Judge, "The Life and Times of the European Union's Co-operation Procedure", *Journal of Common Market Studies*, 35 (1997), 543.

[168] Consolidated TEC, art. 251.

institutions are equally responsible. Under the co-decision procedure, Parliament delivers its opinion on Commission proposals before the Council adopts a common position. Furthermore, Parliament can propose amendments and ultimately veto the final adoption of legislative texts. In case of a disagreement between Council and Parliament, a Conciliation Committee is set up to bridge the differences of view. Bringing the co-decision procedure into practice required a profound change in the EU's legislative culture.[169] From the 1950s until the Maastricht Treaty's entry into force in November 1993, the Council had been responsible for law-making on its own. This changed quickly. Between November 1993 and April 1999, no less than 165 co-decision procedures were completed.[170] Conciliation meetings between Parliament and Council were needed in 66 of these 165 cases, representing 40%. Parliament soon sent Council the message that it had an interest in negotiating seriously.[171] Of the 913 amendments adopted by Parliament in co-decision (between November 1993 and April 1999), 74% were accepted by the Council either unchanged or in compromise form.[172] Another 4% were deemed already covered by another part of the common position. Under the co-operation procedure – which also allowed Parliament to introduce amendments, but without Conciliation Committee or veto right – the Council had adopted only 21% of Parliament's amendments (between July 1987 and July 1997).[173]

During the negotiations of the Treaty of Amsterdam, Parliament succeeded in securing a significant extension of the subject matters falling under the co-decision procedure. This was again the case at Nice.

D. The Role of National Parliaments

Since 1979, MEPs are no longer appointed by their national parliaments. The organic link that existed between national parliaments and the European integration process before 1979 has thus disappeared.[174] Ever since, the French government has insisted on a greater role for the national

---

[169] Richard Corbett, "Academic Modelling of the Codecision Procedure: a Practitioner's Puzzled Reaction", *European Union Politics*, 1 (2000) 373; Michael Shackleton, "The Politics of Codecision", *Journal of Common Market Studies*, 38 (2000) 325.

[170] For a statistical overview, see Fontaine, Imbeni and Verde i Aldea, "Codecision Procedure under Article 189b of the Treaty of Maastricht", Annex II. See also Ricardo Gosalbo Bono, "Co-Decision: an Appraisal of Experience of the European Parliament as Co-Legislator", *Yearbook of European Law*, 14 (1994) 21.

[171] In July 1994, Parliament vetoed the Council's position on voice telephony as the conciliation had not produced agreement.

[172] These are second reading amendments.

[173] Maurer, "(Co-)Governing after Maastricht", 25.

[174] Bernhard Wessels and Richard S. Katz (eds.), *The European Parliament, National Parliaments and European Integration* (Oxford, Oxford University Press, 1999).

parliaments in the EU's decision-making procedure, possibly through the creation of a new EU body composed of representatives of the national assemblies. Against this background, it is no surprise that French Prime Minister Lionel Jospin in May 2001 proposed the establishment of a permanent conference of parliaments or "Congress". It would meet in regular sessions, monitor Community institutions' compliance with subsidiarity, hold annual state of the Union debates and play a role in amending technical Treaty rules.[175] During the IGC 2000, UK Prime Minister Tony Blair expressed support for similar ideas.[176] German Foreign Minister Joschka Fischer's federal project also included the suggestion for a European chamber composed of members who are also national parliamentarians.[177]

A Declaration had already been adopted at Maastricht providing for a Conference of Parliaments that would be composed of delegates from the national parliaments and the European Parliament to discuss the major aspects of European integration.[178] After Maastricht, the Conference never gathered in practice.[179] Of more practical importance is the Conference of European Affairs Committees of the National Parliaments (generally known under its French abbreviation COSAC). COSAC has been meeting twice yearly since 1989. The Amsterdam Protocol on the role of National Parliaments in the EU stipulates that COSAC is authorised to address contributions on the EU's legislative proposals to the European Parliament, Council and Commission.[180]

At Amsterdam, the Member States also agreed that national parliaments needed to be informed in a timely fashion in order to enable them to exercise their right of control.[181] National parliaments have, indeed, an important role to play in controlling the position of their national governments in the Council of Ministers. The degree to which national parliamentary control is actually taking place differs from one Member State to Member the next.[182] The Nice Declaration on the Future of the

---

[175] Lionel Jospin, "L'Avenir de l'Europe Elargie", Paris, May 28, 2001, 16.

[176] Tony Blair, "Prime Minister's Speech to the Polish Stock Exchange", Warsaw, October 6, 2000, 9-10.

[177] Joschka Fischer, "From Confederacy to Federation – Thoughts on the Finality of European Integration", Speech at the Humboldt University, Berlin, May 12, 2000, 6.

[178] Maastricht Declaration 14 on the Conference of Parliaments.

[179] The Conference of Parliament had met in November 1990 before the start of the Maastricht IGCs.

[180] Amsterdam Protocol on the Role of National Parliaments in the European Union, para. 4.

[181] Amsterdam Protocol on the Role of National Parliaments in the European Union, paras. 1-3.

[182] Fabrice Hourquebie, *Les Organes Spécialisés dans les Affaires Communautaires des Parlements Nationaux: les Cas Français et Allemands* (Paris, L'Harmattan, 1999);

Union specified that the reflection process leading to a new round of Treaty reform foreseen for 2004 should notably address "the role of national parliaments in the European architecture".[183]

VI. Between Legislative Harmonisation, Policy Co-ordination and Resource Allocation

A. Community Legislation

In contrast with most international organisations that are merely able to produce resolutions or recommend draft treaties for ratification to their members, the Community produces binding secondary legislation that has precedence over national law. Community legislation takes the form of regulations or directives.[184] Regulations are binding in their entirety for all Member States and their citizens. They are directly applicable without "transposition" into national law and are used in areas of strong Community competence such as external trade, agriculture and competition policy. Directives on the other hand are only binding as to the result to be achieved. National authorities have the choice of form and method in implementing directives. They are used to promote the harmonisation of legislation among the Member States in such areas as the Internal Market and the protection of the environment.[185] In 2001 alone, the Community adopted a total of 752 regulations and 63 directives.[186]

Since 1985, the Community has also been using so-called "new approach" directives whereby the Community merely sets out a number of essential requirements for the placing of products on the Internal Market. Business has the choice as to how to comply with these obligations. Within this framework, the European standards organisations have the task of drafting technical specifications which would offer one way

---

Timothy Pratt, "The Role of National Parliaments in the Making of European Law", *Cambridge Yearbook of European Legal Studies 1998*, 1 (1999) 217.

[183] Nice Declaration 23 on the Future of the Union. See also The European Convention, "Final Report of Working Group IV on the Role of National Parliaments", CONV 353/02, October 22, 2002. For the European Parliament's viewpoint on the role of national parliaments, see Giorgio Napolitano, "Report on Relations between the European Parliament and the National Parliaments in European Integration", European Parliament Session Document, January 23, 2002.

[184] For the definition of regulations and directives, see Consolidated TEC Treaty, art. 249.

[185] Sacha Prechal, *Directives in European Community Law. A Study of Directives and their Enforcement in National Courts* (Oxford, Clarendon Press, 1995); Denys Simon, *La Directive Européenne* (Paris, Dalloz, 1997); Christiaan Timmermans, "Community Directives Revisited", *Yearbook of European Law*, 17 (1999) 1.

[186] Gen. Rep. EU 2001, para. 1239.

of complying with the directives.[187] The "new approach" directives are
an example of the EU's attempt at supplementing more traditional Community legislation with more creative forms of governance.[188]

In the environmental area, the Commission has been pushing self-
and co-regulatory arrangements, including voluntary measures by industry, as more "appropriate and flexible means of addressing environmental issues".[189]

B. Non-legislative Forms of Policy Co-ordination

In addition to legislative action, the Community is increasingly relying
on non-legislative forms of policy co-ordination to stimulate integration.
Two kinds of policy co-ordination can be distinguished: (1) compulsory
co-ordination of national policies; and (2) non-binding co-ordination of
national policies. The broad economic policy guidelines and employment
guidelines are an example of compulsory co-ordination. These guidelines
are formally adopted by the Council, upon a Commission proposal,
according to a procedure outlined in the EC Treaty. They serve as the
benchmark for a peer review process during which the economic and
employment policies of each Member State are assessed in the
Council.[190] This review process can lead to the adoption of formal
recommendations addressed to the Member States.

In addition, the Community has developed mechanisms of national
policy co-ordination without a Treaty basis. The Lisbon European
Council in March 2000, for instance, decided to introduce a "new open

---

187   Commission of the European Communities, "Interim Report from the Commission to
      the Stockholm European Council. Improving and Simplifying the Regulatory
      Environment", COM (2001) 130 final, March 7, 2001, 12. For the political instru-
      ments used in the creation of the Internal Market, see Michelle Egan, *Constructing a
      European Market. Standards, Regulation and Governance* (Oxford, Oxford
      University Press, 2001).

188   See Commission of the European Communities, "European Governance. A White
      Paper", Brussels, COM(2001) 428, July 25, 2001, 18.

189   See Philippe Renaudière, "Phénomènes et Instruments 'Consensuels' ou Non-
      Contraignants en Droit Communautaire de l'Environnement", *Aménagement-Envi-
      ronnement* (Special Issue, 1997) 3; Marc Pallemaerts, "The Decline of Law as an
      Instrument of Community Environmental Policy", *Law and European Affairs*, 9
      (1999) 338; Axel Friedrich, Matthias Tappe and Rudiger K. W. Wurzel, "A New
      Approach to EU Environmental Policy-Making? The Auto-Oil I Programme",
      Journal of European Public Policy, 7 (2000) 593. The Commission intends to conti-
      nue with this practice, see Commission of the European Communities, "Communi-
      cation to the Council, the European Parliament, the Economic and Social Committee
      and the Committee of the Regions on the Sixth Environmental Action Programme of
      the European Community: Environment 2010: Our Future, Our Choice", COM
      (2001) 31 final, January 24, 2001, 61.

190   Consolidated TEC, art. 99 and 128.

method of co-ordination at all levels" to implement the EU's strategic goal "to become the most competitive and dynamic knowledge-based economy in the world capable of sustainable economic growth with more and better jobs and greater social cohesion".[191] The open co-ordination method is based on the following components: (1) the development of policy objectives and indicators in common accord by the Member States; (2) the exchange of best practices among Member States; (3) the regular reporting by the Member States on progress made: and (4) the development of public monitoring mechanisms such as scoreboards allowing the performance of the Member States to be compared and graded. Although they remain formally in charge of the policy fields that are the subject of open co-ordination, Member States that fail to move towards the common policy objectives know they will be subject to public criticism. The open co-ordination method is currently used in several policy fields including the European strategy against social exclusion.[192]

The recent boom of non-legislative policy co-ordination in the EU can be explained in several ways. First, governments generally perceive non-legislative policy co-ordination as less "intrusive" than binding Community legislation which can be used by the citizens in national courts to attack incompatible national laws and practices. Non-legislative policy co-ordination respects formal sovereignty and, in theory, leaves the national governments in charge. Second, non-legislative co-ordination can be used in policy fields that are primarily under the competence of the Member States and where the EU is merely in charge of stimulating co-operation. Third, non-legislative policy co-ordination is able to push integration in quickly changing social and economic areas where the creation of law would be regarded as excessively rigid.

Non-legislative policy co-ordination is often used in an attempt to stimulate "positive co-operation" in areas as social policy, beyond the free movement of goods, services and capital and competition policy. As such, it underscores the difference in approach with the EU's successful drive for the elimination of barriers to the free movement between the Member States ("negative integration").[193] The EU's free movement process has been based on clear Treaty prohibitions that are directly

---

[191] Lisbon European Council, "Presidency Conclusions", March 23-24, 2000, para. 7.

[192] For a systematic overview table of the use of the open co-ordination method, see Dermot Hodson and Imelda Maher, "The Open Method as a New Mode of Governance: The Case of Soft Economic Policy Co-ordination", *Journal of Common Market Studies*, 39 (2001) 726.

[193] On this imbalance, see Fritz Scharpf, *Governing Europe: Effective and Democratic?* (Oxford, Oxford University Press, 1999), 43; Mark A. Pollack, "Neoliberalism and Regulated Capitalism in the Treaty of Amsterdam", University of Wisconsin Working Paper on European Studies No. 2 (1998) 5.

applicable and can therefore be invoked by citizens before their national courts against incompatible legislation of their Member States.[194] Treaty rules in such fields as social and taxation policy, in contrast, include only few directly applicable prohibitions. In addition, these Treaty rules do not define the concrete substance of the actions to be taken. Furthermore, the adoption of secondary legislation in these areas often requires a unanimous vote in the Council. This difficult institutional context explains in part why more flexible forms of governance are nevertheless being tested to advance "positive co-operation". Non-legislative instruments cannot engender, however, the legal dynamic that was fundamental to the success of the free movement drive. In this context, it is not entirely surprising that the European Parliament has on various occasions emphasised that Community legislation would often be a more appropriate tool than non-legislative co-ordination, for instance, to guarantee minimum social rights in the EU.[195]

The non-legislative co-ordination method has also become a subject for discussion because it erodes to some degree the European Parliament's newly developed co-decision powers. Parliament has warned explicitly that the open method of co-ordination "must under no circumstances lead to hidden parallel legislation by circumventing the legislative procedures established in the EC Treaty".[196] Also, while the legislative process leads to Community acts that can be challenged before the European Court of Justice, no such judicial protection exists over the open co-ordination method.

---

[194] René Barents, "The Community and the Unity of the Common Market: Some Reflections on the Economic Constitution of the Community", *German Yearbook of International Law*, 33 (1990) 9; Miguel Poiares Maduro, *We the Court. The European Court of Justice and the European Economic Constitution. A Critical Reading of Article 30 of the EC Treaty* (Oxford, Hart, 1998); Wolf Sauter, "The Economic Constitution of the European Union", *Columbia Journal of European Law*, 4 (1998) 27; Manfred E. Streit and Werner Mussler, "The Economic Constitution of the European Community – From Rome to Maastricht", in Francis Snyder (ed.), *Constitutional Dimensions of European Economic Integration* (The Hague, Kluwer Law International, 1996), 109.

[195] European Parliament, "Resolution on the Commission Communication to the Council, the European Parliament, the Economic and Social Committee and the Committee of the Regions on the Social Policy Agenda", Minutes of the Plenary Session, October 25, 2000, para. 9. See also European Parliament, "Resolution on the Commission's draft Joint Employment Report 1999", Minutes of the Plenary Session, November 4, 1999, para. 19.

[196] European Parliament, "Resolution on the Commission White Paper on European Governance", Minutes of the Plenary Session, November 29, 2001, para. 37.

C. Resource Allocation

In addition to its regulatory task via legislation and policy co-ordination, the EU has increasingly become involved in resource allocation on a scale not foreseen by the Community's founders. As part of the Common Agricultural Policy, the original six Member States had in 1962 set up a European Agricultural Guidance and Guarantee Fund covering expenditure incurred to finance structural adaptations (the Guidance section) and interventions in agricultural markets (the Guarantee section). With the launch of the European Social Fund in 1971 and the European Regional Development Fund in 1975, the EU began developing a policy to foster social and economic cohesion on a European scale. Cohesion policy was strengthened in the Single European Act and beefed up with the Maastricht Treaty's Cohesion Fund. In addition, during the 1990s, numerous important multi-annual programmes have been added to the EU budget relating to both internal policies (such as Esprit, Leonardo, Socrates, Media, Raphael, Kaleidoscope, Ariane) and external activities (such as Phare, Tacis, Meda, Cards, EDF, humanitarian aid). As a result, the financial management tasks conferred on the Commission grew almost exponentially. While the number of tasks increased, the Member States refused to provide the Commission with the necessary staff to manage the new responsibilities. Moreover, the available Commission staff – recruited for legislative, regulatory and external policy tasks – was not always fully equipped and trained to manage significant budgets.[197] While a heavy burden on the Commission, the budgetary significance of the EU's distributive policies should not be overstated. These programmes are, indeed, severely constrained by the EU's low overall budgetary ceiling.[198]

---

[197] Commission of the European Communities, "Reforming the Commission. Consultative Document", COM (2000) 10 final, January 18, 2000.

[198] See Chapter VI. II.

CHAPTER IV

The Rule of Law, Freedom, Security and Justice in the EU

After multiple attempts to achieve European unity *manu militari*, the EU can be interpreted as a unique project to foster European integration *manu legis*. The grand political compromises at the start of the Communities were turned into legally binding Treaties to improve their chances for both survival and correct application. But the Communities were not only based on law, they were also equipped to create law and to ensure its implementation. As the Community's only weapon is the law it creates, Commission President Walter Hallstein already warned in the 1960s that its mission would be doomed if it were no longer able to ensure the binding and uniform nature of Community law in all Member States.[1]

Since the Community's foundation, the Court of Justice of the European Communities, based in Luxembourg, has been in charge of ensuring that in the interpretation and application of the Treaty the law is observed.[2] In October 1988, the decision was taken to attach a Court of

---

[1] Walter Hallstein, "Primauté du Droit Communautaire", Address before the European Parliament, June 17, 1965. For a current perspective, see Maria Luisa Fernandez Esteban, *The Rule of Law in the European Constitution* (The Hague, Kluwer Law International, 1999).

[2] On the role and functioning of the Court of Justice, see Anthony Arnull, *The European Union and its Court of Justice* (Oxford, Oxford University Press, 1999); L. Neville Brown and Tom Kennedy, *The Court of Justice of the European Communities* (London, Sweet & Maxwell, 2000); Henry G. Schermers and Denis F. Waelbroeck, *Judicial Protection in the European Union* (The Hague, Kluwer Law International, 2001); Grainne de Burca and J. H. H. Weiler (eds.), *The European Court of Justice* (Oxford, Oxford University, 2001); David O'Keeffe (ed.), *Judicial Review in European Union Law. Liber Amicorum in Honour of Lord Slyn of Hadley* (The Hague, Kluwer Law International, 2000), Volume 1. For the political impact of the Court, see Alec Stone Sweet and James A. Caporaso, "From Free Trade to Supranational Polity: The European Court and Integration", in Wayne Sandholz and Alec Stone Sweet (eds.), *European Integration and Supranational Governance* (Oxford, Oxford University Press, 1998), 92; Eric Stein, "Lawyers, Judges, and the Making of a Transnational Constitution", *American Journal of International Law*, 75 (1981) 1; J. H. H. Weiler, "Journey to an Unknown Destination: A Retrospective and Prospective of the European Court of Justice in the Area of Political Integration",

First Instance to the Court of Justice with jurisdiction to hear at first instance certain classes of action.[3] This was made necessary by the constant increase in the number of cases. In 1975, 130 cases were lodged at the Court of Justice. In 1988, 385 cases were lodged with 605 cases pending. In 1999, 543 cases were lodged before the Court of Justice and 384 before the Court of First Instance. In 2000, 896 cases were pending before the Court and 732 before the Court of First Instance.[4] The increase in cases is due to three important factors: the EU's growing number of Member States; the expanding scope and quantity of Community legislation; and the fact that lawyers have gradually become more familiar with Community law.[5] Improving the efficiency of the European Court system in view of both the increasing number of cases and the prospect of enlargement was a central concern during the negotiations of the Treaty of Nice.

I. Between the Primacy of EC Law and National Defiance

In the 1950s, it was entirely uncertain how the new legal system created by the Community Treaties would function in practice. Particularly unclear was whether Community law would be uniformly binding and enforceable in all Member States.[6] Only in the Netherlands and Luxembourg was the primacy of international treaties over national law well established. Germany and Italy, on the contrary, had a dualist legal tradition which implied that international agreements had to be transformed into the national legal order by an act of parliament. Transformed treaties took precedence only over earlier national legisla-

---

Journal of Common Market Studies, 31 (1993) 418. For a reconsideration of the Court's often presumed judicial activism see David T. Keeling, "In Praise of Judicial Activism. But What Does it Mean? And Has the European Court of Justice ever Practiced it?", in *Scritti in Onore di Guiseppe Federico Manchini. Vol. II: Diritto dell'Unione Europea* (Milano, Dott. A. Guiffré Editore, 1998), 505; Takis Tridimas, "The Court of Justice and Judicial Activism", *European Law Review*, 21 (1996) 199.

3   Consolidated TEC, art. 225; "Council Decision of 24 October 1988 establishing a Court of First Instance of the European Communities (88/591/ECSC, EEC, Euratom)", O.J. C 215, 21.8.1989, 1. On the functioning of the Court of First Instance, see Georges Vandersanden, "Le Tribunal de Première Instance des Communautés Européennes: Dix Ans d'Existence", in Magnette and Remacle (eds.), *Le Nouveau Modèle Européen*, 105.

4   Court of Justice of the European Communities, "The EC Court of Justice and the Institutional Reform of the European Union", April 2000, 2.

5   Court of Justice of the European Communities, "The EC Court of Justice and the Institutional Reform of the European Union", April 2000, 3.

6   On the reception of EC law in the Member States, see Jürgen Schwarze (ed.), *National Constitutional Law vis-à-vis European Integration. FIDE Kongress, Vol. I* (Baden-Baden, Nomos, 1996); Jyränki (ed.), *National Constitutions in the Era of Integration.*

tion, but could be superseded by later legislative acts. The French Constitution recognised the supremacy of international treaty law over subsequent national legislation, but the prevailing doctrine in French courts was that they were not allowed to set aside French laws conflicting with earlier international agreements. The Belgian legal situation was unclear.[7]

Already during the 1960s, the European Court of Justice established the principle of the absolute primacy of Community law, also over national constitutions.[8] Thus, whenever the law of a Member State conflicts with Community law, the latter will prevail in court. This also implies that national Constitutional Courts cannot call into question the validity of Community law on the basis of national constitutional standards. Allowing national Constitutional Courts to assess the validity of Community law would, according to the European Court of Justice, gravely affect the European law's unity and efficacy. For the European Court, "the validity of a Community measure or its effect within a Member State cannot be affected by allegations that it runs counter to either fundamental rights as formulated by the Constitution of that State or the principles of a national constitutional structure".[9]

Still, the Italian Constitutional Court, the German Federal Constitutional Court and the Danish Supreme Court – in acts of defiance – have all three declared they would nevertheless be competent to control the consistency of Community law with the fundamental principles of their respective constitutions.[10] According to these three national Constitutional Courts, their ultimate obligation is, indeed, to protect their own

---

[7] This paragraph is based on Bruno de Witte, "Direct Effect, Supremacy and the Nature of the Legal Order", in Craig and de Burca (eds.), *The Evolution of EU Law*, 179.

[8] Case 6/64, Costa v. ENEL, E.C.R. 1964, 585. On the acceptance of the primacy of Community law in the Member States, see Karen Alter, *Establishing the Supremacy of European Law. The Making of an International Rule of Law in Europe* (Oxford, Oxford University Press, 2001).

[9] Case 11/70, Internationale Handelsgesellschaft mbH v. Einfuhr- und Vorratstelle für Getreide und Futtermittel, E.C.R. 1970, 1125 at 1134.

[10] See Bruno de Witte, "Sovereignty and European Integration: The Weight of Legal Tradition", *Maastricht Journal of European and Comparative Law*, 2 (1995) 145; Ulrich Everling, "The Maastricht Judgment of the German Federal Constitutional Court and its Significance for the Development of the European Union", *Yearbook of European Law*, 14 (1994) 1; Matthias Heregen, "Maastricht and the German Constitutional Court: Constitutional Restraints for an 'Ever Closer Union'", *Common Market Law Review*, 31 (1994) 235; Stephan Hobe, "The Long and Difficult Road Towards Integration: The Legal Debate on the Maastricht Treaty in Germany and the Judgment of the German Constitutional Court of October 12, 1993", *Leiden Journal of International Law*, 7 (1994) 23; Mattias Kumm, "Who is the Final Arbiter of Constitutionality in Europe?: Three Conceptions of the Relationship between the German Federal Constitutional Court and the European Court of Justice", *Common Market Law Review*, 36 (1999) 315.

national constitutional system. As Sten Harck and Henrik Palmer Olsen have put it, the problem is that the European Court of Justice, the German Constitutional Court, the Danish Supreme Court and the Italian Constitutional Court all see themselves as the final arbiter of the validity of Community regulatory acts, each deriving its authority from a different constitutive instrument.[11]

Resistance to the supremacy of the European Court of Justice was also visible during the negotiation of the Treaty of Amsterdam. The blunt attack against the Court by the UK's Major government – in wake of the dispute on the working time directive of 1993 – was unsuccessful. Prime Minister John Major had announced that he wanted to limit the impact of the Court's judgements in view of their "disproportionate costs on governments or business".[12] Still, the Amsterdam Treaty did contain a dangerous precedent with regard to the primacy of Community law. In the new Community Title on visas, asylum, immigration and other policies related to the free movement of persons, the European Court of Justice was granted only limited jurisdiction which could not be related to measures concerning the maintenance of law and order and the safeguarding of internal security. The Council, the Commission or a Member State may request Court of Justice rulings on the interpretation of this Title. However, such interpretations shall not affect judgements of Member State courts which have become *res judicata*, thus in practice undercutting the primacy principle.[13]

II. Between a Centralised and a Decentralised Law Enforcement Regime

A. *Composition of the Court of Justice and Court of First Instance*

Traditionally, the European Court of Justice and the Court of First Instance have always included at least as many judges as Member States, with one judge coming from each. In light of enlargement, the Court has

---

[11] Sten Harck and Henrik Palmer Olsen, "Decision concerning the Maastricht Treaty, Supreme Court of Denmark, April 6, 1998", *American Journal of International Law*, 93 (1999) 209.

[12] United Kingdom, *A Partnership of Nations. The British Approach to the European Union Intergovernmental Conference* (London, HMSO, 1996), 16-17.

[13] Consolidated TEU, art. 68. See also Albertina Albors-Llorens, "Changes in the Jurisdiction of the European Court of Justice under the Treaty of Amsterdam", *Common Market Law Review*, 35 (1998) 1273; Anthony Arnull, "Taming the Beast? The Treaty of Amsterdam and the Court of Justice", in O'Keeffe and Twomey (eds.), *Legal Issues of the Amsterdam Treaty*, 109; Ole Due, "The Impact of the Amsterdam Treaty upon the Court of Justice", *Fordham International Law Journal*, 22 (1999) 548.

expressed doubt whether it would be appropriate to maintain this practice. During the negotiations of the Treaty of Nice, the Court drew attention "to the risk inherent in a large increase in the number of judges which could entail the Court being transformed from a judicial collegiate body to something like a deliberative assembly. The majority of cases would have to be decided by smaller chambers of judges, thus jeopardising the coherence of the case law".[14]

During the Nice IGC, the great majority of delegations nevertheless considered it essential that the Court's composition would reflect the national legal systems of all Member States.[15] Instead of continuing with the practice to fix the exact number of judges in the Treaty after each accession, the negotiators decided to redraft the Treaty so that the number of judges would automatically change with the number of Member States.[16] With respect to the Court of First Instance, the nego-tiators believed it could be useful at some point for the number of members to exceed the number of Member States. This could be made necessary in light of the increased powers for the Court of First Instance and the foreseeable increase in its caseload that would result from the Treaty of Nice.[17] The number of judges would be determined by the Statute of the Court of Justice. At present their number is fixed at fifteen.[18]

Given that the Member States wanted the number of judges to grow with the number of Member States, the Court's functioning risked becoming extremely unwieldy with a number of judges approaching 25 after accession.[19] Precisely as the Court had predicted in its critical comment referred to above, the Member States specified at Nice that the Court should normally sit in chambers or in a Grand Chamber.[20] Chambers are composed of three or five judges.[21] The Grand Chamber consists of eleven judges and sits when a Member State or a Community institution that is party to the proceedings so requests.[22] The Court of

---

[14] Court of Justice of the European Communities, "The EC Court of Justice and the Institutional Reform of the European Union", April 2000, 1.

[15] CONFER 4729/00, 10. On the judicial reforms of the Treaty of Nice, see Angus Johnston, "Judicial Reform and the Treaty of Nice", *Common Market Law Review*, 38 (2001) 499; Marianne Dony and Emmanuelle Bribosia (eds.), *L'Avenir du Système Jurisdictionnel de l'Union Européenne* (Bruxelles, Ed. de l'Université de Bruxelles, 2002).

[16] Treaty of Nice, art. 2(27) amending Consolidated TEC, art. 221.

[17] CONFER 4729/00, 11.

[18] Nice Protocol on the Statute of the Court of Justice, art. 48.

[19] CONFER 4743, 4.

[20] Treaty of Nice, art. 2(27) amending Consolidated TEC, art. 221.

[21] Nice Protocol on the Statute of the Court of Justice, art. 16.

[22] *Ibid.*

Justice sits in plenary session only in the exceptional situation where
cases are brought before it regarding the compulsory retirement of a
Commissioner, a member of the Court of Auditors or the Ombudsman.[23]
The Court of First Instance continues the practice of sitting in chambers
of three or five judges.[24]

B. Indirect Actions before the Court: Preliminary Rulings

The Treaty of Rome foresaw two major roads of access to the Court:
indirect and direct actions. Indirect actions concern questions on the
validity and interpretation of Community law that are brought before the
European Court of Justice by national courts or tribunals. Whenever a
national court is confronted with the necessity to pronounce itself on the
validity or interpretation of Community law, it may refer the issue to the
European Court of Justice. National courts against whose decisions there
is no judicial remedy under national law are obliged to bring those
questions before the European Court.[25] These questions often concern a
conflict between national and Community law. The Court's so-called
preliminary rulings are binding on the national judges. The purpose of
the system of preliminary rulings is to preserve a high degree of unity
and coherence in the interpretation of European law throughout Member
States.

During the first half of the 1960s, the Court used the system of
preliminary rulings to establish a strong Community legal order that was
years ahead of European political integration. The two building blocks of
the Court's Community legal order were the principles of direct effect
and primacy.[26] As discussed above, primacy means that in conflicts
between the law of a Member State and Community law, the latter has
precedence. Direct effect implies that individuals (and companies) can

---

[23] *Ibid.*

[24] Nice Protocol on the Statute of the Court of Justice, art. 50.

[25] Consolidated TEC Treaty, art. 234. See Henry G. Schermers, Christiaan W. A.
     Timmermans, Alfred E. Kellermann and J. Steward Watson (eds.), *Article 177 EEC:
     Experiences and Problems* (Amsterdam, North-Holland, 1987); Thomas de la Mare,
     "Article 177 in Social and Political Context", in Craig and de Burca (eds.), *The
     Evolution of EU Law*, 215. On the statistical importance of this provision, see Alec
     Stone Sweet and Thomas L. Brunell, "The European Court and the National Courts:
     a Statistical Analysis of Preliminary References, 1961-95", *Journal of European
     Public Policy*, 5 (1998) 66. On the political importance of this procedure, see Walter
     Mattli and Anne-Marie Slaughter, "Revisiting the European Court of Justice",
     International Organization, 52 (1998) 177.

[26] For an excellent overview, see Bruno de Witte, "Direct Effect, Supremacy, and the
     Nature of the Legal Order", in Craig and de Burca, *The Evolution of EU Law*, 177;
     Pavlos Eleftheriadis, "The Direct Effect of Community Laws: Conceptual Issues",
     Yearbook of European Law, 16 (1996) 205; Sacha Prechal, "Does Direct Effect Still
     Matter?", *Common Market Law Review*, 37 (2000) 1047.

rely on Community law before national courts to challenge the law of their Member State. Both principles were enunciated in the framework of preliminary questions. This was certainly not what the governments of the Member States had been aiming for. During the famous Van Gend and Loos case of 1963, the Dutch, Belgian and German governments all submitted observations to the Court arguing against the direct effect of EEC Treaty provisions.[27] Similarly, during the Costa versus ENEL pleadings, the Italian government argued unsuccessfully against the primacy of EEC law over national law.[28] Both principles were nevertheless well-established as *acquis communautaire* when the Community went through its first enlargement from the Six to the Nine in 1973.

According to the negotiators of the Treaty of Nice, the ever-increasing volume of references for preliminary rulings has caused the Court of Justice to be overburdened.[29] In 1990, 209 preliminary references were pending before the Court. This had grown to 413 cases in 1998.[30] The volume of requests for preliminary rulings also affected the length of time taken to deal with each of them. In 1975, the average time taken to deal with a preliminary reference was just over six months. This increased to 17 months in 1988 and over 23 months in 1999.[31] This time must be added to the time taken for these cases to go through the national courts. For the Court of Justice, it was essential to reduce this period of time "because the effectiveness of the preliminary reference procedure depends on the time the Court takes to give a ruling. If the Court takes too long, national courts will be put off from asking preliminary questions".[32] To improve the efficiency of the Court system of dealing with preliminary rulings, the Member States agreed at Nice to grant the Court of First Instance jurisdiction in principle to hear and determine questions referred for a preliminary ruling. Where there is a serious risk of the unity or consistency of Community law being affected, decisions given by the Court of First Instance in preliminary cases can exceptionally be

---

[27] Case 26/62, Van Gend & Loos v. Nederlandse Administratie der Belastingen, E.C.R. 1963, 1.

[28] Case 6/64, Costa v. ENEL, E.C.R. 1964, 585.

[29] Conference of the Representatives of the Governments of the Member States, "Presidency Note: IGC 2000: Other amendments to be made to the Treaties with regard to the institutions", CONFER 4743, May 19, 2000, 5.

[30] Court of Justice of the European Communities, "The Future of the Judicial System of the European Union. Proposals and Reflections", 1999, 29.

[31] Court of Justice of the European Communities, "The EC Court of Justice and the Institutional Reform of the European Union", April 2000, 2.

[32] *Ibid.*

subject to review by the Court of Justice. This allows the Court of Justice to concentrate on the really important preliminary questions.[33]

Keeping the system of preliminary rulings in good working order is of particular relevance in the perspective of enlargement. Via the mechanism of preliminary rulings, the Community's founders ensured that the Community's newly created legal order would be coherently applied in all Member States, while allowing citizens to bring cases involving the interpretation of Community law before national courts. After the accession of the Central and Eastern European countries, preliminary rulings will be the main mechanism to extend the uniform interpretation of Community law to the new Member States. At the same time, preliminary rulings, in combination with the direct effect and primacy of Community law, will be essential instruments in the societal transformation of the new Member States.

C. Direct Actions before the Court

Direct actions are those cases that do not transit via a national court or tribunal, but are brought directly before the European Court system. In this area too, the Court of Justice insisted on Treaty adaptations at Nice to ensure that, in spite of the increasing case-load, it will still be able to concentrate on its most important functions.[34]

Direct actions include cases brought before the Court to review the legality of Community acts,[35] for failure by a Community institution to act,[36] for compensation for damage caused by the Community institutions or officials,[37] in disputes between the Community and its officials[38] and pursuant to arbitration clauses contained in contracts concluded by the Community.[39] In all these cases, the Treaty of Nice stipulated that the Court of First Instance has jurisdiction at first instance.[40] Decisions given by the Court of First Instance are subject to a right of appeal to the Court of Justice on points of law only.[41] By way of an exception listed in the Court's Statute, the Court of Justice maintains jurisdiction in actions brought by the Community institutions, by the European Central Bank

---

[33] The Treaty of Nice explicitly foresaw that such important preliminary questions can be referred by the Court of First Instance to the Court of Justice.

[34] Court of Justice of the European Communities, "The Future of the Judicial System of the European Union. Proposals and Reflections", 1999, 8.

[35] Consolidated TEC, art. 230.

[36] Consolidated TEC, art. 232.

[37] Consolidated TEC, art. 235.

[38] Consolidated TEC, art. 236.

[39] Consolidated TEC, art. 238.

[40] Treaty of Nice, art. 2(31) amending Consolidated TEC, art. 225.

[41] Treaty of Nice, art. 2(31) amending Consolidated TEC, art. 225(1).

and by the Member States.[42] This leaves the Court of First Instance with cases brought by natural or legal persons. By listing the exceptions to the jurisdiction of the Court of First Instance in the Statute, a change does not require a Treaty revision but can be made by the Council acting unanimously. In a Declaration to the Nice Final Act, the negotiators called on the Court of Justice and the Commission to give overall consideration to the division of competence between the Court of Justice and the Court of First Instance as soon as possible.[43]

Direct actions also include the possibility for the Commission or a Member State to bring another Member State before the Court for failure to fulfil its Treaty obligations.[44] This procedure has become more threatening to the Member States since the Maastricht Treaty granted the Court the power to impose penalty payments on Member States that have failed to comply with earlier judgements.[45] In 2001, the Commission started 1050 infringement proceedings and referred 162 cases to the Court of Justice.[46] After Nice, direct actions whereby Member States are brought before the Court for failure to fulfil their Treaty obligations remain under the exclusive jurisdiction of the Court of Justice.[47]

D. Judicial Panels

In addition to the new division of labour between the Court of Justice and the Court of First Instance, the Treaty of Nice also foresaw in the creation of judicial panels that are attached to the Court of First Instance.[48] Judicial panels determine at first instance certain classes of action brought in specific areas. All Member States agreed that such a judicial panel should be set up as soon as possible to deal with litigation between the Community and its officials arising under the staff regulations.[49] The establishment of these judicial panels was a suggestion from the Court to free itself from specialised litigation which is, or might become, considerable.[50] The creation of judicial panels requires a unanimous Council decision on a proposal of the Commission or on a request of the Court of Justice and after consulting the European Parliament. The

---

[42] Nice Protocol on the Statute of the Court of Justice, art. 51.
[43] Nice Declaration 12 on Article 225 of the Treaty establishing the European Community.
[44] Consolidated TEC, arts. 226 and 227.
[45] Consolidated TEC, art. 228.
[46] Gen. Rep. EU 2001, para. 1177.
[47] Consolidated TEC, art. 226.
[48] Treaty of Nice, art. 2(26) and (32) amending Consolidated TEC, arts. 220 and 225a.
[49] CONFER 4743, 5; Nice Declaration 16 on Article 225a of the Treaty establishing the European Community.
[50] CONFER 4743, 5.

members of judicial panels are appointed by the Council acting unanimously. Decisions given by judicial panels are subject to a right of appeal before the Court of First Instance.

E. The Decentralisation in the Enforcement of the Community's Antitrust Law

In addition to the Court, the European Commission also plays a crucial role in the enforcement of Community law. This is particularly the case in the field of antitrust policy.[51] In November 2002, the Council reached a political agreement on the reform of the Community's antitrust enforcement procedures.[52] The new system enters into force as from May 1, 2004. Via the modernisation of the antitrust enforcement procedures, the Community tries to combine the coherence of the Community's competition policy with greater decentralisation in the enforcement.[53] This reform is therefore of particular relevance from an institutional perspective.

The Treaty of Rome's antitrust rules form an essential part of the Internal Market *acquis*. The Treaty prohibits the abuse of a dominant market position by a company.[54] The Treaty also prohibits anti-competitive agreements and concerted practices between companies which may affect trade between the Member States.[55] Examples are agreements whereby companies try to deny their consumers the benefit of competition by fixing prices or partition markets. The prohibition of restrictive agreements is not absolute. The Treaty recognises that exemptions are possible for restrictive agreements that contribute to improving the production or distribution of goods or to promoting technical or economic progress, while allowing consumers a fair share of the resulting benefit and not imposing indispensable restrictions.[56] To implement these Treaty rules, the Council adopted Regulation 17 of 1962.[57] It reserved the power to apply the exemption provisions with respect to

---

[51]   See Consolidated EC Treaty, art. 85 and art. 88.

[52]   Competitiveness Council, "Press Release", November 26, 2002, 25.

[53]   Commission of the European Communities, "Proposal for a Council Regulation on the Implementation of the Rules on Competition laid down in articles 81 and 82 of the Treaty and amending Regulations (EEC) No. 1017/68, (EEC) No. 2988/74, (EEC) No. 4056/86 and (EEC) No. 3975/87", COM(2000) 582 final, September 27, 2000; Commission of the European Communities, "White Paper on Modernisation of the Rules Implementing Articles 85 and 86 of the EC Treaty", April, 28, 1999.

[54]   Consolidated TEC, art. 82.

[55]   Consolidated TEC, art. 81(1).

[56]   Consolidated TEC, art. 81(3).

[57]   "Regulation No. 17. First Regulation Implementing Articles 85 and 86 of the Treaty", O.J. 21.2.1962, P 13, 204.

restrictive agreements to the European Commission. Regulation 17 thus established a highly centralised authorisation system for all restrictive agreements requiring exemptions. Applications for such exemptions had to be notified to the Commission.

According to the Commission, providing it with the exclusive right to apply the exemption possibility with respect to restrictive agreements was well suited for a Community of six Member States in which the coherence of competition law and policy still had to be established. The Commission's monopoly on granting exemptions allowed the consistent application of competition policy throughout the Community. However, after more than 40 years of practice, the Commission was of the opinion that the centralised notification regime which it had to run in view of the granting of exemptions, constituted a heavy administrative burden, only rarely revealing cases posing a real threat to competition. In view of the amount of work involved, the notification system also prevented the Commission from using its scarce human resources in an optimal manner for the detection and punishment of the most serious infringements. Furthermore, the Commission's monopoly on the application of the exemption possibility was seen as a significant obstacle to the effective application of Community antitrust discipline by national competition authorities and courts. According to the Commission, the perspective of enlargement of the Community made a modernisation of the procedures even more urgent. "In a Union with over 20 Member States, it will no longer be possible to retain a centralised prior authorisation system in Brussels, involving the individual assessment of thousands of cases".[58]

In order to remedy the drawbacks of the current system, the Council agreed, upon a Commission proposal, to reform the system. This will allow the national authorities and courts to apply not only the prohibition provision against anti-competitive agreements between companies, but also the exemption possibility. A core element of the new system is that the Commission and the national competition authorities form a network that provides for a mutual exchange of information and assistance. The network also ensures an efficient allocation of cases, based on the principle that they must be dealt with by the best placed authority. This will allow the Commission to concentrate on the detection of the most serious infringements with a Community dimension.[59]

---

[58]   Commission of the European Communities, "White Paper on Modernisation of the Rules Implementing Articles 85 and 86 of the EC Treaty", April, 28, 1999, 18.

[59]   For an analysis of the Commission's proposal for the modernisation of the antitrust procedures, see Koen Lenaerts *et al.*, "Le Livre Blanc de la Commission sur la Modernisation des Règles de Concurrence", *Cahiers de Droit Européen*, 35 (2001) 133; José Rivas and Margot Horspool (eds.), *Modernisation and Decentralisation of EC Competition Law* (The Hague, Kluwer Law International, 2000; Wouter P. J.

While pushing for a decentralisation of antitrust enforcement, the Commission at the same time wanted to prevent a renationalisation of the policy behind competition law. National competition authorities and courts will be under the obligation to use every effort not to contradict a Commission decision. National authorities and courts will continue to work within the framework of the Community block exemption regulations, Commission guidelines and case-law of the Court of Justice and the Court of First Instance. To further ensure consistency, the application of Community competition rules by national courts will be subject to the preliminary reference procedure.

The modernisation of Community antitrust procedures shares a number of important objectives with the reform of the Court system at Nice. Both try to ensure that Court of Justice and Commission are able to focus on the most significant cases with a Community dimension. In the perspective of enlargement, both try to prevent the Court and the Commission from being "snowed under" by a constantly increasing load of less important cases. Furthermore, both reforms build on the strong foundations of the Community method, including primacy of Community law, direct effect and preliminary rulings, to ensure the continuing coherence in the interpretation and application of the law.

III. Between Solemn Declarations and Directly Applicable Fundamental Rights

A. Judicial Protection of Fundamental Rights in the EU

The original Treaty of Rome did not explicitly refer to respect for fundamental human rights. This is not entirely surprising. First, the EEC Treaty contained mainly economic provisions. In this framework it prohibited "any discrimination on grounds of nationality"[60] and provided for "the principle that men and women should receive equal pay for equal work".[61] Second, the six original Member States were also all party to the Council of Europe's European Convention for the Protection of

---

Wils, "The Modernisation of the Enforcement of Articles 81 and 82 EC: a Legal and Economic Analysis of the Community's Proposal for a new Council Regulation replacing Regulation No. 17", in Barry E. Hawk (ed.), *2000 Annual Proceedings of the Fordham Corporate Law Institute Conference on International Antitrust Law and Policy* (New York, Fordham Corporate Law Institute, 2001), 313).

[60] EEC Treaty, art. 6. For a good overview of the issue, see Emmanuelle Bribosia, Emmanuelle Dardenne, Paul Magnette and Anne Weyembergh (eds.), *Union Européenne et Nationalités: le Principe de Non-Discrimination et ses Limites* (Brussels, Bruylant, 1999).

[61] EEC Treaty, art. 119. For the recent evolution of the case-law in this area, see Evelyn Ellis, "The Recent Jurisprudence of the Court of Justice in the Field of Sex Equality", *Common Market Law Review*, 37 (2000) 1403.

Human Rights and Fundamental Freedoms of 1950. There seemed no need to duplicate the Council of Europe's advanced protection mechanism that had entered into force in 1953.

Still, the Court of Justice recognised early on that Community law does create rights and obligations not only for the Member States but also directly for European citizens, and this in contrast with most international treaties. In the Van Gend and Loos judgement of 1963, the European Court of Justice emphasised that the Treaty of Rome

> is more than an agreement which merely creates mutual obligations between the contracting states ... Independently of the legislation of the Member States, Community law ... not only imposes obligations on individuals but is also intended to confer upon them rights which become part of their legal heritage.[62]

At the end of the 1960s and the beginning of the 1970s, the Court confirmed that such rights included fundamental human rights and stated unambiguously that these rights formed an integral part of the general principles of law whose observance it observed.[63] In Maastricht and Amsterdam, the link between the EU, its citizens and the protection of their fundamental rights was substantially strengthened. The Treaty of Maastricht notably created the concept of the "citizenship of the Union", explicitly adding that the "[c]itizens of the Union shall enjoy the rights conferred by the Treaty and shall be subject to the duties imposed thereby".[64] The Treaty thus formalised the relationship between the

---

[62]   Case 26/62, Van Gend & Loos, E.C.R. 1963, 1 at 12.

[63]   See Case 29/69, Stauder v. City of Ulm, E.C.R. 1969, 419 at 425; Case 11/70 Internationale Handelsgesellschaft mbH v. Einfuhr- und Vorratsstelle für Getreide und Futtermittel, E.C.R. 1970, 1125 at 1134; Case 4/73 J. Nold Kohlen- und Baustoff-grosshandlung v. Commission, E.C.R. 1974, 491 at 507-508. For the evolution of the case-law since the 1960s, see Gérard Cohen-Jonathan, "La Protection des Droits Fondamentaux par la Cour de Justice des Communautés européennes", in Roland Bieber, Karel De Gucht, Koen Lenaerts and Joseph Weiler (eds.), *In the Name of the Peoples of Europe: A Catalogue of Fundamental Rights* (Baden-Baden, Nomos, 1996), 44; Koen Lenaerts, "Le Respect des Droits Fondamentaux en tant que Principe Constitutionnel de l'Union Européenne", in Marianne Dony (ed.), *Mélanges en Hommage à Michel Waelbroeck* (Brussels, Bruylant, 1999), 423; Gil Carlos Rodriguez Iglesias, "The Protection of Fundamental Rights in the Case Law of the Court of Justice of the European Communities", *Columbia Journal of European Law*, 1 (1994-5) 169; J. H. H. Weiler and Nicolas J. S. Lockhart, "'Taking Rights Seriously' Seriously: The European Court of Justice and its Fundamental Rights Jurisprudence", *Common Market Law Review*, 32 (1995) 51 and 579.

[64]   Consolidated TEC, art. 17. On European citizenship, see Klaus Eder and Bernhard Giesen (eds.), *European Citizenship between National Legacies and Postnational Projects* (Oxford, Oxford University Press, 2001); Marie José Garot, *La Citoyenneté de l'Union Européenne* (Paris, L'Harmattan, 1999); Paul Magnette, *La Citoyenneté Européenne* (Brussels, Ed. de l'Université de Bruxelles, 1999); Siofra O'Leary, *The Evolving Concept of Community Citizenship: From Free Movement of Persons to*

citizens and the Union, complementing but not replacing the relationship between the citizens and their Member States. Even the German Federal Constitutional Court, in its famous Maastricht judgement of 1993, came to the conclusion that "with the establishment of Union citizenship ... a legal bond is formed between the nationals of the individual Member States which ... provides a legally binding expression of the degree of the *de facto* community already in existence".[65] The Treaty of Amsterdam further strengthened the Community's legal basis for the protection of human rights, notably by granting the Community an explicit competence to take appropriate action in combating discrimination based on sex, racial or ethnic origin, religion or belief, disability, age, and sexual orientation.[66]

While adding new references to citizens rights, the Member States ensured, however, that they would keep full control over the implementation of the anti-discrimination provision. Action can only be taken by unanimity in the Council. As such, the anti-discrimination clause does not have direct effect. This implies that individuals cannot rely on its provisions to obtain rights before national courts.

Direct effect was also excluded with regard to the legal instruments (framework decisions) foreseen by the Treaty of Amsterdam in the area of police and judicial co-operation in criminal matters.[67] The Member States feared actions by individuals before domestic courts against their national police and judicial practices. Furthermore, while Council, Commission and Member States may request Court of Justice rulings on the interpretation of the EC Treaty's provisions on visas, asylum, immigration and other policies related to free movement of persons, the Treaty of Amsterdam made sure that individuals cannot do so.[68] While

---

Union Citizenship (The Hague, Kluwer Law International, 1996); Linda Hiljemark, "A Voyage around Article 8: An Historical and Comparative Evaluation of the Fate of European Citizenship", *Yearbook of European Law*, 17 (1997) 135; Helen Toner, "Judicial Interpretation of European Union Citizenship: Transformation or Consolidation?", *Maastricht Journal of European and Comparative Law*, 7 (2000) 158.

[65]   Entscheidungen des Bundesferfassungsgerichts (German Federal Constitutional Court), October 12, 1993, C.M.L.R. 1, 1994, 57, para. 39.

[66]   Consolidated TEC, art. 13. See also Catherine Barnard, "Article 13: Through the Looking Glass of Union Citizenship", in O'Keeffe and Twomey (eds.), *Legal Issues of the Amsterdam Treaty*, 375; Mark Bell, "The New Article 13 EC Treaty: A Sound Basis for European Anti-Discrimination Law?", *Maastricht Journal of European and Comparative Law*, 6 (1999) 5; Leo Flynn, "The Implications of Article 13 EC – After Amsterdam, Will Some Forms of Discrimination be More Equal than Others?", *Common Market Law Review*, 36 (1999) 1127.

[67]   Consolidated TEU, art. 34. In addition, preliminary rulings with respect to the EU's third pillar are possible only if the Member States concerned have explicitly accepted the jurisdiction of the Court of Justice. See Consolidated TEU, art. 35(2).

[68]   Consolidated TEC, art. 68.

the formal recognition of the citizen's fundamental rights in the EU framework was largely the result of the Court's case-law, often in cases started before national courts, the Member States showed great reluctance to allow the further evolution of the law via direct effect in areas that touch the fundamental rights and obligations of individuals.

B. The Charter of Fundamental Rights of the European Union

While the Treaties of Maastricht and Amsterdam brought the EU under the explicit obligation to "respect fundamental rights, as guaranteed by the Council of Europe's European Convention for the Protection of Human Rights and Fundamental Freedoms",[69] the EU's direct accession to the Council of Europe's Convention was ruled out by the Court's Opinion 2/94 of 1996.[70] The Court held that accession to the Council of Europe's Convention would entail such a substantial change in the Community's system for human rights that it went beyond the scope of the existing Treaty provisions. According to Koen Lenaerts, Judge at the Court of First Instance, this was a "thinly veiled appeal to the Community's legal order's constituent powers to assume its responsibilities by amending the "constitutional charter" of that legal order".[71]

At Amsterdam, the Member States failed, however, to make the necessary Treaty changes that would allow for the EU's accession to the Council of Europe's Convention. Instead, the Cologne European Council of June 1999 took the decision that the EU would itself draw up a Charter of Fundamental Rights.[72] It was elaborated by a body composed of 15 representatives of the Heads of State or Government, a Commission representative, 16 Members of the European Parliament and 30 rep-

---

[69] Consolidated TEU, art. 6.s

[70] Opinion 2/94, E.C.R. 1996, I-1759. See Johan Ludwig Duvigneau, "From Advisory Opinion 2/94 to the Amsterdam Treaty: Human Rights Protection in the European Union", *Legal Issues of European Integration*, 25 (1998) 61; Olivier De Schutter and Yves Lejeune, "L'Adhésion de la Communauté à la Convention des Droits de l'Homme. A Propos de l'Avis 2/94 de la Cour de Justice des Communautés", *Cahiers de Droit Européen*, 32 (1996) 555; Sandrine Mathieu, "L'Adhésion de la Communauté à la CEDH: un Problème de Compétence ou un Problème de Soumission?", *Revue du Marché Commun et de l'Union Européenne*, (1998) 31; Noreen Burrows, "Question of Community Accession to the European Convention Determined", *European Law Review*, 22 (1997) 58; Patrick Wachtsmann, "L'Avis 2/94 de la Cour de Justice Relatif à l'Adhésion de la Communauté Européenne à la Convention de Sauvegarde des Droits de l'Homme et des Libertés Fondamentales", *Revue Trimestrielle de Droit Européen*, 32 (1996) 467; Florence Chaltiel, "L'Union Européenne doit-elle Adhérer à la Convention Européenne des Droits de l'Homme?", *Revue du Marché Commun et de l'Union Européenne*, (1997) 34.

[71] Koen Lenaerts, "Fundamental Rights in the European Union", *European Law Review*, 25 (2000) 575.

[72] Cologne European Council, "Presidency Conclusions", June 3-4, 1999, para. 64.

resentatives of the national parliaments.[73] The resulting Charter contains the fundamental rights and fundamental freedoms as well as the basic procedural rights guaranteed by the Council of Europe's Convention and derived from the constitutional traditions common to the Member States.[74] There was no consensus among the Member States to incorporate the Charter in the Treaty. The United Kingdom, supported by Ireland, Denmark and Sweden, expressed absolute determination to avoid the Charter becoming legally binding as it could form the basis for a European Constitution.[75] The European Parliament's proposal that the Charter should at least be referred to in Article 6 of the Consolidated Treaty on European Union was also rejected.[76] As a result, the Charter has the status of a non-binding solemn declaration, reaffirming the rights which are enshrined in other fundamental rights instruments.[77] While welcoming the proclamation of the Charter, the European Parliament explicitly regretted "the fact that it has neither been incorporated nor even referred to in the new Treaty".[78]

The Nice European Council decided that the Charter's status should be reviewed during the IGC that is foreseen for 2004.[79] In preparation for this new round of Treaty reform, the European Convention's Working Group on the Charter considered essential that the Charter of Fundamental Rights would be incorporated into the Constitutional Treaty. The Working Group also suggested that a legal basis be created to make the

---

[73]   On the negotiating process leading to the Charter, see de Burca, "The Drafting of the European Union Charter of Fundamental Rights"; Deloche-Gaudez, *La Convention pour l'Elaboration de la Charte des Droits Fondamentaux.*

[74]   O.J. C 364, 2000, 1.

[75]   *European Report*, October 18, 2000, I-8; *European Report*, December 6, 2000, I-4.

[76]   Conference of the Representatives of the Governments of the Member States, "Presidency: IGC 2000: Incorporation of the Charter of Fundamental Rights into Article 6 TEU", CONFER 4804/00, November 16, 2000, 1.

[77]   For an analysis of the Charter, see Kim Feus (ed.), *The EU Charter of Fundamental Rights – Text and Commentaries* (London, Federal Trust, Constitution for Europe Series 1, 2000); Koen Lenaerts and Eddy De Smijter, "A "Bill of Rights" for the European Union", *Common Market Law Review*, 38 (2001) 273; Piet Eeckhout, "The EU Charter of Fundamental Rights and the Federal Question", *Common Market Law Review*, 39 (2002) 945 and the interesting contributions in the Special Issue on the EU Charter of Fundamental Rights in the *Maastricht Journal of European and Comparative Law*, 8 (2001) 1.

[78]   European Parliament, "Resolution on the Outcome of the European Council on 7-11 December 2000 in Nice", Minutes of the Plenary Session of December 14, 2000, para. 3. For the European Parliament's view on the Charter, see European Parliament, "Decision Approving the Draft Charter of Fundamental Rights of the European Union", Minutes of the Plenary Session of 14 November 2000.

[79]   Nice Declaration 23 on the Future of the Union, para. 5.

EU's accession to the Council of Europe's Convention on Human Rights possible.[80]

C. Surveillance over the Member States: The Austrian Crisis and the EU's Alarm and Sanction Mechanism

At Amsterdam, the Heads of State or Government had decided to list "liberty, democracy, respect for human rights and fundamental freedoms, and the rule of law" as the principles on which the EU was founded.[81] Respect for these principles became an explicit precondition for applying for EU membership.[82] In addition, a two-step sanction procedure was created. Following the determination by the Council of the "existence of a serious and persistent breach" of the above-mentioned principles by a Member State,[83] certain rights of the Member State in question could be suspended.[84]

The Amsterdam procedure did not, however, foresee any early warning ahead of the introduction of sanctions. Following the "Austrian crisis", the need for a surveillance and warning mechanism was catapulted on the agenda of the Nice Treaty negotiations.[85] In February 2000, a coalition government had been formed between the Austrian People's Party (ÖVP) and the Austrian Freedom Party (FPÖ). The FPÖ was notorious for its extreme right-wing programme and for "the insulting, xenophobic, racist statements" by its leader Jörg Haider.[86] The fourteen Heads of State or Government of the EU's other Member States immediately "informed the Austrian authorities that there would be no

---

[80]   The European Convention, "Final Report of Working Group II : Incorporation of the Charter/Accession to the ECHR", CONV 354/02, October 22 , 2002.

[81]   Consolidated TEU, art. 6.

[82]   Consolidated TEU, art. 49.

[83]   Consolidated TEU, art. 7(1), has become art. 7(2) following the entry into force of the Treaty of Nice. The Council can take this decision meeting in the composition of the Heads of State or Government and acting by unanimity on a proposal by one third of the Member States or by the Commission and after obtaining the assent of the European Parliament. The vote of the Member State in question shall not be taken into account.

[84]   Consolidated TEU art. 7(2), has become art. 7(3) following the entry into force of the Treaty of Nice. The Council can take this decision, acting by qualified majority without taking into account the vote of the Member State in question.

[85]   On the Austrian episode, see Michael Merlinger, Cas Mudde and Ulrich Sedelmeier, "European Norms, Domestic Politics and Sanctions Against Austria", *Journal of Common Market Studies*, 39 (2001) 59.

[86]   This is how the European Parliament characterised the statements by Jörg Haider. See European Parliament, "Resolution on the Legislative Elections in Austria and the Proposal to form a Coalition Government between the ÖVP (Austrian People's Party) and the FPÖ (Austrian Freedom Party)", Minutes of the Plenary Session of February 3, 2000, para. 1.

business as usual in the bilateral relations with a Government integrating the FPÖ".[87] As there had not been any evidence of a "serious and persistent breach" of fundamental rights by Austria, there was no legal basis, however, for sanctions at the EU level. On request of the French Council Presidency, the President of the European Court of Human Rights, in July 2000, appointed a committee of three Wise Men to exa-mine the political and human rights record in Austria.[88] The Wise Men Report, issued on September 8, 2000, found no evidence that the Austrian government had breached the European Convention for the Protection of Human Rights and Fundamental Freedoms or significantly altered Austria's policy towards refugees, immigrants or ethnic mino-rities.[89] A few days later, Austria's EU partners decided to lift their bilateral sanctions.[90]

The Presidency statement lifting the bilateral sanctions against Austria mentioned that it would be appropriate to continue the reflection process within the EU on the best way to act in similar situations.[91] During the negotiations of the Treaty of Nice, Belgium (the Member State that had been leading the push for bilateral sanctions against Austria), Austria, the Portuguese Presidency and the European Commis-sion all made proposals to introduce an early warning mechanism ahead of penalties.[92] In the end, it was agreed to create a procedure in two stages. Since the entry into force of the Treaty of Nice, the Council first assesses whether there exists "a clear *risk*" of a serious breach of the EU's fundamental principles. Only thereafter can the Council conclude

---

[87]   "Statement from the Portuguese Presidency of the European Union on Behalf of XIV Member States", January 31, 2000. The statement did include the following sanctions against the Austrian government:
   – Governments of XIV Member States will not promote or accept any bilateral offi-cial contacts at political level with an Austrian Government integrating the FPÖ;
   – There will be no support in favour of Austrian candidates seeking positions in international organisations;
   – Austrian Ambassadors in EU capitals will only be received at a technical level.

[88]   The members of the committee were Martti Ahtisaari, former President of Finland, Marcelino Oreja, former Spanish Minister of Foreign Affairs and former European Commissioner and Jochen Frowein, a German lawyer.

[89]   Martti Ahtisaari, Jochen Frowein and Marcelino Oreja, "Report on the Austrian Government's Commitment to the Common European Values, in Particular Concerning the Rights of Minorities, Refugees and Immigrants and the Evolution of the Political Nature of the FPÖ (The Wise Men Report)", *International Legal Materials*, 40 (2001) 101.

[90]   For the statement by the French Presidency announcing the decision to lift the sanctions, see *Le Monde*, September 14, 2000, 2.

[91]   *Le Monde*, September 14, 2000, 2.

[92]   Conference of the Representatives of the Governments of the Member States, "Presi-dency: IGC 2000: Article 7 of the TEU", CONFER 4782/00, October 5, 2000, 1.

that there is a persistent *breach*.[93] In a case of "risk", the Council is able to "address appropriate recommendations to that State".[94] Before making a declaration of risk, the Council may call on independent persons to submit a report on the situation in the Member State in question.[95]

IV. Between a Pro-active and a Reactive Approach to the Creation of an Area of Freedom, Security and Justice in the EU

Since the entry into force of the Treaty of Amsterdam, the creation of an area of freedom, security and justice is one of the EU's key objectives.[96] The progressive establishment of an area of freedom, security and justice can be found in two different parts of the EU Treaty framework. First, it is the objective of the new provisions on "visas, asylum, immigration and other policies related to free movement of persons" in the Treaty establishing the European Community.[97] Second, providing citizens with a high level of safety within an area of freedom, security and justice is the central purpose under the provisions on police and judicial co-operation in criminal matters (the EU's amended third pillar).[98]

The Treaty of Maastricht's third pillar provisions on Co-operation in the fields of Justice and Home Affairs (JHA) had initially covered both fields (with the exception of the pure free movement of persons and visa questions which were already part of the European Community pillar).[99] The set-up of the Maastricht Treaty's third pillar was intergovernmen-

---

[93] Treaty of Nice, art. 1(1) amending Consolidated TEU, art. 7(1). The Treaty of Nice requires that Council decisions in this area are made by a majority of four fifths of its Members and after obtaining the assent of the European Parliament, on a reasoned proposal by one third of the Member States, by the European Parliament or by the Commission. Belgium had proposed Council decision-making by qualified majority, the Commission proposed a two thirds Council majority, the Portuguese Presidency a majority of nine tenths and Austria unanimity.

[94] Treaty of Nice, art. 1(1) amending Consolidated TEU, art. 7(1).

[95] *Ibid.*

[96] See Jörg Monar, "Justice and Home Affairs after Amsterdam: the Treaty Reforms and the Challenge of their Implementation", in Jörg Monar and Wolfgang Wessels (eds.), *The European Union after the Treaty of Amsterdam* (London, Continuum, 2001), 267; Steve Peers, *EU Justice and Home Affairs Law* (London, Longman, 2000).

[97] Consolidated TEC, Title IV, Visas, asylum, immigration and other policies related to free movement of persons.

[98] Consolidated TEU, Title VI, Provisions on police and judicial co-operation in criminal matters.

[99] Treaty on European Union, Title VI, Provisions on co-operation in the fields of justice and home affairs.

tal.[100] At the start of the negotiations of the Treaty of Amsterdam, the Member States realised that little had been achieved under Maastricht's third pillar. This was considered as worrying, in particular in light of enlargement which was believed to necessitate "a qualitative change in the need to guarantee the internal security of citizens of the Union more effectively".[101] According to the report of the Reflection Group that had been put in charge of preparing the Amsterdam IGC, "the Group ... concluded unanimously that the magnitude of the challenges [in JHA] is not matched by the results achieved so far in response to them".[102] The Reflection Group Report further clarified that "many" of its members took "the view that, in order to act more efficiently, we need to put fully under Community competence matters concerning third country nationals, such as immigration, asylum and visa policy, as well as common rules for external border controls".[103] Other members of the Reflection Group disagreed. They argued that the "separation of 'pillars' is essential in order to respect the intergovernmental management of these matters that are so closely linked with national sovereignty".[104] In the end, the Treaty of Amsterdam left police and judicial co-operation in criminal matters in the intergovernmental third pillar. The other topics under Maastricht's JHA provisions were transferred to the Community pillar.

The Treaty of Amsterdam's Community title on free movement of persons, asylum and immigration is to ensure intra-EU free movement of persons within five years following its entry into force in 1999.[105] The

---

[100] On Maastricht's JHA provisions, see Jörg Monar and Roger Morgan (eds.), *The Third Pillar of the European Union: Cooperation in the Fields of Justice and Home Affairs* (Brussels, European Interuniversity Press, 1994); Roland Bieber and Jörg Monar (eds.), *Justice and Home Affairs in the European Union: Development of the Third Pillar* (Brussels, European Interuniversity Press, 1995).

[101] *Reflection Group Report*, para. 45. See also Jörg Monar, "The Justice and Home Affairs Dimension of EU Enlargement", *International Spectator*, 36 (2001/3) 37.

[102] *Reflection Group Report*, para. 46.

[103] *Reflection Group Report*, 23.

[104] *Reflection Group Report*, para. 50.

[105] Consolidated TEC, art. 61(1). This also involved the integration of the Schengen *acquis* in the EU framework. Schengen refers to the Agreement on the gradual abolition of checks at common borders of June 14, 1985 and the Convention implementing the Schengen Agreement of June 19, 1990, initially signed by the States of the Benelux Economic Union (Belgium, Luxembourg and the Netherlands), Germany and France and later extended to Denmark, Greece, Italy, Spain, Portugal, Austria, Finland and Sweden (as well as to non-Member States Norway and Iceland). Amsterdam Protocol 2 integrating the Schengen *acquis* into the framework of the European Union recognises that UK and Ireland are not bound by the Schengen *acquis*, but may at any time request to take part in some or all of the provisions of this *acquis*. All new Member States have to accept the Schengen *acquis* in full. For the text of the Schengen Agreement, the Convention implementing the Schengen Agreement and the Schengen *acquis*, see O.J. L 239, 22.9.2000, 1. For a comment,

Treaty foresees that this should be accompanied by measures regulating the crossing of the EU's external borders, asylum and immigration.[106] In practice, "progress has been slower and less substantial than expected".[107] Initial Presidency texts during the Amsterdam negotiations on the free movement of persons, asylum and immigration foresaw an automatic passage from unanimity to qualified majority voting after a three-year transition period. However, under pressure from the sixteen German Länder, which share responsibility for immigration with the German Federal government, Chancellor Helmut Kohl insisted, during the final days of the negotiations, on greater caution. Recalling that Germany had over the last decade taken in an average of 45 to 60% of all refugees who have sought asylum in the Union, Kohl saw it as a national duty and a matter of self-preservation to ensure that Germany kept a right to veto in the area.[108] At Nice, Germany again proved to be the most difficult partner with respect to majority voting in this Treaty title. Chancellor Kohl's successor, Gerhard Schröder, ensured that a gradual move towards qualified majority voting on immigration and asylum policy will be possible only after common rules and basic principles have been defined by unanimity.[109] Decision-making in this new Community pillar title therefore remains largely intergovernmental. During the first

---

see Monica den Boer, "Not Merely a Matter of Moving House: Police Co-operation from Schengen to the TEU", *Maastricht Journal of European and Comparative Law*, 7 (2000) 336; P. J. Kuijper, "Some Legal Problems associated with the Communautarization of Policy on Visas, Asylum and Immigration under the Amsterdam Treaty and Incorporation of the Schengen Acquis", *Common Market Law Review*, 37 (2000) 345; Steve Peers, "Caveat Emptor? Integrating the Schengen Acquis into the European Union Legal Order", *Cambridge Yearbook of European Legal Studies 1999*, 2 (2000) 87.

[106] With Prime Minister Blair insisting on the UK's special island status and right to keep border control checks, the UK and Ireland obtained two Protocols to the Treaty of Amsterdam. The first recognises the Common Travel Area between the UK and Ireland and their right to exercise border controls (Amsterdam Protocol 3 on the application of certain aspects of Article 7a of the Treaty establishing the European Community to the United Kingdom and to Ireland). The second Protocol provides the UK and Ireland with an opt-out of the free movement of persons, with the possibility for participation following a notification of the wish to take part in a decision (Amsterdam Protocol 4 on the position of the United Kingdom and Ireland). Another Protocol deals with the special position of Denmark, providing for an opt-out of the free movement of persons title and of any decisions with defence implications (Amsterdam Protocol 5 on the position of Denmark). See Jaap W. de Zwaan, "Opting In and Opting Out of Rules concerning the Free Movement of Persons. Problems and Practical Arrangements", *Cambridge Yearbook of European Legal Studies 1998*, 1 (1999) 107.

[107] Laeken European Council, "Presidency Conclusions", December 14-15, 2001, para. 38.

[108] Devuyst, "Treaty Reform in the European Union", 621.

[109] Treaty of Nice, art. 2(4) amending Consolidated TEC, art. 67(5).

five years after the entry into force of the Treaty of Amsterdam, the right of legislative initiative is shared between Member States and the Commission.[110] This is a major exception to the Commission's exclusive right of the initiative in the Community pillar. The role of the European Parliament is limited to consultation. Following the five-year transition period after the entry into force of the Amsterdam Treaty, the Commission will receive the exclusive right of initiative. The Council shall then decide by unanimity on the parts of this title that will be dealt with through the co-decision procedure, including qualified majority in the Council.[111]

The remaining third pillar provisions on police and judicial co-operation in criminal matters also underwent a limited institutional adaptation.[112] The Amsterdam negotiators in particular tried to provide the third pillar with more effective policy instruments.[113] "Framework decisions" were created for the purpose of approximating Member State laws. They are binding upon the Member States as to the result to be achieved, but leave choice of form and methods to the Member States (cf. Community directives). "Decisions" are binding and can be implemented through "measures" adopted by qualified majority. For all other third pillar decisions, the Treaty of Amsterdam maintained the unanimity rule. The European Court of Justice was granted limited jurisdiction for third pillar issues not related to the validity or proportionality of law and order enforcement in the Member States.[114]

To give concrete shape to the implementation of the Treaty of Amsterdam's provisions on the creation of an area of freedom, security and justice, the European Council held a special meeting in October 1999 in Tampere, Finland. The European Council established an ambitious set of pro-active political guidelines for the development of a common EU policy asylum and migration policy, a genuine European area of justice, a unionwide fight against crime and stronger external action in the fields of justice and home affairs.[115] The Tampere European Council notably agreed on the reinforcement of the fight against serious

---

[110] Consolidated TEC, art. 67(1).

[111] Consolidated TEC, art. 67(2).

[112] Eugene Regan (ed.), *The New Third Pillar. Cooperation against Crime in the European Union* (Dublin, Institute of European Affairs, 2000).

[113] Consolidated TEU, art. 34(2).

[114] Consolidated TEU, art. 35. On the level of parliamentary and judicial control over third pillar issues, see the interesting analysis by Brendan Smith and William Wallace, "Constitutional Deficits of EU Justice and Home Affairs: Transparency, Accountability and Judicial Control", in Monar and Wessels (eds.), *The European Union after the Treaty of Amsterdam*, 125.

[115] Tampere European Council, "Presidency Conclusions", October 15-16, 1999.

organised crime by setting up a European Judicial Co-operation unit, also called Eurojust. Eurojust is composed of one national member seconded by each Member State in accordance with its legal system, being a prosecutor, judge or police officer of equivalent competence. It has the task of facilitating the proper co-ordination of national prosecuting authorities, of supporting criminal investigations particularly in organised crime cases and of co-operating closely with the European Judicial Network.[116] The creation of Eurojust was formalised by the Treaty of Nice.[117] In the absence of an overall agreement on the seat of certain Community agencies, the Laeken European Council decided that Eurojust would begin operations in The Hague.[118]

While the Tampere European Council had underlined that it would keep under constant review progress made towards implementing the area of freedom, security and justice, concrete policy achievements were relatively modest when, on September 11, 2001, the terrorist attacks on the World Trade Centre (WTC) and the Pentagon shocked the EU into rapid action.[119] By September 19, the Commission had tabled two proposals for Council framework decisions. The first proposal was intended to provide the EU with a common definition of terrorist offences and establish a set of minimum penalties for some of them. The second proposal concerned the European arrest warrant. Its objective was the replacement of the current system of extradition between the Member States, with a new system based on the principle of quasi-automatic recognition of judicial orders for arrest made in another Member State. The Brussels European Council, meeting in extraordinary session on September 21, adopted a plan of action, "instructing" the Justice and Home Affairs Council to implement as quickly as possible the entire package of measures decided at the Tampere European Council. The Justice and Home Affairs Council was further "directed" to flesh out an agreement on the European arrest warrant as a matter of urgency and at the latest at its meeting in December 2001.[120]

By the Laeken European Council of December 14-15, 2001, political agreement had, indeed, been reached on both the European arrest warrant and the common definition of terrorist offences and minimum sen-

---

[116] Tampere European Council, "Presidency Conclusions", October 15-16, 1999, para. 46.

[117] Treaty of Nice, art. 1(7) and (8) amending Consolidated TEU, art. 29 and 31.

[118] Laeken European Council, "Presidency Conclusions", December 14-15, 2001, para. 57.

[119] The following summary of the EU's response to the attacks of September 11, 2001 is based on Gen Rep. 2001, paras 502 ff.

[120] Brussels Extraordinary European Council, "Conclusions and Plan of Action", September 21, 2001, para. 2.1.

tences.[121] The terrorist attacks played a crucial role in creating the necessary momentum for the quick adoption of these decisions. Nevertheless, the EU was able to move forward with great speed only because the Commission had taken the initiative to start preparing the necessary texts with the other institutions several years before September 2001. On September 5, a week before the terrorist attacks, the European Parliament had recommended – on the basis of earlier Commission proposals – that the Council should adopt a common definition of terrorist offences, penalties for such offences, mutual recognition of decisions in criminal matters and a European search and arrest warrant. However, before the attacks of September 2001, it had never been possible to get the agreement of all Member States on such proposals. Even in the context of the terrorist attacks, it took a massive diplomatic effort to bring a very reluctant Italian Prime Minister Berlusconi on board for the European arrest warrant. That the attacks of September 11, 2001 were necessary to move co-operation in police and judicial co-operation forward can therefore be seen as an illustration of the weakness of the intergovernmental third pillar system which requires unanimity among all Member States before any operational decision can be taken.

---

[121] The formal legal texts were adopted by the Council, in written procedure, on December 27, 2001. See O.J. L 344, 28.12.2001.

CHAPTER V

The External Relations of the EU

In the words of Walter Hallstein, "one reason for creating the European Community [wa]s to enable Europe to play its full part in world affairs".[1] The first Commission President emphasised that it was "vital for the Community to be able to speak with one voice and to act as one in its economic relations with the rest of the world".[2] The essential characteristic of the EU's foreign policy has been the attempt to foster political stability and economic development in the neighbouring regions, thereby actively contributing to conflict prevention.[3] In its attempt to fulfil this mission, the EU has "exported" several components of its own integration model. The most significant components of the EU's international engagement can be summarised in four points.

First, the EU has created an extensive network of bilateral international agreements.[4] Such agreements have, for instance, been concluded with the remaining EFTA States (the European Economic Area – EEA), the Central and Eastern European countries (the Europe Agreements), the countries of the western Balkans (the Stabilisation and Association Agreements) and the Mediterranean countries (the Euro-Mediterranean Agreements). These agreements either extend the Internal Market (in the case of the EEA) or allow for the development of a free trade regime, in addition to some degree of legislative approximation and political and economic dialogue. In addition to the agreements with the neighbouring countries, the EU has concluded agreements that contain, or offer a perspective for, preferential trade relations with countries that are at a greater distance such as the African, Caribbean and Pacific (ACP) countries, South Africa, Mexico, Chile and Mercosur. Since the 1995, such Community agreements with third countries all include a clause

---

[1] Walter Hallstein, *United Europe,* 79.

[2] *Ibid.*

[3] For the central role of conflict prevention in the EU's external relations, see Christopher Hill, "The EU's Capacity for Conflict Prevention", *European Foreign Affairs Review,* 6 (2001) 315.

[4] For an overview of this network, see Christopher Piening, *Global Europe. The European Union in World Affairs* (Boulder, Lynne Rienner, 1997); Hazel Smith, *European Union Foreign Policy. What it Is and What it Does* (London, Pluto Press, 2002).

permitting the suspension of the agreements if human rights and democratic principles are not respected.[5]

Second, the EU has set up important financial assistance programmes for third countries. These programmes are designed to support economic development, the strengthening of democracy, the rule of law, civil society, independent media and gender equality. Examples of such financial support programmes are PHARE (for the Central and Eastern European countries),[6] TACIS (for the former Soviet Republics and Mongolia),[7] CARDS (for the western Balkans),[8] MEDA (for the Mediterranean countries),[9] ALA (for the countries in Asia and Latin America)[10] and the European Development Fund (for the ACP countries).[11] These programmes have made the EU the world's largest donor of development aid. In 1998-1999, the EU contributed 47.5% of world-wide development aid, against 27.2% for Japan and 16.2% for the United States.

Third, the EU is actively engaged in fostering regional integration around the world. The ACP-EU Partnership Agreement signed in Cotonou on 23 June 2000, for instance, is specifically designed to stimulate the development of integration among regional groups of ACP countries. Furthermore, the EU pushes for further regional integration in its dialogues with such organisations as the Association of South-East Asian Nations (ASEAN), the Andean Community, Mercosur and the Gulf Co-operation Council. The purpose is to increase economic interde-

---

5   Karen E. Smith, "The EU, Human Rights and Relations with Third Countries: 'Foreign Policy' with an Ethical Dimension?", in Karen E. Smith and Margot Light (eds.), *Ethics and Foreign Policy* (Cambridge, Cambridge University Press, 2001), 185.

6   "Council Regulation (EEC) 3906/89 of 18 December 1989 on economic aid to the Republic of Hungary and the Polish People's Republic", O.J. L 375, 23.12.1989, 1. PHARE support has since been extended to all candidate countries from Central and Eastern Europe, see "Council Regulation (EC) 2666/2000", O.J. L 306, 7.12.2000, 1.

7   "Council Regulation (EC, Euratom) 1279/96 of 25 June 1996 concerning the provision of assistance to economic reform and recovery in the New Independent States and Mongolia", O.J. L 165, 4.7.1996, 1.

8   "Council Regulation 2666/2000 on assistance for Albania, Bosnia and Herzegovina, Croatia, the Federal Republic of Yugoslavia, and the Former Yugoslav Republic of Macedonia", O.J. L 306, 7.12.2000, 1.

9   "Council Regulation (EC) 1488/96 of 23 July 1996 on financial and technical measures to accompany (MEDA) the reform of economic and social structures in the framework of the Euro-Mediterranean partnership", O.J. L 189, 30.7.1996, 1

10   "Council Regulation (EEC) 443/92 of 25 February 1992 on financial and technical assistance to, and economic cooperation with, the developing countries in Asia and Latin America", O.J. L 52, 27.2.1992, 1.

11   Fourth ACP-EEC Convention, O.J. L 229, 17.8.1991, 3; Convention as amended by the Agreement signed at Mauritius on November 4, 1995, O.J. L 156, 29.5.1998, 3.

pendence, stimulate mutual confidence and decrease political tensions between the participants.

Fourth, the EU tries to stimulate a multilateral liberalisation of trade. As one of the world's most important trading powers, the EU sees such liberalisation as being in its own interest. In 2000, the EU was the world's largest exporter of goods and the most important foreign investor in the world. At the same time, the EU was also the largest importer of products from the developing countries. In 1999, the EU imported 55% of developing country exports (in comparison with 38% for the United States and 6% for Japan). To foster the integration of developing countries in the world economy, products from developing countries are granted preferential access on the Internal Market.[12] Since 2001, products originating in the least developed countries enjoy duty-free access in the EU, without any quantitative restrictions. Other developing countries respecting international social and environmental standard. benefit from the Community's scheme of generalised tariff preferences. This scheme includes special incentive arrangements for developing countries respecting international social and environmental standards.[13]

As to the future of the EU's external relations, particular attention is going to the creation of a renewed neighbourhood policy that is expected to address the whole arc of the regions around the Union, from the Maghreb countries to Russia. Both the preliminary draft Constitutional Treaty and the conclusions of the Copenhagen European Council of 2002 included particular provisions on the EU and its neighbours.[14] This is not surprising. As Javier Solana, the High Representative for the CFSP, has explained the reunification of Europe has enormous geopolitical implications.[15] When all current candidate countries, including Turkey, are EU members, the EU will have a population of 500 million and it will share borders with Russia, Belarus, Ukraine, Moldova, Georgia,

---

[12] See Carol Cosgrove-Sacks (ed.), *Europe, Diplomacy and Development. New Issues in EU Relations with Developing Countries* (Basingstoke, Palgrave, 2001); Martin Holland, *The European Union and the Third World* (Basingstoke, Palgrave, 2002). For interesting older perspectives, see Enzo R. Grilli, *The European Community and the Developing Countries* (Cambridge, Cambridge University Press, 1993) and Philip Mishalani, Annette Robert, Christopher Stevens and Ann Weston, "The Pyramid of Privilege", in Christopher Stevens (ed.), *EEC and the Third World: A Survey 1* (London, Hodder and Stoughton, 1981), 60.

[13] "Council Regulation (EC) No. 2501/2001 of 10 December 2001 applying a scheme of generalised tariff preferences for the period from 1 January 2002 to 31 December 2004", O.J. L 346, 31.12.2001, 1.

[14] The European Convention, "Preliminary Draft Constitutional Treaty", CONV 369/02, October 28, 2002, art. 42 ; Seville European Council, "Presidency Conclusions", December 12-13, 2002, para. 22.

[15] Javier Solana, "Lecture at the Inauguration of the Diplomatic Academy of the Ministry of Foreign Affairs of the Republic of Poland", Warsaw, October 16, 2002, 5.

Armenia, Azerbaijan, Iran, Iraq and Syria. The EU's attempt to create, what Commission President Romano Prodi has called, a "ring of friends" is the logical consequence of the EU's own interests.[16] Indeed, Europe's wealth and stability depend to a considerable degree on what is happening in neighbouring areas such as the Eurasian region, the south bank of the Mediterranean and the Middle East.[17]

While the EU's enlargement thus increases its geopolitical role as a factor in international relations, the EU's institutional framework in the field of external relations is extremely complex. As the following pages will highlight, the EU's institutional set-up is a crucial factor determining the its ability to speak with a single voice on world affairs.

I. Between *de jure* and *de facto* International Legal Personality

From the start, the Treaties of Paris and Rome granted explicit legal personality to the three Communities.[18] In addition, the EEC Treaty included clear provisions on the conclusion of international agreements between the Community and one or more States or international organisations.[19] In simplified terms, the Commission acts as the Community's negotiator after having received the authorisation from the Council. The Commission conducts the negotiations within the framework of such directives as the Council may issue to it. During the negotiations, the Commission must regularly consult with a special committee of Member State representatives gathering in the framework of the Council. In the end, it is the Council that concludes international agreements resulting from the negotiations. In principle, the Council acts by qualified majority. Unanimity applies when an agreement covers a field for which unanimity is required for the adoption of internal rules and for the conclusion of association agreements. In general, the European Parliament must be consulted before the Council can conclude agreements.[20] The most

---

[16]   Romano Prodi, "A Wider Europe: A Proximity Policy as a Key to Stability", Speech at the Sixth ECSA World Conference, Brussels, December 5-6, 2002, 5. See also Romano Prodi, "Europe and the Mediterranean: Time for Action", Speech at the Université Catholique de Louvain-la-Neuve, November 26, 2002, 3.

[17]   Solana, "Lecture at the Inauguration of the Diplomatic Academy", 5.

[18]   EEC Treaty, art. 210 currently Consolidated TEC, art. 281. See also ECSC Treaty, art. 6 and Euratom Treaty, art. 184.

[19]   EEC Treaty, art. 228, now Consolidated TEC, art. 300. See also Koen Lenaerts and Eddy De Smijter, "The European Community's Treaty-Making Competence", *Yearbook of European Law*, 16 (1996) 1.

[20]   The consultation procedure leads to non-binding recommendations from Parliament. Consultation of Parliament is not formally required for agreements under the common commercial policy. However, in 1973, the Commission committed itself to

important international agreements can be adopted only after the assent of the European Parliament has been obtained.[21]

While the three European Communities were explicitly granted legal personality, the EU Treaty framework has never explicitly conferred such legal personality on the European Union. This does not imply, however, that no international agreements can be concluded in the context of the CFSP or police and judicial co-operation in criminal matters. Since the Treaty of Amsterdam, it has been explicitly recognised that international agreements with third countries or international organisations can be concluded in implementation of the CFSP and police and judicial co-operation in criminal matters.[22] The decision-making rules for such agreements differ from the Community practice. The intergovernmental nature of the second and third pillars implies that agreements in these fields are negotiated by the Presidency, "assisted by the Commission as appropriate". Before it can start negotiations, the Presidency must be authorised to do so by the Council, acting unanimously. Agreements are concluded by the Council acting unanimously on a recommendation from the Presidency.[23]

As a sign of transparency and good faith *vis-à-vis* third parties, the Legal Adviser to the Nice IGC suggested it would be useful to mark

---

consulting the European Parliament with regard to all measures based on the common commercial policy, except in special cases. See Bull. EC, 10-1973, paras. 24-27.

[21] Under the assent procedure, the agreement of Parliament is required before the agreement can enter into force. Agreements requiring the assent of the European Parliament are association agreements, agreements establishing a specific institutional framework by organising co-operation procedures, agreements having important budgetary implications for the Community and agreements entailing amendment of an act adopted under the co-decision procedure. See Consolidated TEC, art. 300(3).

[22] Consolidated TEU, art. 24. This provision has been used to conclude the "Agreement between the European Union and the Federal Republic of Yugoslavia (FRY) on the Activities of the European Union Monitoring Mission (EUMM) in the FRY", O.J. L 125, 5.5.2001, 1 and the "Agreement between the European Union and the Former Federal Republic of Macedonia (FYROM) on the activities of the European Union Monitoring Mission (EUMM) in FYROM", O.J. L 241, 11.9.2001, 1. On December 10, 2002, the Council adopted Agreements under TEU, art. 24 with Bulgaria, Cyprus, the Czech Republic, Estonia, Hungary, Iceland, Latvia, Lithuania, Norway, Romania, Slovakia, Slovenia, Switzerland, Turkey and Ukraine on their participation in the European Union Police Mission (EUPM) in Bosnia and Herzegovina. On December 19, 2002, the Council adopted a similar Agreement with Poland. See Justice and Home Affairs Council, "Press Release", December 19, 2002, XI.

[23] Consolidated TEU, art. 24. The Treaty of Nice stipulated that the Council would be able to act by qualified majority for CFSP agreements implementing a joint action or common position (Treaty of Nice, art. 1(4) amending Consolidated TEU, art. 24(3)). and for agreements in the field of police and judicial co-operation covering issues for which qualified majority applies for the adoption of internal decisions or measures Treaty of Nice, art. 1(4) amending Consolidated TEU, art. 24(3)).

clearly in the Treaty that these agreements are concluded on behalf of the Union as such and not on behalf of its Member States.[24] In this context, the Treaty of Nice does make clear that international agreements concluded under the CFSP and also in the framework of police and judicial co-operation in criminal matters shall be binding on the institutions of the Union.[25]

The Treaty of Nice did not remedy the lack of an explicit provision on the legal personality of the EU. Following the criteria used by the International Court of Justice for the recognition of the legal personality of the United Nations,[26] the Legal Adviser to the Nice Treaty negotiations came to the conclusion that – in view of international legal and diplomatic reality – it was already clear that "the Union exists" and "that it exists legally".[27] First, the EU Treaty already included as one of the Union's objectives "to assert its identity on the international scene, in particular through the implementation of a common foreign and security policy". The CFSP, in turn, was given the objectives "to safeguard the independence and integrity of the Union" and "to strengthen the security of the Union".[28] Second, the EU's international legal existence was, according to the IGC's Legal Adviser, confirmed by the EU's diplomatic practice. The EU has notably effected a multiplicity of declarations and *démarches* on its own behalf. Furthermore, it has conducted a large number of political dialogues with third countries on its own behalf and through its own institutions. Third, the Legal Adviser emphasised how experience demonstrated that third countries and international organisations accept as such the positions taken by the EU, accept and sometimes seek political commitments by the EU without casting any doubt upon its capacity to respect them, and often describe their missions in Brussels as being accredited "to the European Union". In this light, he felt it was not

---

[24] SN 5332/1/00, 7.

[25] Treaty of Nice, art. 1(4) amending Consolidated TEU, art. 24(6).

[26] International Court of Justice, "Advisory Opinion: Reparation for Injuries Suffered in the Service of the United Nations", *Reports 1949*, 178. Although the Charter is silent as to the legal personality of the United Nations, the International Court of Justice came to the conclusion that it is clear from the Charter and from practice that the United Nations does, indeed, have a legal personality.

[27] Conference of Representatives of the Governments of the Member States, The Legal Adviser: Comments on the draft amendments to Article 24 TEU, SN 5332/1/00, 24 November 2000, 1. See also Martti Koskenniemi (ed.), *International Law Aspects of the European Union* (The Hague, Kluwer Law International, 1998); Koen Lenaerts and Eddy De Smijter, "The EU as an Actor in International Law", *Yearbook of European Law*, 19 (1999/2000) 95; Esa Paasivirta, "The European Union: From an Aggregate of States to a Legal Person?", *Hofstra Law & Policy Symposium*, 2 (1997) 37.

[28] SN 5332/1/00, 2.

necessary to add new provisions to the Treaty on the EU's international legal personality. This opinion was followed by the Member States.

The decision at Nice not to grant a legal personality to the Union was received with some relief by the proponents of an intergovernmental Europe of States. In their view, "granting the European Union a legal personality, that is creating an overarching legal framework common to the three pillars, cannot be understood in any other way ... but as a means of starting to unify the pillars from the top down and eliminating the independent presence of States on the international stage".[29] For the European Parliament's *rapporteur* on the issue, on the contrary, the failure of the negotiators at Nice to grant legal personality to the EU constituted a major shortcoming. His argument was that giving the Union legal personality "constitutes the prerequisite for legal clarity of the status of political Union and the European Constitution".[30] While arguing that legal personality would facilitate the EU's political and contractual activities at bilateral and multilateral level and increase the EU's visibility for the citizens, the Parliament's *rapporteur* also emphasised that a single, full legal personality for the EU would help "remedy the dysfunctions caused by the pillar structure".[31] The European Convention's Working Group on Legal Personality reached a similar conclusion. It recommended that the EU must explicitly have legal personality that replaces the existing legal personalities of the Communities.[32]

II. Between a Single Community Voice and a Fragmented External Economic Representation

According to Walter Hallstein, it was for the Commission to represent the interests of the Community as a whole *vis-à-vis* the outside world, "for the Community must speak with one voice and not with six or ten".[33] In practice, maintaining the Community's unity in external representation has been more difficult than initially imagined.

---

[29] "Minority Opinion by Mr Georges Berthu", in Carlos Carnero Gonzalez, "Report on the Legal Personality of the European Union", European Parliament Session Document, November 21, 2001, 16.

[30] Carlos Carnero Gonzalez, "Report on the Legal Personality of the European Union", European Parliament Session Document, November 21, 2001, 7.

[31] *Ibid.*, 8.

[32] The European Convention, "Final Report of Working Group III on Legal Personality", CONV 305/02, October 1, 2002.

[33] Hallstein, *Europe in the Making*, 57.

A. The Common Commercial Policy

It is useful to recall that the Community – as a customs union – has established a common customs tariff in relations with third countries. The common customs tariff was integrally applied in 1968 for industrial products and by 1970 for the remaining agricultural products. As the logical corollary of the customs union's common customs tariff, the Community also established a common commercial policy. By the end of the so-called transitional period, on January 1, 1970, the Community's common commercial policy was to be based on uniform principles and to be implemented by the Community's institutions in accordance with the EEC Treaty's Article 113 (now renumbered as Consolidated TEC, Article 133). Where an agreement falling under the scope of the common commercial policy needs to be negotiated with third countries, the Commission conducts the negotiations within the framework of such directives as the Council may issue to it. During the negotiations, the Commission consults with the trade policy experts of the Member States in the framework of the so-called Committee 133.[34] In the end, the Council decides whether or not to conclude the agreement. Throughout this procedure, the Council acts by qualified majority. Since the Community's commercial policy powers have a so-called "exclusive" nature, the Member States are no longer competent to act on their own in the fields covered by the common commercial policy.[35]

In view of its exclusive nature, the definition of the common commercial policy is particularly important. Still, both the Treaty of Rome's original Article 113 and the Treaty of Amsterdam's redrafted Article 133 merely included a non-exhaustive list of examples of topics to be dealt with under the common commercial policy:

> changes in tariff rates, the conclusion of tariff and trade agreements, the achievement of uniformity in measures of liberalisation, export policy and measures to protect trade such as those to be taken in case of dumping or subsidies.

---

[34]   Michael Johnson, *European Community Trade Policy and the Article 113 Committee* (London, Royal Institute of International Affairs, 1998).

[35]   For an introduction to the common commercial policy see E. L. M. Völker (ed.), *Protectionism and the European Community* (Deventer, Kluwer, 1987); Marc Maresceau (ed.), *The Community's Commercial Policy after 1992: the Legal Dimension* (Dordrecht, Martinus Nijhoff, 1993); Nicholas Emiliou and David O'Keeffe (eds.), *The European Union and World Trade Law* (Chichester, John Wiley & Sons, 1996); Alan Dashwood and Christophe Hillion (eds.), *The General Law of E.C. External Relations* (London, Sweet & Maxwell, 2000); Stephen Woolcock, "European Trade Policy", in Wallace and Wallace (eds.), *Policy-Making in the European Union* (2000, 4th edition), 373.

Because of the lack of a precise definition, the scope of the common commercial policy has been the subject of a persistent controversy between the Commission's broad and the Member States' restrictive point of view.[36] In the framework of the old General Agreement on Tariffs and Trade (GATT) of 1947, the Community's problems posed by the lack of a clear definition of the common commercial policy were relatively limited. GATT dealt exclusively with trade in goods and there was little controversy that this fell under the common commercial policy. As a result, it was the Commission that spoke in GATT bodies on behalf of the Community even though the Member States had formally remained GATT Contracting Parties. The Community as such had never formally gained the status of a GATT Contracting Party.[37] This situation was explicitly recognised by the GATT Council. In 1988, during an open conflict with the Commission in the GATT Council, France invoked its status as a GATT Contracting Party in an attempt to block the formation of a dispute settlement panel in the oilseeds case. The Commission representative replied that commercial policy was the exclusive competence of the Community, which – in the GATT Council – was represented by the Commission and that France could not raise objections concerning something that no longer belonged to its competence. The Commission representative also stressed that Community responsibility for trade policy served as a guarantee and security for the other Contracting Parties. To take French views into consideration would put in question all existing Community obligations and rights. For these reasons, the Commission official concluded that, even when France spoke as a Contracting Party, its views as to trade policy were to be considered as null and void. The Chairman of the GATT Council confirmed this view.[38]

---

[36] On the definition of EEC Treaty, art. 113 see Claus D. Ehlermann, "The Scope of Article 113 of the EEC Treaty", in *Etudes de Droit des Communautés Européennes: Mélanges offerts à Pierre-Henri Teitgen* (Paris, Pedone, 1984), 147 and Jacques H. J. Bourgeois, "The Common Commercial Policy – Scope and Nature of the Powers", in E. L. M. Völker (ed.), *Protectionism*, 3. During the negotiations of the Maastricht Treaty, the issue was not clarified, see Youri Devuyst, "The EC's Common Commercial Policy and the Treaty of European Union: An Overview of the Negotiations", *World Competition*, 16 (1992) 67; Marc Maresceau, "The Concept 'Common Commercial Policy' and the Difficult Road to Maastricht", in Maresceau (ed.), *The Community's Commercial Policy*, 3.

[37] On the Community's *ad hoc* status in the GATT 1947, see Ernst-Ulrich Petersmann, "Participation of the European Communities in the GATT: International Law and Community Law Aspects", in David O'Keeffe and Henry G. Schermers (eds.), *Mixed Agreements* (Deventer, Kluwer, 1983), 167; Ernst-Ulrich Petersmann, "The EEC as a GATT Member – Legal Conflicts between GATT Law and European Community Law", in Meinhard Hilf, Francis G. Jacobs and Ernst-Ulrich Petersmann, *The European Community and GATT* (Deventer, Kluwer, 1986), 23.

[38] GATT Council, Minutes of Meeting held on 16 June 1988, C/M/222, 13.

In the framework of the World Trade Organisation (WTO) which started functioning in 1995, the situation with respect to the division of powers between the Community and its Member States was less clear. The WTO was created in the context of the Uruguay Round negotiations.[39] In contrast with the old GATT 1947, the Uruguay Round's Final Act covered not only trade in goods, but also trade in services and trade-related aspects of intellectual property protection. The Member States were determined to protect their own prerogatives in the two latter fields and denied exclusive Community competence. In its landmark Opinion 1/94, the European Court of Justice clarified the situation.[40] According to the Court, which followed a narrow interpretation of the implied external powers doctrine, the following aspects of the Uruguay Round's Final Act fell under the Community's exclusive competence:

- trade in goods (i.e. the entire General Agreement on Tariffs and Trade – GATT);
- cross-frontier trade in services, but only where it did not involve any movement of persons (thereby excluding from the Community's exclusive competence the important parts of the Uruguay Round's General Agreement on Trade in Services – GATS – involving consumption abroad, commercial presence through subsidiary or branch and presence of natural persons abroad); and
- measures taken at the external frontiers of the Community regarding the prohibition of the release into free circulation of counterfeit goods (excluding practically the entire Uruguay Round's Agreement on Trade-Related Intellectual Property measures – TRIPs – from the Community's exclusive competence).

The Court's Opinion was disappointing from the Commission's perspective because it prevented the simple extension of the traditional Community method to the "new" trade topics. Instead, trade in services and the trade-related aspects of the protection of intellectual property had to be treated as so-called shared or mixed competences. This means that their subject-matter covers both Community and Member States

---

[39]   On the Uruguay Round and the creation of the WTO, see Hugo Paemen and Alexandra Bensch, *From the GATT to the WTO. The European Community in the Uruguay Round* (Leuven, Leuven University Press, 1995); Ernest H. Preeg, *Traders in a Brave New World: The Uruguay Round and the Future of the International Trading System.* (Chicago, Chicago University Press, 1995).

[40]   Opinion 1/94, E.C.R. 1994, I-5267. For an interpretation of this opinion see Jacques H. J. Bourgeois, "The EC in the WTO and Advisory Opinion 1/94: an Echternach Procession", *Common Market Law Review*, 32 (1995) 763; Meinhard Hilf, "The ECJ's Opinion 1/94 on the WTO – No Surprize, but Wise?", *European Journal of International Law*, 6 (1995) 245; Pierre Pescatore, "Opinion 1/94 on "Conclusion" of the WTO Agreement: is there an Escape from a Programmed Disaster", *Common Market Law Review*, 36 (1999) 387.

competences. In areas of shared or mixed competence, close co-operation between Member States and Community institutions is essential to ensure the Community's unity of external representation. Decision-making in areas of shared competence is cumbersome as it requires unanimity among the Member States. Moreover, international agreements covering mixed issues must be ratified by all Member States before they can enter into force. To third countries, the resulting EU decision-making process lacked clarity and efficiency. Ambassador Charlene Barshefsky, the Clinton administration's Trade Representative, characterised the EU's trade policy regime as "an opaque system", involving "unclear lines of authority between the Commission and the Member States".[41]

For the Commission, the confirmation of the mixed character of the Uruguay Round Final Act risked harming the Community in future WTO negotiations. The Commission notably recalled the "disastrous" experience within the Food and Agriculture Organisation (FAO), where Community and Member States are to agree before each meeting on a declaration of competence addressed to the other FAO partners regarding every single item on the agenda.[42] This practice has obliged the Community to enter into difficult and lengthy internal discussions before every FAO meeting. Moreover, according to the Commission, third countries quickly learned how to take advantage of this situation in trying to divide the Member States.[43] As to the WTO, although the Commission and the Member States tried to formalise their duty to co-operate in the form of a broad Code of Conduct regulating the representation in that framework, no agreement could be reached. For the Commission, it was essential to maintain the unity of the Community's representation through its monopoly of taking the floor in the WTO.

---

[41] Charlene Barshefsky, "Reflections at a Moment of Transition: the Transatlantic Relationship and its Future", Speech at the European-American Business Council, Washington, D.C., January 17, 2001, 4.

[42] For the Community's position in the FAO, see Rachel Frid, "The European Community – A Member of a Specialized Agency of the United Nations", *European Journal of International Law*, 4 (1993) 239; Antonio Tavares de Pinho, "L'Admission de la Communauté Economique Européenne comme Membre de l'Organisation des Nations Unies pour l'Alimentation et l'Agriculture (FAO)", *Revue du Marché Commun et de l'Union Européenne,* 370 (1993) 656; Jacques Schwob, "L'Amendement de l'Acte Constitutif de la FAO visant à Permettre l'Admission en Qualité de Membres d'Organisations d'Intégration Economique Régionale et la Communauté Economique Européenne", *Revue Trimestrielle de Droit Européen,* 29 (1993) 1; Beate Rudolf, "Commission of the European Communities v. Council of the European Union. Case C-25/94", *American Journal of International Law,* 91 (1997) 349.

[43] Commission of the European Communities, "Community Participation in United Nations Organs and Conferences", March 3, 1993, 8.

Since a number of Member States wanted to ensure their own right to speak in the areas under their competence, in the absence of a consensus position, the negotiations on a Code of Conduct post-Opinion 1/94 failed.

During the negotiations of the Treaty of Amsterdam, the Commission proposed an explicit extension of the common commercial policy to trade in services, intellectual property protection and foreign investment. The Commission emphasised that it was not trying to expand its powers artificially. Its purpose was merely to avoid the complications inherent to situations of mixed or shared competence and guarantee a consistent and effective Community policy in the field of external trade relations. The Commission's suggestion met with resistance from a significant number of Member States. In the end, the negotiators of the Treaty of Amsterdam simply agreed that the Council, acting unanimously on a proposal from the Commission and after consulting the European Parliament, would be enabled to extend the application of the common commercial policy to international negotiations on services and intellectual property.[44] The Council has so far not made use of this possibility.

From the start of the negotiations leading up to the Treaty of Nice, the Commission again put the extension of the common commercial policy to include trade in services and trade-related aspects of intellectual property protection on the agenda.[45] The French government, which held the Council Presidency during the negotiations of the Treaty of Nice, was reticent. Following the Uruguay Round pre-agreement on agriculture

---

[44]   For a detailed treatment of the common commercial policy after Amsterdam, see Marianne Dony (ed.), *L'Union Européenne et le Monde après Amsterdam* (Brussels, Ed. de l'Université de Bruxelles, 1999); Marise Cremona, "EC External Commercial Policy after Amsterdam: Authority and Interpretation within Interconnected Legal Orders", in J. H. H. Weiler (ed.), *The EU, the WTO, and the NAFTA. Towards a Common Law of International Trade?* (Oxford, Oxford University Press, 2000), 5; Sophie Meunier and Kalypso Nicolaïdes, "Who Speaks for Europe? The Delegation of Trade Authority in the European Union", *Journal of Common Market Studies*, 37 (1999) 477; Sophie Meunier and Kalypso Nicolaïdes, "EU Trade Policy: The 'Exclusive' vs. Shared Competence Debate", in Maria Green Cowles and Michael Smith (eds.), *The State of the European Union. Vol. 5: Risks, Reforms, Resistance or Revival?* (Oxford, Oxford University Press, 2001), 325; Eleftheria Neframi, "Quelques Réflexions sur la Réforme de la Politique Commerciale par le Traité d'Amsterdam: le Maintien du Status Quo et l'Unité de la Représentation Internationale de la Communauté", *Cahiers de Droit Européen*, 34 (1998) 137.

[45]   For an introduction to the negotiations on the common commercial policy at Nice, see Sophie Meunier and Kalypso Nicolaïdes, "Trade Competence in the Nice Treaty", *ECSA Review*, 14:2 (2001) 7; Christoph W. Hermann, "Common Commercial Policy after Nice: Sisyphus Would Have Done a Better Job", *Common Market Law Review*, 39 (2002) 7; Horst Günter Krenzler and Christian Pitschas, "Progress or Stagnation?: The Common Commercial Policy after Nice", *European Foreign Affairs Review*, 6 (2001) 291.

concluded between the United States government and the Commission at Blair House in 1992, France argued that the Member States needed to keep the Commission under closer scrutiny during international trade negotiations.[46] France therefore suggested that the Presidency should accompany the Commission during trade negotiations whenever the Council would consider it appropriate.[47] Furthermore, France also wanted to maintain the unanimity rule with respect to trade negotiations in cultural and audio-visual services.[48] Greece, with the support of Denmark, wanted to avoid the inclusion of maritime services in the common commercial policy.[49] In the end, a complex Finnish compromise was agreed to.[50] For Finnish Prime Minister Paavo Lipponen, the issue was crucial:

> The Community used to be a driving force in global trade negotiations for many years. Now over 60% of all trade is in the field of services, where the Community does not have exclusive competence. Consequently our status as an effective negotiator has declined dramatically. The Union must re-establish its position. We can do this only if we are able to agree on the communautarisation of trade in services, intellectual property and investments in the ongoing IGC.[51]

As a general principle, the Treaty of Nice stated that the provisions on the common commercial policy also apply to the negotiation and conclusion of agreements related to trade in services and the commercial aspects of intellectual property.[52] By way of derogation, agreements relating to trade in cultural and audio-visual services, educational services, and social and human health services continue to fall within the shared competences of the Community and its Member States.[53] The

---

[46] On the Blair House episode, see Stephen Woolcock and Michael Hodges, "EU Policy in the Uruguay Round", in Wallace and Wallace (eds.), *Policy-Making in the European Union* (1996, 3rd ed.), 317; Paemen and Bensch, *From the GATT to the WTO*, 215.

[47] Conference of the Representatives of the Governments of the Member States, "Presidency, Presidency: IGC 2000: Extension of Qualified Majority Voting", CONFER 4789/00, October 26, 2000, 4; Conference of the Representatives of the Governments of the Member States, "Presidency, Presidency: IGC 2000: Extension of Qualified Majority Voting", CONFER 4800/00, November 16, 2000, 5.

[48] *European Report*, October 18, 2000, I-5; *European Report*, December 6, 2000, I-2; *European Report*, December 13, 2000, I-7.

[49] *Ibid.*

[50] Finnish delegation, "Meeting document: Article 133", SN 526/00, December 10, 2000.

[51] Paavo Lipponen, "Address at the College of Europe", Bruges, Nov. 10, 2000, s.p.

[52] Treaty of Nice, art. 2(8) amending Consolidated TEC, art. 133(5).

[53] Treaty of Nice, art. 2(8) amending Consolidated TEC, art. 133(6).

common commercial policy rules do not apply to the negotiation and conclusion of international agreements in the field of transport.[54]

As a general rule, the Treaty of Nice prescribed that decisions under the common commercial policy shall be taken by qualified majority.[55] However, a list of exceptions complicates this picture. When negotiating and concluding agreements on trade in services and the commercial aspects of intellectual property the Council must, by derogation, act unanimously where the agreements include provisions for which una-nimity is also required for the adoption of internal rules or where agreements relate to a field in which the Community has not yet adopted internal rules.[56] In a rather vague provision, the Treaty of Nice specified that the Council also acts unanimously with respect to the negotiation and conclusion of so-called "horizontal agreements".[57] Horizontal agree-ments are not precisely defined in the Treaty, but seem to be those inter-national treaties that cover both common commercial policy provisions where qualified majority is the rule and aspects of trade policy where unanimity applies.[58] It is not clear whether the scope of unanimity for decision-making with regard to horizontal agreements will also reach to those areas that should normally come under qualified majority voting.[59]

The Treaty of Nice also made clear that an international agreement may not be concluded by the Council if it includes provisions which go beyond the Community's internal powers.[60] This provision aims in particular at agreements that would lead to a harmonisation of the laws and regulations of the Member States in an area for which the Treaty rules out such harmonisation.[61] The French suggestion to have the Presi-dency accompany the Commission during international trade negotia-tions was not retained. Instead, the Treaty underlined that the Commis-sion has to report regularly to the trade policy experts of the Member States in the Committee 133 on the progress of the negotiations.[62]

In his evaluation of the Treaty of Nice's compromise on the common commercial policy, the Commission's former Director General for External Economic Relations, Horst G. Krenzler, expressed a severe judgement:

---

[54] *Ibid.*

[55] Treaty of Nice, art. 2(8) amending Consolidated TEC, art. 133(4).

[56] Treaty of Nice, art. 2(8) amending Consolidated TEC, art. 133(5).

[57] *Ibid.*

[58] *Ibid.*

[59] *European Report*, December 13, 2000, I-7.

[60] Treaty of Nice, art. 2(8) amending Consolidated TEC, art. 133(6).

[61] *Ibid.*

[62] Treaty of Nice, art. 2(8) amending Consolidated TEC, art. 133(3).

The requirement of unanimity [in the Treaty of Nice's exceptions to qualified majority voting on trade issues] gives a tool to each and every Member State in the internal decision-shaping procedure on the conclusion of international agreements to demand concessions that are non-related to trade. Furthermore, it enables third countries to exert influence on single Member States; this could be detrimental to an enlarged Community's capacity to act internationally. National sovereignty has gained the upper hand over efficiency in foreign trade. The result of Nice in the area of the EC's common commercial policy corresponds to the overall outcome of this summit: the aim was not to make the Community better capable of acting internationally but to ensure the possibility of single Member States to block this capacity.[63]

In practice, the complex institutional situation has often made it very difficult for the Community to present a single policy line during international trade negotiations.[64] Internal side-payments, to compensate specific economic sectors or particular Member States that claim damage as a result of international trade deals, have often been essential to obtain the necessary unanimity within the Community.[65] Enlargement will make such internal bargains only more difficult. Still, in spite of the complex internal political processes, the Community has to a very large extent been able to maintain the unity of its representation in the WTO and play a major role in world trade policy. In areas of mixed competence, the co-ordination between the Community and the Member States has, in practice, been guided by a short Code of Conduct agreed in May 1994 between the Council, its Member States and the Commission on the post-Uruguay Round negotiations of services. This is not the broad Code of Conduct that the Commission and the Member States failed to conclude on their representation in the WTO after the European Court of Justice issued its Opinion 1/94 that was already referred to above. The Code of Conduct of May 1994 predates the Opinion 1/94. It stipulates that the Commission should continue – as during the Uruguay Round – to negotiate on behalf of the Community and its Member States.

---

[63]   Krenzler and Pitschas, "Progress or Stagnation?", 313.

[64]   See Youri Devuyst, "European Unity in Transatlantic Commercial Diplomacy", in Eric Philippart and Pascaline Winand (eds.), *Ever Closer Partnership. Policy-Making in US-EU Relations* (Brussels, P.I.E.–Peter Lang, 2001), 283. For a different viewpoint, see Sophie Meunier, "Divided but United: European Trade Policy Integration and EC-US Agricultural Negotiations in the Uruguay Round", in Carolyn Rhodes (ed.), *The European Union in the World Community* (Boulder, Lynne Rienner, 1998), 193.

[65]   For examples, see Youri Devuyst, "The European Community and the Conclusion of the Uruguay Round", in Carolyn Rhodes and Sonia Mazey (eds.), *The State of the European Union. Vol. 3: Building a European Polity?* (Boulder, Lynne Rienner, 1995), 449; Devuyst, "European Unity in Transatlantic Commercial Diplomacy", 307.

The Community's position is systematically discussed with the Member States in the framework of the 133 Committee where the Commission needs to gather a consensus behind its policy lines on all issues of mixed competence.[66]

B. The External Dimension of EC Competition Policy

The Treaty of Rome made clear that the Commission was to play the key role in ensuring the application of the antitrust principles on the Internal Market. A number of Council regulations have been adopted laying down the detailed rules defining the Commission's implementing powers. The basic regulation in the antitrust sector dates from 1962.[67] It enables the Commission to independently investigate, decide and impose fines in the case of anti-competitive concerted practices between companies or abuse of a dominant market position. The Commission is also in charge of independently deciding whether or not to authorise mergers on a Community level.[68] The representatives of the Member States are consulted in an Advisory Committee before any decision is taken. The Advisory Committee delivers a non-binding opinion. Commission decisions can be appealed before the Court of First Instance. These supranational procedures have ensured efficiency and have allowed the Commission to become a respected player on the international antitrust scene.

It is well-established that the Community's antitrust enforcement powers are not restricted to anti-competitive practices by European companies. In its Wood Pulp ruling of 1988, the European Court of Justice confirmed that the Commission has jurisdiction to apply the EC's competition disciplines against non-European firms registered outside the EC if they "implement" an anti-competitive agreement reached outside the EC by selling their products to purchasers inside the EC.[69] For mergers, the Court of First Instance clarified in the Gencor judgement of 1999 that the application of the EC's merger regulation by the Commission is justified under public international law – even in cases of mergers between non-EC companies – "when it is foreseeable that a proposed concentration will have an immediate and substantial

---

[66] General Affairs Council, "Press Release", May 16-17, 1994, 11. See also General Affairs Council, "Press Release", March 6, 1995, 1.

[67] O.J. P 13, 21.2.1962, 204.

[68] O.J. L 395, 30.12.1989, 1 and O.J. L 180, 9.7.1997, 1.

[69] Cases 89/85 (Wood Pulp), ECR (1988) 5193, para. 16. For a comment, see Dieter G. F. Lange and John Byron Sandage, "The Wood Pulp Decision and its Implications for the Scope of EC Competition Law", *Common Market Law Review*, 26 (1989) 137; Walter Van Gerven, "EC Jurisdiction in Antitrust Matters: the Wood Pulp Judgement", in Barry E. Hawk (ed.), *Annual Proceedings of the Fordham Corporate Law Institute International Antitrust Law and Policy Conference* (New York: Fordham Corporate Law Institute, 1990), 451.

effect in the Community".[70] In 2001, the Commission made use of this doctrine to prohibit the merger between American giants General Electric and Honeywell.[71] Already in 1997, the Commission had signalled its existence as an effective international competition regulator by imposing conditions on the merger between American aircraft manufacturers Boeing and McDonnell Douglas.[72]

Very few sectors have escaped coverage by the antitrust implementing regulations granting full enforcement powers to the Commission. The most significant exception is situated in the field of aviation. The Commission currently has full powers to apply the antitrust rules directly to intra-Community routes only. For the application of competition rules to routes between the EC and non-member countries, the Commission must resort to the more basic transitional provisions foreseen by the Treaty in the early days of the Community.[73] To remedy this situation in light of the globalisation of air transport markets, the Commission has in 1989 and 1997 proposed the necessary implementing Council regulations that would increase its efficiency in the application of the competition rules to air transport between the EC and non-member countries.[74] Both attempts have so far been unsuccessful, illustrating the reluctance of the Member States to proceed with the supranational aspects of the Community method, even in areas where it has proven its efficiency.

While the Treaty does not explicitly include a provision on external relations in the competition field, the European Court of Justice has

---

[70] Case T-102/96 (Gencor), ECR II (1999) 753, para. 90. For a comment, see Antonio F. Bavasso, "Gencor: A Judicial Review of the Commission's Policy and Practice. Many Lights and Some Shadows", *World Competition*, 22 (1999/4) 45; Ariel Ezrachi, "Limitations on the Extraterritorial Reach of the European Merger Regulation", *European Competition Law Review*, 22 (2001) 137; Eleanor Fox, "The Merger Regulation and its Territorial Reach: Gencor Ltd. v. Commission", *European Competition Law Review*, 20 (1999) 334; Francisco Enrique Gonzalez-Diaz, "Recent Developments in EC Merger Control Law. The Gencor Judgment", *World Competition*, 22 (1999/3), 3; Yves van Gerven and Lorelien Hoet, "Gencor: Some Notes on Transnational Competition Law Issues", *Legal Issues of Economic Integration*, 28 (2001) 195.

[71] See Dimitri Giotakos *et al.*, "General Electric/Honeywell – An Insight into the Commission's Investigation and Decision", *Competition Policy Newsletter* (2001/3) 5.

[72] Chad Damro, "Building an International Identity: the EU and Extraterritorial Competition Policy", *Journal of European Public Policy*, 8 (2001) 208; Thomas L. Boeder, "The Boeing-McDonnell Douglas Merger", in Simon Evenett, Alexander Lehmann and Benn Steil (eds.), *Antitrust Goes Global. What Future for Transatlantic Cooperation?* (Washington, D.C., Brookings Institution, 2000), 139.

[73] Consolidated TEC, art. 85.

[74] *European Community Competition Policy 1997: 27th Report on Competition Policy* (Luxembourg, Office for Official Publication of the European Communities, 1998), paras. 87-88.

confirmed that the Community can conclude international agreements in this area. It follows from the implied external powers doctrine, as developed by the Court in the ERTA case and Opinion 1/76, that the Community's authority to enter into international agreements arises not only from an express attribution by the Treaty, but also from other provisions of the Treaty and measures taken pursuant to those provisions by the Community institutions.[75] Consequently, the Court concluded that the Community was empowered, under the competition rules in the Community Treaty and measures implementing those rules, to conclude international agreements in this field.[76]

Initially, it was not entirely clear whether such international competition agreements could be concluded by the European Commission, or needed approval by the Council. In 1991, the Commission tried to conclude the first bilateral competition agreement with the United States under its own administrative implementing powers. This caused France to initiate a case before the Court of Justice to oppose the conclusion of the agreement.[77] The Court confirmed France's view that the Commission lacked the competence to conclude such an international agreement on its own. As a result, the agreement was declared void.[78] The same agreement was subsequently concluded by the Council under the proper procedures and was allowed to enter into force in 1995.[79] A similar bilateral competition agreement was concluded in 1999 between the Community and Canada.

In conclusion, the Community has been very effective in establishing itself as an important international actor in the competition field. This is largely due to the independent powers attributed to the Commission. The Member States have shown reluctance, however, to extend these effective procedures to new areas.

---

[75] Opinion 1/92, ECR I (1992) 2821, para. 39.

[76] *Ibid.*, para. 40.

[77] On the bilateral competition agreement of 1991, see Allard D. Ham, "International Cooperation in the Anti-Trust Field and in Particular the Agreement between the United States of America and the Commission of the European Communities", *Common Market Law Review*, 30 (1993) 571.

[78] Case C-327/91, ECR I (1994) 3641.

[79] O.J. L 95, 27.4.1995, 47; O.J. L 131, 15.6.1995, 38. On the developments within the framework of this agreement since 1995, see Youri Devuyst, "Transatlantic Competition Relations", in Mark A. Pollack and Gregory C. Shaffer (eds.), *Transatlantic Governance in the Global Economy* (Lanham, Rowman & Littlefield, 2001), 127; Merit E. Janow, "Transatlantic Cooperation on Competition Policy", in Evenett, Lehmann and Steil (eds.), *Antitrust Goes Global,* 253.

C. The External Representation of the Euro

One example of an area where the Member States have been most hesitant to pursue the logic of the Community method is the external representation of the Euro.[80] While agreeing on the way forward to the single European currency, the negotiators of the Treaty of Maastricht were unable to come to a concrete arrangement on the Community's representation during international monetary negotiations. The Maastricht Treaty merely stated that the Community needs to express a single position and that the Commission should be fully associated with any international negotiations.[81] By mentioning that the Commission would be "fully associated", the Member States indicated they were not inclined to grant the Commission the task of speaking on behalf of the Community.

At the Vienna European Council in December 1998, just days before the entry into force of the Euro as the EU's single currency in January 1999,[82] the Heads of State or Government were finally able to endorse the Council's report on a general framework for EMU's external representation. As a general principle, it was decided that the Community would be represented at both ministerial level and central banking level. The Commission would merely be involved in the Community's external representation "to the extent required to enable it to perform the role assigned to it in the Treaty".[83]

---

[80]   See Box 4 on the institutional introduction to the Eurosystem.

[81]   Consolidated TEC, art. 111. On the external dimension of EMU, see Jacqueline Dutheil de la Rochère, "EMU: Constitutional Aspects and External Representation", *Yearbook of European Law*, 19 (1999/2000) 427; Barbara Dutzler, "EMU and the Representation of the Community in International Organisations", in Stefan Griller and Birgit Weidel (eds.), *External Economic Relations and Foreign Policy in the European Union* (Wien, Springer Verlag, 2002), 445; Joël Lebullenger, "La Projection Externe de la Zone Euro", *Revue Trimestrielle de Droit Européen*, 34 (1998) 459; Chiara Zilioli and Martin Selmayr, "The External Relations of the Euro Area: Legal Aspects", *Common Market Law Review*, 36 (1999) 273.

[82]   The United Kingdom, Denmark, Sweden and Greece did not participate when the Euro was launched in 1999. Since January 1, 2001, Greece participates in the final phase of the single currency project.

[83]   Vienna European Council, "Presidency Conclusions", December 11-12, 1998, Annex II, para. 5.

Box 4: Institutional Introduction to the Eurosystem

On January 1, 1999 the final stage of EMU commenced. This included the irrevocable fixing of the exchange rates of the currencies of the Member States participating in Monetary Union (Austria, Belgium, Germany, Finland, France, Ireland, Italy, Luxembourg, the Netherlands, Portugal and Spain, joined in 2001 by Greece). The conduct of a single monetary policy became the exclusive responsibility of the European Central Bank (ECB). On January 1, 2002 Euro banknotes and coins were put in circulation in the participating Member States.

The European System of Central Banks (ESCB) is composed of the European Central Bank (ECB) and the national central banks of all Member States. The Eurosystem is the term used to refer to the ECB and the national central banks of the Member States which have adopted the Euro.

The Eurosystem is governed by the decision-making bodies of the ECB, namely the Executive Board and the Governing Council.

– The Executive Board comprises the ECB's President, Vice-President and four other members. They are appointed by common accord of the governments of the Member States, implement monetary policy as formulated by the Governing Council and manage day-to-day business of the ECB.
– The Governing Council includes all members of the Executive Board and the governors of the national central banks of the Member States which have adopted the Euro. It is the highest decision-making body of the ECB. The main responsibility of the Governing Council is to formulate the monetary policy of the Euro area. Its primary objective is to maintain price stability.

The members of the decision-making bodies of the Eurosystem must perform their tasks in an independent way. They may neither seek nor take instructions from any external body.

While monetary policy-making in the Eurosystem is centralised at the European level, general economic policy, fiscal policy and employment policy have remained the primary responsibility of the Member States. In these areas, Member States co-ordinate their policies in the framework of the Council. The Finance Ministers of the Euro Member States meet regularly in the framework of the Euro Group.

Pragmatic solutions were worked out for the Community's representation at the G7 and the International Monetary Fund (IMF). During the meetings of G7 Finance Ministers and Central Bank Governors, the President of the European Central Bank (ECB) attends the discussions relating to EMU. Representation at ministerial level is ensured by the President of the Euro Group, who attends the G7 meetings in addition to the Euro's members with a traditional G7 presence, i.e. the French, German and Italian Finance Ministers. The Commissioner in charge of Economic and Monetary Affairs is invited to take part in some G7 meetings as a member of the Community delegation "in the capacity of providing assistance" to the Euro Group Presidency.

For representation in the IMF, the Council agreed not to propose solutions that would require a change in the IMF's Articles of Agreement. In doing so, Germany and France – two of the IMF members who each have the permanent right to appoint one of the 24 Executive Directors on the IMF's Executive Board – were able to keep their privileged position. Avoiding a change in the Articles of Agreement also enabled Belgium, the Netherlands, Spain and Italy to maintain their Executive Directors on the Board via the system of election through multinational groups of member countries.[84] The ECB was granted an observer position at the Board. The Community's views are presented by the relevant member of the Executive Director's office of the Member State holding the Euro Group Presidency. He is assisted by a Commission representative. The Commissioner in charge of Economic and Monetary Affairs takes part, as observer, in the IMF's International Monetary and Financial Committee as well as in the Development Committee of the IMF and the World Bank.

The compromise on EMU's external representation has been severely criticised by the Commission and some of the smaller Member States.[85] "For the sake of its credibility", the Finnish Prime Minister argued, "the Euro needs to have a single voice in all international *fora*. The Council has now opted for an informal structure, without the Commission. It is very important to rectify the situation".[86] At Nice, hardly any substantive changes were agreed with respect to this issue.[87] In the European

---

[84] On December 30, 2002, EU Member State representation in the IMF's Executive Board was arranged as follows:
 – Germany, France and the United Kingdom each have their own Executive Director;
 – the Belgian Executive Director (with an Austrian Alternate) represents Austria, Belarus, Belgium, the Czech Republic, Hungary, Kazakhstan, Luxembourg, the Slovak Republic, Slovenia and Turkey;
 – the Dutch Executive Director represents Armenia, Bosnia and Herzegovina, Bulgaria, Croatia, Cyprus, Georgia, Israel, Macedonia, Moldova, the Netherlands, Romania and the Ukraine;
 – the Italian Executive Director (with a Greek Alternate) represents Albania, Greece, Italy, Malta, Portugal and San Marino;
 – Spain is member of a group represented by an Executive Director from Venezuela;
 – Denmark has an Alternate Director in a group represented by an Executive Director from Iceland. Finland and Sweden are also member of this group;
 – Ireland has an Alternate Director in a group represented by a Canadian Executive Director.
 See <http://www.imf.org/external/np/sec/memdir/eds.htm>.

[85] Romano Prodi, "Pour une Europe Forte, Dotée d'un Grand Projet et de Moyens d'Action", Speech at the Institut d'Etudes Politiques, Paris, May 29, 2001, 8; Guy Verhofstadt, "A Vision of Europe", Speech at the European Policy Center, Brussels, September 21, 2000, 4.

[86] Paavo Lipponen, "Address at the College of Europe", Bruges, November 10, 2000, s.p.

[87] Treaty of Nice, art. 2(6) amending Consolidated TEC, art. 111(4) ; Nice Declaration 7 on Article 111 on the Treaty on the Establishment of the European Community.

Convention's Working Group on the EU's external action, the Eurozone members expressed support for a single representation of the Eurozone in international financial institutions.[88]

III. Between Intergovernmental Declarations and Community Action in Foreign and Security Policy

The original European Communities dealt exclusively with economic questions. This was also reflected in the external relations field. It took the Member States until 1970 before they decided to set up a co-ordination mechanism between the Ministries of Foreign Affairs to discuss traditional foreign policy topics.[89] This co-ordination mechanism, known as European Political Co-operation (EPC), initially functioned outside the Treaty framework.[90] EPC received a legal basis in the Single European Act of 1986[91] and was transformed into the Common Foreign and Security Policy (CFSP) at Maastricht.[92] The idea to develop a real European foreign policy at Maastricht was pushed – following a Belgian initiative – by French President François Mitterrand and German Chancellor Helmut Kohl.[93] They strongly believed that the end of the Cold War and German unification required a reinforced European Political Union.[94] After World War II, the problem of security "against"

---

[88]   The European Convention, "Final Report of Working Group VII on External Action", CONV 459/02, December 16, 2002, 10.

[89]   This mechanism was based on the network of European Correspondents in the Ministries of Foreign Affairs, linked through the Coreu telex system. For the origins and development of EPC, see Simon J. Nuttall, *European Political Cooperation* (Oxford, Oxford University Press, 1992); David Allen, Reinhardt Rummel and Wolfgang Wessels (ed.), *European Political Cooperation. Towards a Foreign Policy for Western Europe* (London, Butterworth, 1982); Alfred Pijpers, Elfriede Regelsberger and Wolfgang Wessels (eds.), *European Political Cooperation in the 1980s. A Common Foreign Policy for Western Europe?* (Dordrecht, Nijhoff, 1988).

[90]   EPC was based on the Luxembourg report of 1970 (also called the Davignon report, Bull. EC, 1-1970, 7); the Copenhagen report of 1973 (Bull. EC, 9-1973, 14); the London report of 1981 (Bull. EC, S.3-1981, 14); and the Stuttgart Solemn Declaration on European Union of 1983 (Bull. EC, 6-1983, 24).

[91]   SEA, art. 30.

[92]   TEU, art. J-J(11).

[93]   For the origins of the CFSP, see Simon J. Nuttall, *European Foreign Policy* (Oxford, Oxford University Press, 2000); Finn Laursen and Sophie Vanhoonacker (eds.), *The Intergovernmental Conference on Political Union* (Maastricht, European Institute of Public Administration, 1992).

[94]   German unification not only pushed Political Union but also EMU. See Kenneth Dyson and Kevin Featherstone, *The Road to Maastricht. Negotiating Economic and Monetary Union* (Oxford, Oxford University Press, 1999); John T. Wooley, "Linking Political and Monetary Union: The Maastricht Agenda and German Domestic Politics", in Barry Eichengreen and Jeffry Frieden (eds.), *The Political Economy of European Monetary Unification* (Boulder, Westview Press, 1994) 67.

Germany had been solved by creating a system of security "with" Germany.[95] Germany had been economically integrated in the Community and militarily in the Atlantic Alliance. In this context, Germany's "relative economic superiority did not have a dominating effect but proved beneficial for all".[96] With the end of the Cold War, the survival of this stable system was not guaranteed. President Mitterrand feared the dominant geopolitical power that would emerge in the centre of Europe following Germany's unification. In this context, Mitterrand considered the creation of a European Political Union, with a CFSP, as a necessity to prevent a united Germany from upsetting stability in the post-Cold War system.[97] Chancellor Kohl hardly needed convincing.[98] Much like Adenauer after World War II, Kohl realised that a new step in the "normalisation" of Germany required a strengthened European framework as anchor.[99]

While moving towards CFSP, Germany and the Benelux countries tried to convince their partners that the Maastricht Treaty had to move foreign policy co-operation beyond the intergovernmental working methods of EPC. This proved unacceptable, in particular to France and the United Kingdom. The resulting CFSP structure remained primarily intergovernmental and Council-based.[100] It resembled in large measure

---

[95] CDU/CSU Parliamentary Group, "Reflections on European Policy", *Agence Europe Documents*, September 7, 1994, 2.

[96] CDU/CSU Parliamentary Group, 2.

[97] François Mitterrand, *De l'Allemagne, de la France* (Paris, Odile Jacob, 1997); Hubert Védrine, *Les Mondes de François Mitterrand* (Paris, Fayard, 1996), 423; Lacouture, *Mitterrand*, Vol. 2, 359. For the diplomacy behind German unification, see Philip Zelikow and Condoleeza Rice, *Germany Unified and Europe Transformed. A Study in Statecraft* (Cambridge, Mass.: Harvard University Press, 1995).

[98] For Kohl's own perspective, see Helmut Kohl with Kai Diekmann and Ralf-Georg Reuth, *Ich Wollte Deutschlands Einheit* (Berlin, Ullstein Buchverlag/Propyläen Verlag, 1996).

[99] Simon Bulmer, Charlie Jeffery and William E. Patterson, *Germany's European Diplomacy. Shaping the Regional Milieu* (Manchester, Manchester University Press, 2000); Douglas Webber (ed.), "New Europe, New Germany, Old Foreign Policy? German Foreign Policy since Unification", *German Politics* (Special Issue), 10 (2001) 1; Simon Bulmer and William E. Paterson, "Germany in the European Union: Gentle Giant or Emergent Leader", *International Affairs*, 72 (1996) 9; William E. Paterson, "Helmut Kohl, "The Vision Thing" and Escaping the Semi-Sovereignty Trap", in Clay Clemens and William E. Paterson (eds.), *The Kohl Chancellorship* (London, Frank Cass, 1998), 28; Thomas Banchoff, "History and Memory: German Policy towards the European Union", *German Politics*, 6 (1997) 60.

[100] For the CFSP's current functioning, see John Peterson and Helene Sjursen (eds.) *A Common Foreign Policy for Europe?* (London, Routledge, 1998); Kjell A. Eliassen (ed.), *Foreign and Security Policy in the European Union* (London, Sage, 1998); Elfriede Regelsberger, Philippe de Schoutheete and Wolfgang Wessels (eds.), *Foreign Policy of the European Union: From EPC to CFSP and Beyond* (Boulder, Lynne Rienner, 1997); Anthony Forster and William Wallace, "Common Foreign

the intergovernmental design put forward in the Fouchet proposals of French President Charles De Gaulle.[101] The European Council was put in charge of defining the principles and general guidelines for the CFSP.[102] The necessary decisions were, in principle, to be taken by unanimity in the Council.[103] Representation of the EU in CFSP matters was left to the Council Presidency.[104] The Commission was "fully associated" with the work carried out in the CFSP.[105] Together with the Council, the Commission was given responsibility for ensuring the consistency of the EU's external activities as a whole.[106] Parliament was merely to be kept informed.[107]

The Member States' intention to proceed with a Council-based structure for the CFSP, separate from the Community method, was confirmed by the Treaty of Amsterdam.[108] It turned the Council Secretary General into the High Representative for the CFSP.[109] In addition, the

---

and Security Policy. From Shadow to Substance?", in Wallace and Wallace (eds.), *Policy-Making in the European Union* (2000, 4th ed.), 461.

[101] For an excellent comparison between the intergovernmental structure of the CFSP pillar and De Gaulle's Fouchet proposals, see C. W. A. Timmermans, "The Uneasy Relationship between the Communities and the Second Union Pillar: Back to the 'Plan Fouchet'?", *Legal Issues of European Integration* (1996/1) 61.

[102] Consolidated TEU, art. 13 (1) and (2).

[103] Consolidated TEU, art. 23(1).

– Since the Treaty of Amsterdam, qualified majority voting can be applied for CFSP matters when the Council adopts joint actions, common positions or other decisions or the basis of a common strategy decided by unanimity in the European Council and when adopting a decision implementing a joint action or a common position. Consolidated TEU, art. 23(2).

– The Treaty of Amsterdam also created the possibility for constructive abstention in CFSP decision-making. When abstaining in a vote, any member of the Council may qualify its abstention by making a formal declaration. In that case, the Member State in question shall not be obliged to apply the decision, but shall accept that the decision commits the Union. Consolidated TEU, art. 23(1).

[104] Consolidated TEU, art. 18(1).

[105] Consolidated TEU, art. 27.

[106] Consolidated TEU, art. 3.

[107] Consolidated TEU, art. 21: "The Presidency shall consult the European Parliament on the main aspects and the basic choices of the common foreign and security policy and shall ensure that the views of the European Parliament are duly taken into consideration. The European Parliament shall be kept regularly informed ... The European Parliament may ask questions of the Council or make recommendations to it...".

[108] Alan Dashwood, "External Relations Provisions of the Amsterdam Treaty", *Common Market Law Review*, 35 (1998) 1019; Jörg Monar, "The European Union's Foreign Affairs System after the Treaty of Amsterdam: A 'Strengthened Capacity for External Action'?", *European Foreign Affairs Review*, 2 (1997) 423.

[109] Consolidated TEU, art. 18(3): "The Presidency shall be assisted by the Secretary General of the Council who shall exercise the function of High Representative for the

Amsterdam negotiators decided to establish a CFSP Early Warning and Planning Unit in the framework of the Council Secretariat, not in the Commission's external relations services.[110]

In the course of the negotiations of the Treaty of Nice, the Member States were frequently reminded that the CFSP needed a greater political commitment to turn it into an effective vehicle for common action. In June 2000, External Relations Commissioner Christopher Patten presented an analysis devoid of any diplomatic phraseology:

> The Member States ... claim to want a muscular Common Foreign and Security Policy. But they often resent or seek to deny the sovereignty implications of that choice (i.e. that it implies limits on national freedom of action). The lack of consensus on what the EU really is, and what it should aspire to be, has particularly acute repercussions in the external field;
> Partly in consequence, CFSP still lacks beef. "Joint actions" and "Common strategies" were designed to inject substance into common policy – but they have not yet achieved much in practice;[111]

---

common foreign and security policy". The tasks of the High Representative are defined in Consolidated TEU, art. 26: "The Secretary General of the Council, High Representative for the common foreign and security policy, shall assist the Council in matters coming within the scope of the common foreign and security policy, in particular through contributing to the formulation, preparation and implementation of policy decisions, and, when appropriate and acting on behalf of the Council at the request of the Presidency, through conducting political dialogue with third parties."

[110] Amsterdam Declaration 6 on the Establishment of a Policy Planning and Early Warning Unit. This Unit is currently know as the Policy Unit.

[111] The CFSP works through the following instruments:

– Common strategies: the European Council can decide on common strategies to be implemented by the Union in areas where the Member States have important interests in common. Common strategies shall set out their objectives, duration and the means made available by the Union and the Member States. The Council shall implement common strategies, in particular by adopting joint actions and common positions (Consolidated TEU, art. 13);

– Joint actions: the Council can adopt joint actions. Joint actions shall address specific situations where operational action by the Union is deemed to be required. They shall lay down their objectives, scope, the means to be made available to the Union, if necessary their duration, and the conditions for their implementation. Joint actions shall commit the Member States in the positions they adopt and in the conduct of their activity. The Council may request the Commission to submit to it any appropriate proposals relating to the CFSP to ensure the implementation of a joint action (Consolidated TEU, art. 14);

– Common positions: the Council can adopt common positions. Common positions shall define the approach of the Union to a particular matter of a geographical or thematic nature. Member States shall ensure that their national positions conform to the common positions (Consolidated TEU, art. 15);

– Decisions: the Council may adopt CFSP decisions that are binding on the Member States (Consolidated TEU, art. 23);

Our contribution is hampered by the Commission's limited "foreign policy" role. We operate through institutional structures, in the external political field, that are still embryonic. There is an unresolved tension between inter-governmentalism and Community powers (*e.g.* in mixed agreements);

The – welcome – creation of the CFSP High Representative doubling as Council Secretary General has not helped to resolve this tension. Indeed it has given rise to some new institutional complications. It may also have increased the tendency for CFSP to usurp functions which should be the responsibility of the Commission ...;

Ministers and Heads of Government make ringing political declarations, which they are subsequently reluctant to underwrite in money and staff. The Commission is left to wrestle with the contradictions, and blamed for inadequate outcomes ...[112]

While presenting this blunt analysis, the Prodi Commission simultaneously prepared a series of concrete measures to increase the efficiency of the EU's external relations through the more systematic use of Community instruments.[113] Already in the past, the CFSP relied in large measure on the use of Community instruments.[114] CFSP Common Positions frequently included calls for "corresponding expeditious action by the Community ... in order to implement the measures cited".[115] In other cases, CFSP Decisions explicitly included a Commission commitment that it had "agreed to take on certain duties necessary for the implementation of this Decision"[116] or that it "intends to direct its action towards

---

– International agreements: the Council can conclude agreements with one or more States or international organisations in implementation of the CFSP Title of the Treaty (Consolidated TEU, art. 24);

– Declarations: the Council or the Council Presidency can adopt declarations that give public expression to a position, request or expectation of the European Union *vis-à-vis* a third country or an international issue. They are entitled "Declaration by the European Union" where the Council meets and adopts a position on an international issue and "Declaration by the Presidency on behalf of the European Union" where the Council does not meet.

[112] Christopher Patten, "External Relations: Demands, Constraints and Priorities", *Agence Europe*, June 10, 2000, 28-29.

[113] I thank David Spence for pointing this out. The following paragraphs are in large measure the result of David Spence's stimulating comments on the developments in the CFSP.

[114] See Ramses A. Wessel, *The European Union's Foreign and Security Policy. A Legal Institutional Perspective* (The Hague, Kluwer Law International, 1999).

[115] See for instance, "Council Common Position of 3 September 1999 amending Common Position 1999/273/CFSP concerning a ban on the supply and sale of petroleum and petroleum products to the Federal Republic of Yugoslavia (FRY)", and "Common Position 1999/318/CFSP concerning additional restrictive measures against the Federal Republic of Yugoslavia (1999/604/CFSP)", O.J. 7. 9. 1999, L 236, 1.

[116] See, for instance, "Council Decision of 14 December 2000 implementing Joint Action 1999/34/CFSP with a view to a European Union contribution to combating

achieving the objectives and the priorities of this Common Position, where appropriate by pertinent Community measures".[117] On Commissioner Patten's initiative, the Commission has proposed a more systematic and co-ordinated use of Community instruments in the EU's external relations. In February 2001, following a Commission proposal, the Council created a Rapid Reaction Mechanism designed to allow the Community to respond in a rapid, efficient and flexible manner to situations of urgency or crisis.[118] The regulation draws on existing Community instruments for the alleviation of crises through human rights work, election monitoring, institution building, media support, border management, humanitarian missions, police training and the provision of police equipment, civil emergency assistance, rehabilitation, reconstruction, pacification, resettlement and mediation.[119] The Rapid Reaction Mechanism has its own budget line, reinforced by the authority of the Commission to decide quickly on urgent interventions. In a similar vein, in April 2001, the Commission presented a Communication on conflict prevention, recommending the more effective integration of Community actions and programmes in the EU's external action.[120]

The terrorist attacks of September 11, 2001 against the World Trade Centre and the Pentagon constituted a major test for the CFSP mechanisms and instruments. The Brussels and Ghent European Councils in September and October 2001 were quick to express their solidarity with the United States. While supporting military action in Afghanistan, the European Council also underlined the central role of the United Nations in building an effective global framework against terrorism and in finding a political solution to the situation in Afghanistan. Several high level EU Troika missions were sent to the Middle East, Pakistan and India. At the same time, the EU provided important amounts of additional financial and humanitarian support for Afghanistan, Pakistan and the Palestinian Authority.[121] In spite of these efforts, the EU seemed to exercise little concrete influence on military and diplomatic develop-

---

the destabilising accumulation and spread of small arms and light weapons in South Ossetia (2000/803/CFSP)", O.J. 22. 12. 2000, L 326, 1.

[117] See, for instance, "Council Common Position of 22 January 2001 on Afghanistan (2001/56/CFSP)", O.J. 23.1.2001, L 21, 1.

[118] "Council Regulation (EC) 381/2001 of 26 February 2001 creating a Rapid Reaction Mechanism", O.J. 27.2.2001, L 57, 5.

[119] The Annex to the Regulation 381/2001 lists the various geographical and sectoral Regulations and Decisions that form the legal basis for Community action in these fields. See O.J. 27.2.2001, L 57, 8.

[120] Commission of the European Communities, "Communication on Conflict Prevention", COM(2001) 211 final, April 11, 2001.

[121] See Commission of the European Communities, "EU Response to 11 September: The Diplomatic Front", http://europa.eu.int/comm/external_relations/news.

ments in Afghanistan and the Middle East in the wake of the terrorist attacks of September 2001.

In practice, the EU's response to the terrorist attacks showed several signs of weakness.[122] Immediately after September 11, political leaders of all large Member States raced to the White House for individual photo opportunities with President George W. Bush. With French President Jacques Chirac, British Prime Minister Tony Blair and German Chancellor Gerhard Schröder holding bilateral meetings in the Oval Office and pledging national military assets, the EU did not project an image of unity in external representation. In the wake of the terrorist attacks, Prime Minister Blair in particular focused heavily on his special relationship with Washington, making projects for European foreign and military co-operation look of only secondary importance. The perception of heterogeneity was reinforced by two European mini-summits on Afghanistan. The first one, between Chirac, Blair and Schröder, preceded the Ghent European Council of October 19, 2001.[123] The second mini-summit of November 4, 2001 in London was initially intended to involve only the United Kingdom, France and Germany, but was extended at the last minute when the Belgian Council Presidency and the High Representative for the CFSP as well as the Italian, Spanish and Dutch Prime Ministers showed up.[124] The European Commission was absent on both occasions.

Austrian Chancellor Wolfgang Schüssel, representing the smaller Member States that were absent in London, approached the Belgian Council Presidency stating that "the European idea [was being] undermined" by the mini-summits and that all EU Member States had to be treated as "equal members".[125] This was not the first occasion during which the smaller Member States complained that the intergovernmental CFSP structure did not fully protect them against old "*directoire*" practices in foreign policy.[126] During the preparations for the Amsterdam

---

[122] Jolyon Howorth, "CESDP after 11 September: From Short-term Confusion to Long-term Cohesion?", in *EUSA Review*, 15 (2002/1) 1.

[123] *European Report*, October 20, 2001, I.4.

[124] *European Report*, November 7, 2001, I.2.

[125] *Agence Europe*, November 11, 2001, 4.

[126] Attempts to form foreign policy "*directoires*" are nothing new in European history. The most famous example in the post-World War II era is French President Charles De Gaulle's memorandum of September 17, 1958 in which he proposed "that an organisation comprising the United States, Great Britain and France should be created and ... would make joint decisions in all political questions affecting global security" as a tripartite directorate steering the Atlantic Alliance. The idea was rejected by President Dwight D. Eisenhower who argued that "[w]e cannot afford to adopt any system which would give to our other Allies, or other Free World countries, the impression that basic decisions affecting their own vital interests are

Treaty negotiations, Belgian Foreign Minister Erik Derycke had been especially critical towards the Contact Group for Bosnia.[127] While the smaller Member States were asked to contribute significant human and financial resources to the EU's peace-keeping efforts in Bosnia, he claimed they were hardly kept informed on the policy orientation that was being pursued.[128] Derycke returned to the issue in 1999 while commenting on the Rambouillet peace conference regarding Kosovo: "if Belgium is excluded from the deliberations ... there is no reason why it should feel obliged to offer solidarity or to participate" in operations to guarantee peace. According to the Belgian Foreign Minister, accepting "directorates of large powers" would for the smaller Member States "mean a return to ... the inevitable role of being cannon fodder".[129]

The institutional problems encountered by the EU in its reaction to the terrorist attacks of September 11, 2001 and the conflict in the Middle East have provided additional ammunition to those favouring structural measures to turn the EU into a more effective foreign policy actor. For the European Parliament, the combination of the office of CFSP High Representative with that of Council Secretary General "inevitably generates conflicts of responsibilities with the Commissioner for External Relations, thus showing up the unsuitable nature of the existing "pillar" structure of the European Union".[130] To remedy this situation, the European Parliament and the Commission proposed that the tasks of the High Representative be entrusted to a Commission Vice-President for

---

being made without their participation". For the text of De Gaulle's memorandum and Eisenhower's reply see Alfred Grosser, *The Western Alliance. Euro-American Relations since 1945* (Basingstoke, Macmillan, 1980), 186-188. For the historical details, see Michael M. Harrison, *The Reluctant Ally. France and Atlantic Security* (Baltimore, Johns Hopkins University Press, 1981), 88; Marc Trachtenberg, *A Constructed Peace. The Making of the European Settlement 1945-1963* (Princeton, Princeton University Press, 1999), 242; Maurice Vaïse, *La Grandeur. Politique Etrangère du Général de Gaulle 1958-1969* (Paris, Fayard, 1998), 114. For De Gaulle's own interpretation, see his *Mémoires d'Espoir: Le Renouveau*, 214. On the "*directoire*" concept in EU politics, see Catherine Gegout, "The Quint", *Journal of Common Market Studies*, 40 (2002) 331; Pierre Pescatore, "L'Executif Communautaire", 396; Philippe de Schoutheete, "The European Community and its Sub-Systems", in William Wallace (ed.), *The Dynamics of European Integration* (London, Pinter, 1990), 113.

[127] The Contact Group countries are France, Germany, Italy, the Russian Federation, the United Kingdom and the United States.

[128] Erik Derycke, "The Present Challenges of the European Union", Address before the Symposium Austria: A New Partner in the European Union, April 3, 1995, 7.

[129] *Agence Europe*, February 10, 1999, 4.

[130] European Parliament, "Resolution on the progress achieved in the implementation of the common foreign and security policy", Minutes of the Plenary Session of November 30, 2000, para. 67.

External Relations.[131] In the European Convention's Working Group on the EU's external action, a majority of the members also suggested that the offices of the High Representative and the External Relations Commissioner be exercised by a single "European External Representative". The European External Representative would be appointed by the Council with the approval of the President of the Commission and endorsement by the European Parliament. The Representative would receive direct mandates from and be accountable to the Council. At the same time, (s)he would be a full member of the Commission.[132]

IV. Between Military Dependence and Autonomous Intervention Capability

An early attempt to move towards a European Defence Community (EDC) failed when the French National Assembly refused to ratify the EDC Treaty in 1954.[133] The EDC had been conceived as an explicitly supranational organisation to enable the rearmament of Germany in a solid European framework.[134] To overcome the non-ratification of the EDC Treaty, a new European cover for German rearmament was found through the development of the Western European Union (WEU) as the successor to the Treaty of Brussels Organisation of 1948.[135] Like the Treaty of Brussels, the WEU was based on a military assistance clause that would be automatically triggered should one of the members be the subject of an attack. The WEU's military structure was entirely integrated in the North Atlantic Treaty Organisation (NATO) framework. In

---

[131] *Ibid.*, para. 68 ; Romano Prodi, "The New Europe in the Transatlantic Partnership", Speech at the European University Institute, Florence, May 9, 2001, 5.

[132] European Convention, "Final Report of Working Group VII on External Action", CONV 459/02, December 16, 2002, 5.

[133] For an excellent historical introduction to European defence co-operation, see Simon Duke, *The Elusive Quest for European Security. From EDC to CFSP* (Basingstoke, Macmillan, 2000).

[134] On the failure of the EDC, see Edward Fursdon, *The European Defence Community: a History* (London, Macmillan, 1980); Raymond Aron and Daniel Lerner (eds.), *France Defeats EDC* (New York, Praeger, 1957).

[135] On the creation of the WEU, see Anne Deighton, "Britain and the Creation of Western European Union, 1954", in Anne Deighton (ed.), *Western European Union 1954-1997. Defence, Security, Integration* (Oxford, St Antony's College, 1997), 11; Silvain Frey, "Aspects de l'Organisation de la Défense Collective en Europe Occidentale", *Travaux et Conférences de la Faculté de Droit de l'Université Libre de Bruxelles* (1962) 110. On the WEU's resurrection from the mid-1980s till the late 1990s, see Anne Deighton and Eric Remacle (eds.), "The Western European Union, 1948-1998", *Studia Diplomatica*, 51 (1998/1-2); André Dumoulin and Eric Remacle, *L'Union de l'Europe Occidentale, Phénix de la Défense Européenne* (Brussels, Bruylant, 1998); Willem van Eekelen, *Debating European Security 1948-1998* (Brussels, Centre for European Policy Studies, 1998).

the early 1960s, President Charles De Gaulle, who resented the Anglo-Saxon dominance in the Atlantic Alliance, tried to push for a French-led European foreign and security policy that would function separately from the United States. As was already mentioned, De Gaulle's ideas took the shape of the so-called Fouchet proposals for a largely intergovernmental Union of States that would have included a common foreign and defence policy.[136] The Fouchet proposals failed because of Dutch and Belgian opposition. The Netherlands in particular feared that De Gaulle's plan would undercut the primacy of the Atlantic Alliance in foreign and defence policy.[137]

Following the failure of the EDC and the Fouchet proposals, the creation of an integrated European approach to security and defence policy became a taboo subject in the Community.[138] In the framework of EPC, the military aspects of security could not be treated.[139] This was changed by the Maastricht Treaty which stipulated as follows:

> The common foreign and security policy shall include all questions related to the security of the Union, including the eventual framing of a common defence policy, which might in time lead to a common defence.[140]

It is only since the Cologne European Council of June 1999 that the development of a Common European Security and Defence Policy (CESDP) has concretely taken shape.[141] The wars in the Balkans served

---

[136] Bloes, *Le Plan Fouchet;* Jouve, *Le Général de Gaulle et la Construction de l'Europe,* 316.

[137] As a pre-condition for their approval of the Fouchet proposals, the Netherlands and Belgium requested the United Kingdom's entry into the Community. This was unacceptable for De Gaulle. In addition, the Netherlands and Belgium insisted on a "Community correction" of the intergovernmental features of the Fouchet proposals. Yves Stelandre, "Les Pays du Benelux, l'Europe Politique et les Négotiations Fouchet (26 juin 1959-17 avril 1962)", *Journal of European Integration History*, 2 (1997) 21.

[138] For a brief overview of this period, see William Wallace, "European Defence Co-operation: The Reopening Debate", *Survival*, 26 (1984) 251.

[139] SEA, art. 30(6)(a) states that "The High Contracting Parties ... are ready to coordinate their positions more closely on the political and economic aspects of security".

[140] TEU, art. J.4(1). This sentence was amended by the Treaty of Amsterdam. See Consolidated TEU, art. 17: "The common foreign and security policy shall include all questions relating to the security of the Union, including the progressive framing of a common defence policy ... which might lead to a common defence, should the European Council so decide ...".

[141] Cologne European Council, "Presidency Conclusions", June 3-4, 1999, Annex III. For a compilation of all the essential documents in the development of the CESDP between 1998 and the end of 2000, see Maartje Rutten (ed.), *From St-Malo to Nice. European Defence: Core Documents* (Paris, Institute of Security Studies of WEU, Chaillot Paper 47, 2001). For the historical background, see Charles G. Cogan, *The Third Option: The Emancipation of European Defence, 1989-2000* (Westport, Praeger, 2001); Jolyon Howorth, "Britain, France and the European Defence

as the catalyst for action. While unable to handle the conflicts in the Bosnia and Kosovo on its own, the EU had to rely on the military power of the United States to restore some degree of stability on the continent.[142]

The Kosovo war convinced in particular British Prime Minister Tony Blair to revise the UK's long-standing reserve *vis-à-vis* the creation of a European military capacity. At the Franco-British Summit of December 1998 at Saint-Malo, the UK joined France in demanding that "the Union must have the capacity for autonomous action, backed up by credible military forces, the means to decide to use them and a readiness to do so, in order to respond to international crises".[143] At the same time, Germany had during the 1990s gradually shifted to a new security policy which, in principle, accepted German military participation in interventions outside NATO's collective defence framework.[144]

As a result of these developments, the Cologne European Council of June 1999 was able to launch the creation of the CESDP.[145] The EU's purpose is to develop an autonomous capacity to decide and conduct EU-

---

Initiative", *Survival*, 42 (2000/2) 33; Jolyon Howorth, *European Integration and Defence: the Ultimate Challenge?* (Paris, Institute for Security Studies of WEU, Chaillot Paper 43, 2000); Alexander Moens, "Developing a European Intervention Force", *International Journal*, 50 (2000) 247. For interesting perspectives on the development of the CESDP, see Anne Deighton, "The Military Security Pool: Towards a New Security Regime for Europe?", *International Spectator*, 35 (2000/4) 41; Karen E. Smith, "The End of Civilian Power EU: a Welcome Demise or Cause for Concern?", *International Spectator*, 35 (2000/2) 11.

[142] According to the European Parliament's report on transatlantic co-operation during the Kosovo crisis, the EU's dependence on American military power did not feel comfortable to the EU's leaders. The United States, while pushing for an air campaign against Serbia, resisted for months European proposals to send in ground troops if a stalemate would be reached in the air campaign. According to the European Parliament's report, the European "feeling of marginalisation" was increased by the fact that Washington did not supply its allies with information on the missions carried out by United States stealth aircraft. See Catherine Lalumière, "Report on the establishment of a common European security and defence policy of the European Union after Cologne and Helsinki", European Parliament Session Document, November 21, 2000, 27.

European uncertainties about the intentions of the new President George W. Bush as regards the American military engagement in Kosovo did not help to dispel doubts in the European capitals about their dependence on US military power. See Ivo H. Daalder and James M. Goldgeier, "Putting Europe First", *Survival*, 43 (2001) 71.

[143] Howorth, "Britain, France and the European Defence Initiative", 43; Margarita Mathiopoulos and Istvan Gyarmati, "Saint Malo and Beyond: toward European Defense", *Washington Quarterly*, 22 (1999/4) 65.

[144] Hanns W. Maull, "Germany and the Use of Force: Still a 'Civilian Power'?", *Survival*, 42 (2000) 56; Hanns W. Maull, "German Foreign Policy, Post-Kosovo: Still a 'Civilian Power'?", *German Politics*, 9 (2000) 1.

[145] Cologne European Council, "Presidency Conclusions", June 3-4, 1999, Annex III.

led military operations in response to international crises where NATO as a whole is not engaged. This process does not imply the creation of a unified European army. The EU's goal is that the Member States must by 2003 be able to deploy within 60 days a Rapid Reaction Force of up to 50,000-60,000 persons. This force should be capable of carrying out the full range of humanitarian and rescue tasks, peace-keeping tasks and tasks of combat forces in crisis management, including peace-making.[146] At the Nice European Council, it was emphasised that the decision by any Member State to commit its armed forces to an EU-led operation remains a sovereign decision of that Member State.[147] The Nice European Council also specified that NATO continues to serve as the basis of the collective defence of its members.[148] Should the EU decide to launch an operation, it will be able to rely to NATO assets and all or part of the EU-command may be drawn from the NATO chain of command.[149] To dispel all fears that the CESDP would grow away from, or eventually compete with, NATO, an agreement was concluded on December 16, 2002 on the establishment of EU-NATO permanent arrangements. In addition, the EU's High Representative for the CFSP Javier Solana went out of his way to emphasise that the EU's purpose was not to achieve European military autonomy at the expense of the coherence in the Atlantic Alliance, but rather to build "a genuine strategic partnership between the EU and NATO in the management of crises with due regard for the two organisations' decision-making autonomy".[150] The EU also

---

[146] Helsinki European Council, "Presidency Conclusions", Annex 1 to Annex IV, 22.

[147] *European Report*, December 13, 2000, I-1. See also Simon Duke, "CESDP: Nice's Overtrumped Success?", *European Foreign Affairs Review*, 6 (2001), 155.

[148] *European Report*, December 13, 2000, I-1. The Clinton and Bush administrations have given their cautious support to the development of a European Security and Defence Policy that would function in the broader framework of the Atlantic Alliance.

The Clinton administration made its support conditional on the guarantee that there would be no *d*uplication of what NATO already does, no *d*iscrimination against NATO allies that are not EU Member States and no *d*ecoupling of Europe's security from that of the United States (these are the famous three "Ds" of Clinton's Secretary of State Madeleine Albright). The three "Ds" were met by the three "Is" of NATO Secretary General George Robertson. For Robertson, EDSI/ESDP should lead to *i*mprovements in European defence capabilities, *i*nclusion of all non-EU NATO allies and an *i*ndivisibility of the transatlantic link.

[149] Already in January 1994, NATO Heads of State or Government had announced that they were "ready to make collective assets of the Alliance available, on the basis of consultations in the North Atlantic Council, for WEU operations undertaken by the European Allies in pursuit of their Common Foreign and Security Policy".

[150] *European Report*, December 13, 2000, I1-I2. In October 1999, the Clinton administration's Deputy Secretary of State Strobe Talbott had warned that the United States did "not want to see an ESDI that comes into being first within NATO, but then grows out of NATO and finally grows away from NATO [and] could eventually

established permanent consultations with the non-EU members of NATO, covering the full range of security, defence and crisis management issues.[151]

While the terrorist attacks of September 11, 2001 had the effect of speeding up the EU's police and judicial co-operation in criminal matters, this did not seem the case in the field of security and defence. In the wake of the attacks, the EU notably saw the controversy over the mini-summits on Afghanistan among the EU's larger Member States. Furthermore, British Prime Minister Tony Blair's focus on military co-operation with the United States made European co-operation look of only secondary importance.

The development of the CESDP has also caused institutional change within the EU's Council structures. Since November 1998, the EU Ministers of Defence have held informal meetings in the EU framework every six months.[152] Since November 1999, the EU's Ministers of Defence have also participated jointly with the Ministers of Foreign Affairs in General Affairs Council sessions.[153] These Council sessions are prepared by the Political and Security Committee (PSC) that has replaced the Political Committee.[154] The Political Committee used to serve as the cornerstone for the co-ordination of the foreign policies of the Member States since the 1970s, both in EPC and the CFSP. It was composed of the Political Directors of the Ministries of Foreign Affairs who were based in the national capitals. The new Political and Security Committee is composed of national representatives of senior or ambassadorial level based in Brussels and deals with all aspects of the CFSP.[155] In addition, the Committee also exercises political control and strategic direction in case of military crisis management operations. It does so under the responsibility of the Council.[156] For military advice, the

---

compete with NATO". See Strobe Talbott, "Transatlantic Ties", *Newsweek*, October 18, 1999, 34. On the CESDP's autonomy from NATO, see Jolyon Howorth, "Franco-British Defence Cooperation and the Compatibility of ESDP with NATO", in Simon Duke (ed.), *Between Vision and Reality. CFSP's Progress on the Path to Maturity* (Maastricht, European Institute of Public Administration, 2000), 35.

[151] Brussels European Council, "Presidency Conclusions", October 24-25, 2002, Annex II : ESDP - Implementation of the Nice Provisions on the Involvement of the Non-EU European Allies.

[152] *Agence Europe*, March 30, 2001, 5.

[153] General Affairs Council, "Press Release", November 15, 1999, 5.

[154] Treaty of Nice, art. 1(5) amending Consolidated TEU, art. 25.

[155] Treaty of Nice, art. 1(5) amending Consolidated TEU, art. 25. For a more detailed description of the role of the Political and Security Committee, see "Council Decision of 22 January 2001 setting up the Political and Security Committee (2001/78/CFSP)", O.J. 30.1.2001, L 27, 1.

[156] Treaty of Nice, art. 1(5) amending Consolidated TEU, art. 25.

Political and Security Committee relies on the EU's new Military Committee, which is composed of the Member States' Chiefs of Staff.[157] The Military Committee provides military direction to the Military Staff. The Staff is composed of military experts seconded by the Member States to the Council Secretariat.[158]

While deciding to move forward with the CESDP, the Cologne European Council in June 1999 also set itself the objective of bringing about "the inclusion [in the EU] of those functions of the WEU which will be necessary for the EU to fulfil its new responsibilities in the area of the Petersberg tasks [i.e. humanitarian and rescue tasks, peace-keeping tasks and tasks of combat forces in crisis management, including peace-making]".[159] Furthermore, the decision was taken to transfer the WEU Satellite Centre and the WEU Institute for Security Studies to the EU.[160] As a result, the WEU retains only a limited number of residual functions, including mutual military assistance among the ten signatory members to the Modified Treaty of Brussels (Article V).[161]

A factor that is complicating the concrete establishment of a common EU defence policy is the important differences in defence status between the Member States. The European Convention's Working Group on defence paid particular attention to these differences.[162] Eleven EU Member States are members of NATO (Belgium, Denmark, France, Germany, Greece, Italy, Luxembourg, the Netherlands, Portugal, Spain and the United Kingdom). With the exception of Denmark, these countries are also members of the WEU and are therefore bound by the collective defence commitments of Article 5 of NATO's Washington Treaty and Article V of the WEU's Modified Brussels Treaty. Denmark, while a NATO member, has negotiated a special status in the EU defence framework. By virtue of a Protocol annexed to the Treaty of Amsterdam, Denmark does not participate in the elaboration and the implementation of decisions and actions of the Union which have defence mplications.[163] Four EU Member States are neutral or non-aligned

---

[157] "Council Decision of 22 January 2001 setting up the Military Committee of the European Union (2001/79/CFSP)", O.J. 30.1.2000, L 27, 4.

[158] "Council Decision of 22 January 2001 on the establishment of the Military Staff of the European Union (2001/80/CFSP)", O.J. 30.1.2001, L 27, 7.

[159] Cologne European Council, "Presidency Conclusions", June 3-4, 1999, Annex III, 35.

[160] Lalumière, "Report on the establishment of a common European security and defence policy", 34.

[161] *Ibid*

[162] The European Convention, "Final Report of Working Group VIII on Defence", CONV 461/02, December 16, 2002, 11. This following paragraph is based on Working Group's report.

[163] Amsterdam Protocol 5 on the Position of Denmark, art. 6.

(Austria, Finland, Ireland and Sweden). They co-operate with NATO under the Partnership for Peace Programme (PPP) and take part in the Euro-Atlantic Parternship Council. They also have observer status in the WEU. With respect to the EU's candidate countries, four of them are already NATO members (the Czech Republic, Hungary, Poland and Turkey). At the same time, they are associate members of the WEU. At NATO's Prague Summit of November 21-22, 2002, Bulgaria, Estonia, Latvia, Lithuania, Romania, Slovakia and Slovenia were invited to join. They have the status of associate partners in the WEU and will become associate members of the WEU once they have joined NATO. Cyprus and Malta remain non-aligned and have declared they will not take part in EU military operations using NATO assets once they have become EU Member States.[164]

The creation of the EU's military crisis intervention capability goes hand in hand with the establishment of civilian crisis response tools. The Member States have undertaken that by 2003 they would be able to provide up to 5,000 police officers for international missions across the range of conflict prevention and crisis management operations. Member States have also undertaken to be able to deploy 1,000 police officers within 30 days.[165] It is in this area that the EU decided to fulfil its first formal crisis management operation. The General Affairs Council of February 2002 agreed that an EU Police Mission, supported by the Community's institution-building programmes, would ensure by January 2003 the follow-up to the United Nations International Police Task Force in Bosnia-Herzegovina.[166] The mission would comprise 466 policemen, 67 civil experts and 289 local agents.

---

[164] Copenhagen European Council, "Presidency Conclusions", December 12-13, 2002, Annex II, para. 3.

[165] Santa Maria da Feira European Council, "Presidency Conclusions", June 19-20, 2000, para. 11.

[166] General Affairs Council, "Press Release", February 18-19, 2002, 16.

CHAPTER VI

Differentiation, Solidarity, Philosophical Openness and the EU's Political Future

The European Convention on the EU's future focuses largely on institutional questions. While the role and composition of the various EU institutions are important issues, the EU's future depends to a much greater degree on the concrete shape which differentiation, solidarity and philosophical openness will take in an enlarged Union.

I. Between Coherent Differentiation and Pick-and-Choose Flexibility

The tension between the need for coherent differentiation and the danger of pick-and-choose flexibility in an enlarged EU was approached as follows in the report on *The Institutional Implications of Enlargement* by Jean-Luc Dehaene, Richard von Weizsäcker and David Simon:

> In a larger and more diverse Union, flexibility in the institutional framework is even more important than at present. Enlargement will increase diversity. This does not imply that Member States should be allowed to opt out of any policy they choose: the European Union would not survive if Member States were allowed to pick-and-choose among obligations of the Union. But it does imply that, in a more heterogeneous aggregate of Member States, some will wish to go further or faster than others ... This seems both legitimate and indispensable.[1]

One of the Community's characteristics was from the start that it incorporated a degree of positive integration going beyond a simple free trade area.[2] EU membership involves rights, but also entails obligations. Maintaining a certain equilibrium between the Member States' rights and obligations – in the sense that they should respect the Community's

---

[1] Dehaene, von Weizsäcker and Simon, *The Institutional Implications of Enlargement*, 7. See also Alex Warleigh, *Flexible Integration : What Model for the European Union ?* (London, Continuum, 2002).

[2] Ugo La Malfa, "The Case for European Integration: Economic Considerations", in C. Grove Haines (ed.), *European Integration* (Baltimore, Johns Hopkins University Press, 1957), 64. See Chapter III. VI for the limits of positive integration in the EU context.

coherence – has often been regarded as essential to keep the integration project sustainable.[3] Throughout the Spaak report of 1956, which formed the starting point for the negotiations leading to the Rome Treaties, this point was underscored, notably on France's demand. While the Spaak report put the emphasis on the free movement of the factors of production as a way to revitalise Europe's economy, it also contained an important chapter on the correction of market distortions and the harmonisation of the laws of the Member States. This last element was seen as essential to preventing the common market from being undermined from within. The Spaak report even touched upon the correction of distortions due to divergent tax and social security systems, and the harmonisation of labour laws, all topics which are still on the agenda today.[4] During the subsequent Treaty of Rome negotiations, France aimed at making a successful harmonisation of social regulations a prerequisite to the final stage of the common market. In the final version of the Treaty, France's idea was watered down significantly.[5] Still, the Treaty of Rome called for "progressively approximating the economic policies of Member States" and provided the possibility for harmonisation of fiscal legislation and the promotion of closer co-operation on social security.[6] While decision-making in these fields required unanimity, the Treaty of Rome nevertheless went much further in the direction of positive integration than any other European agreement of the immediate post World War II era. As such, the Treaty of Rome did provide the basis for a remarkable integration *acquis* in all fields of economic and social life. Since the 1950s, the emphasis on the need for balance in the economic integration process has only grown. In this context, it is interesting to read the complex formulation of the consolidated version of EC Treaty Article 2, as it emerged from the Amsterdam negotiations:

> The Community shall have as its task, by establishing a common market and an economic and monetary union and by implementing common policies or activities ..., to promote throughout the Community a harmonious, balanced and sustainable development of economic activities, a high level of employment and of social protection, equality between men and women, sustainable and non-inflationary growth, a high degree of competitiveness and convergence of economic performance, a high level of protection and improvement of the quality of the environment, the raising of the standard

---

[3]   See for instance Commission, "Opinion to the Intergovernmental Conference 1996. Reinforcing Political Union and Preparing for Enlargement", 21-22.

[4]   Comité Intergouvernemental Crée par la Conférence de Messine, "Rapport des Chefs de Délégation aux Ministres des Affaires Etrangères", 1956, 60.

[5]   On the limited success of French harmonisation demands, see Milward, *The European Rescue of the Nation-State*, 211-217.

[6]   EC Treaty, arts. 2, 99 and 118.

of living and quality of life, and economic and social cohesion and solidarity among Member States.

To date, the most significant challenge to the maintenance of the equilibrium between rights and obligations in the EU resulted from the opt-out formulae obtained by the UK's Conservative government at Maastricht. Via Maastricht's Social Protocol, Prime Minister John Major managed to escape from the constraints of new developments in the EU's social dimension.[7] At Maastricht, Major also obtained a Protocol stating that the UK would not be obliged or committed to participate in EMU.[8] In preparation for the Amsterdam negotiations, Major seemed determined to continue with the opt-out strategy. He explicitly defended greater flexibility in the EU as the only way to achieve a successful enlargement.[9] Labour's election victory in May 1997, just one month before the end of the Amsterdam negotiations, changed the situation. It enabled the negotiators to integrate the Social Protocol into the Treaty's mainstream. This brought an end to what the Commission had called an example of "a 'pick-and-choose Europe' ... which flies in the face of the common European project and the links and bonds which it engenders".[10] At the same time, incoming Prime Minister Tony Blair reversed Major's plea for "easy flexibility" because he saw a danger in the possibility of the other Member States using it to leave the UK behind.[11]

In preparation for the accession of more than ten new Member States, the Treaty of Amsterdam nevertheless provided for a general possibility for closer co-operation among less than all Member States, but within the EU's institutional framework.[12] At the same time, the Treaty of Amsterdam's provisions on closer co-operation reflected Blair's concerns. Closer co-operation could neither affect the competences, rights, obligations and interests of the non-participants, nor the *acquis communautaire*. As ultimate safeguard, any Member State had the possibility of blocking a closer co-operation framework from coming

---

[7]   Maastricht Protocol No. 14 on Social Policy.

[8]   Maastricht Protocol No. 11 on Certain Provisions relating to the United Kingdom of Great Britain and Northern Ireland.

[9]   John Major, "Europe: A Future that Works", William and Mary Lecture at the Universiteit Leiden, September 7, 1994, 6.

[10]   Commission, "Opinion to the Intergovernmental Conference 1996", 21-22.

[11]   *European Report*, May 8, 1997, I-5.

[12]   Consolidated TEU, arts. 43-45. The Amsterdam Treaty's closer co-operation provisions applied to police and judicial co-operation in criminal matters (Consolidated TEU, art. 40) and European Community matters (Consolidated TEC, art. 11).

into being.[13] While the Amsterdam Treaty stipulated that the Council could in principle grant authorisation for closer co-operation by qualified majority, any Member State could prevent that a vote would be taken by invoking "important and stated reasons of national policy".[14] As such, maximum national control was maintained. According to Jean-Luc Dehaene, Richard von Weizsäcker and David Simon, the Amsterdam Treaty's closer co-operation clauses were "so complex and subject to such conditions and criteria that they are unworkable".[15]

During the negotiations of the Treaty of Nice, the Commission,[16] the European Parliament,[17] Belgium[18] and Germany and Italy[19] all proposed to make the closer co-operation provisions more operational. The proponents of a better functioning closer co-operation regime argued that

> in a Union with up to 28 members, it will become indispensable that those Member States willing to move ahead on the path of integration are enabled to do so, with full respect for the common institutional framework and the existing rules and regulations. It should be possible that these Member

---

[13]   On the Treaty of Amsterdam's closer co-operation provisions, see Alexander Stubb, *Negotiating Flexibility in the European Union. Amsterdam, Nice and Beyond* (Basingstoke, Palgrave, 2002); Claus-Dieter Ehlermann, "Retrospective: Differentiation, Flexibility, Closer Co-operation: The New Provisions of the Amsterdam Treaty", *European Law Journal*, 4 (1998) 246; Giorgio Gaja, "How Flexible is Flexibility Under the Amsterdam Treaty?", *Common Market Law Review*, 35 (1998) 855; Helmut Kortenberg, "Closer Cooperation in the Treaty of Amsterdam", *Common Market Law Review*, 35 (1998) 833; Eric Philippart and Geoffrey Edwards, "The Provisions on Closer Co-operation in the Treaty of Amsterdam", *Journal of Common Market Studies*, 37 (1999) 87.

[14]   Consolidated TEU, art. 40; Consolidated TEC, art. 11. The concept of "important reasons of national policy" was vague and put no limits to any Member State's political discretion to hinder other Member States from moving further ahead towards integration. See Conference of the Representatives of the Governments of the Member States, "Position paper from Germany and Italy: IGC 2000: Enhanced cooperation", CONFER 4783/00, October 4, 2000, 4.

[15]   Dehaene, von Weizsäcker and Simon, *The Institutional Implications of Enlargement*, 7. The complexity of the Treaty of Amsterdam's closer co-operation provisions can be explained by the fact that they form a compromise between entirely different viewpoints on flexibility. See Alexander C-G. Stubb, "A Categorization of Differentiated Integration", *Journal of Common Market Studies*, 34 (1996) 283.

[16]   Commission, "Adopting the Institutions to Make a Success of Enlargement", 33.

[17]   European Parliament, "Resolution on closer cooperation", Minutes of the Plenary Session of October 25, 2000. See also José Maria Gil-Robles Gil-Delgado, "Report on reinforced cooperation", European Parliament, Committee on Constitutional Affairs, October 12, 2000.

[18]   Conference of the Representatives of the Governments of the Member States, "IGC 2000: Closer cooperation", CONFER 4765/00, August 28, 2000

[19]   Conference of the Representatives of the Governments of the Member States, "Position paper from Germany and Italy: IGC 2000: Enhanced cooperation", CONFER 4783/00, October 4, 2000.

States can form an open, functional *avant-garde* which serves the process of integration and is fully open to future participation by further Member States.[20]

With reference to the Schengen Agreement, Germany and Italy emphasised that the EU's more recent history had shown that enhanced co-operation, if it would not be able to take place within the institutional framework, would do so outside that framework.[21] For those Member States defending the Community method, such developments outside the EU's framework had to be discouraged because it would prevent the Commission and the European Parliament from playing their role as defenders of the Community's general interest as opposed to individual Member State interests.[22]

The most important achievement in Nice regarding enhanced co-operation concerned the elimination of the veto right in the start-up phase.[23] Any Member State is still able to request that the start of en-

---

[20]   CONFER 4783/00, 3.

[21]   CONFER 4783/00, 3. Consolidated TEC, art. 61(1). The Schengen Agreement on the gradual abolition of checks at common borders of June 14, 1985 and the Convention implementing the Schengen Agreement of June 19, 1990, were initially signed by the States of the Benelux Economic Union (Belgium, Luxembourg and the Netherlands), Germany and France. The Schengen Agreement was later extended to Denmark, Greece, Italy, Spain, Portugal, Austria, Finland and Sweden (as well as to non-Member States Norway and Iceland). The UK and Ireland decided not to take part in the Schengen Agreement. The Schengen Agreement existed outside the EU framework as a way to make progress with regard to the free movement of persons, while circumventing UK negativism. During the negotiations of the Treaty of Amsterdam, the Member States decided to integrate the Schengen *acquis* into the EU framework. Amsterdam Protocol 2 recognises, however, that UK and Ireland are still not bound by the Schengen *acquis*, but may at any time request to take part in some or all of the provisions of this *acquis*. All new Member States have to accept the Schengen *acquis* in full.

[22]   CONFER 4783/00, 3; CONFER 4765/00, 4.

[23]   The Treaty of Nice confirmed that enhanced co-operation in Community matters is possible only on proposal of the Commission following a request by the Member States concerned. In the event of the Commission not submitting a proposal, it is obliged to inform the Member States concerned of the reasons for not doing so (Treaty of Nice, art. 2(1) amending Consolidated TEC, arts. 11(1) and 11(2)). Should the Commission not react positively and start enhanced co-operation relating to police and judicial co-operation in criminal matters, the Treaty of Nice foresaw that the Member States concerned are nevertheless be able to submit an initiative to the Council to obtain authorisation (Treaty of Nice, art. 1(9) amending Consolidated TEU, arts. 40a(1) and 40a(2)). When enhanced co-operation related to Community matters concerns an area covered by the co-decision procedure, the Treaty of Nice stipulated that the assent of the European Parliament is required (Treaty of Nice, art. 2(1) amending Consolidated TEC, art. 11(2)).

hanced co-operation be referred to the European Council.[24] However, in the end, this does not prevent the Council from taking a decision by qualified majority.[25]

To prevent the proliferation of numerous small groups of Member States within the EU, the Treaty of Amsterdam foresaw that closer co-operation frameworks could be authorised only on condition that at least a majority of Member States would participate.[26] In view of enlargement, this threshold was regarded as too high.[27] As Belgium argued, "[i]f the minimum threshold of participants is kept at 'half', i.e. 14 out of 27, there is clearly a risk that closer co-operation could become unworkable after major enlargement".[28] It was therefore decided at Nice to fix the minimum number of Member States at eight.[29] Like the Treaty of Amsterdam, the Treaty of Nice specified that enhanced co-operation frameworks must be open to all Members, subject to their compliance with the decisions in that framework.[30]

Many of the Treaty of Amsterdam's other constraints to closer co-operation were maintained.[31] The Treaty of Nice confirmed that enhanced co-operation would not be allowed to undermine the Internal Market or economic and social cohesion and could not be set up to constitute a barrier to trade or distort competition between the Member

---

[24] Treaty of Nice, art. 1(9) amending Consolidated TEU, art. 40a(2); Treaty of Nice, art. 2(1) amending Consolidated TEC, art. 11(2). An exception to this rule concerns enhanced co-operation in the CFSP. The Treaty of Amsterdam had not foreseen closer co-operation in the CFSP. It had simply created the possibility for constructive abstention whereby individual Member States could refrain from entering into a binding obligation under the CFSP, while not preventing the other Member States from moving ahead. Given the need to maintain the unity of the CFSP, the negotiators at Nice still did not find it appropriate to use closer co-operation to define general policy in the CFSP. A majority of Member States nevertheless believed that enhanced co-operation could be useful in the implementation of specific joint actions or common positions. According to the Treaty of Nice, any member of the Council is still be able to declare that "for important and stated reasons of national policy" it is opposing the start of an enhanced co-operation framework in the CFSP by qualified majority. In the military sphere, the Treaty of Amsterdam allowed closer co-operation on a bilateral basis, in the WEU or in the Atlantic Alliance. At Nice, any additional enhanced co-operation with regard to matters having military or defence implications was explicitly excluded, as requested by the UK.

[25] Treaty of Nice, art. 1(9) amending Consolidated TEU, art. 40a(2); Treaty of Nice, art. 2(1) amending Consolidated TEC, art. 11(2).

[26] Consolidated TEU, art. 43(1)(d).

[27] CONFER 4783/00, 4; CONFER 4765/00, 2.

[28] CONFER 4765/00, 2.

[29] Treaty of Nice, art. 1(11) amending Consolidated TEU, art. 43(g).

[30] *Ibid.*, art. 43b.

[31] CONFER 4765/00, 3.

States. In addition, enhanced co-operation cannot be authorised if it would affect the *acquis communautaire*.[32] Belgium in particular had insisted on this point to avoid enhanced co-operation from being abused to undermine the achievements of Community integration.[33]

The Treaty of Nice did not change the requirement that enhanced co-operation can only be engaged in as a last resort, when it has been established within the Council that the objectives pursued are not attainable within a reasonable period by applying the relevant provisions of the Treaties.[34] Germany and Italy argued that this last resort provision created the risk of juridical disputes on which efforts were required to establish that the Treaty objectives could not be attained without the use of enhanced co-operation, whereas this should largely be a matter of political discretion.[35] Belgium emphasised that the last resort rule should not imply a long wait until the impossibility of proceeding with everybody on board had been proved.[36]

Once started, decision-making in a framework of enhanced co-operation takes place according to the normal Treaty rules. In areas where the Treaty provides for Council decision-making by unanimity, this also applies within the framework of enhanced co-operation.[37] Enhanced co-operation therefore does not lead to a greater degree of supranationalism or majority decision-making. Furthermore, even when a framework of enhanced co-operation has been set up, all members of the Council can take part in the deliberations.[38] Only the participating Member States, however, are able to take part in the adoption of decisions.[39] It remains to be seen whether the provisions of the Treaty of Nice on enhanced co-operation are sufficiently flexible to allow for the further evolution of European integration while maintaining the coherence of the project.

---

[32] *Ibid.*

[33] Belgium (CONFER 4765/00, 3), Germany and Italy (CONFER 4783/00, 4), and the European Parliament (Gil-Robles, "Report on reinforced cooperation", 12) successfully argued to delete the term "interests" from the Amsterdam requirement that closer co-operation would not be allowed to "affect the competences, rights, obligations and interests of those Member States which do not participate". See Treaty of Nice, art. 1(11) amending Consolidated TEU, art. 43(h). According to Parliament's *rapporteur*, the term "interests" was "imprecise and subjective, and could be employed to create serious obstacles to the establishment of reinforced cooperation".

[34] Treaty of Nice, art. 1(11) amending Consolidated TEU, art. 43a.

[35] CONFER 4783/00, 4.

[36] CONFER 4765/00, 3.

[37] Treaty of Nice, art. 1(11) amending Consolidated TEU, art. 44(1).

[38] *Ibid.*

[39] *Ibid.*

In the meantime, a *de facto* differentiation has occurred with the creation of the Euro as the single currency for twelve Member States. For some, the Euro is likely to pave the way for political union among the participating countries. In the words of former French Minister of Finance Laurent Fabius:

> ... the twelve countries that have adopted the Euro are in fact the more pro-European Union countries. We shall probably build something that will be more ambitious than what we have today – at least those twelve nations and maybe a few more ... The finance ministers have a meeting every month called the Euro Group ... At the beginning it was a bit theoretical, but now every month we discuss substantive issues concerning fiscal and social policies. We talk about retirement schemes and redundancy, for example. But what is important is that, step by step, we are building a common culture. At the beginning it is economic, but then it becomes social. And because of the importance of economy in our societies, it leads to discussion of other problems – political problems, cultural problems.[40]

II. Between Long-term Solidarity and Short-term Self-interest

From the start, Schuman insisted that Europe had to be "built by practical actions whose first result will be to create a *de facto* solidarity".[41] In legal terms, solidarity has traditionally been associated with the general principle of Community law according to which Member States and Community institutions "are bound by a duty of mutual loyalty and co-operation".[42] This principle has been derived from what used to be Article 5 of the EEC Treaty.[43] *Stricto sensu*, this Article contains three basic obligations: the Member States must take all necessary measures to ensure fulfilment of the obligations arising out of the Treaty; they must facilitate the achievement of the Community's tasks; and they are to abstain from any measure which could jeopardise the attainment of the objectives of the Treaty. The European Court of Justice, however, has come to interpret these obligations as the expression of a more general principle imposing on Member States and Community institutions mutual duties of genuine co-operation and assistance.[44] Furthermore,

---

[40] "The Future of the European Union. Interview with Laurent Fabius", *Challenge*, 44 (2001/2) 7.

[41] Schuman, "Declaration of May 9, 1950", 76.

[42] Giorgio Gaja, "Identifying the Status of General Principles in European Community Law", in *Scritti in Onore di Giuseppe Federico Manchini. Vol. II*, 450.

[43] Currently Consolidated TEC, art. 10.

[44] For an excellent overview of the case-law, see Marc Blanquet, *L'Article 5 du Traité CEE: Recherche sur les Obligations de Fidélité des Etats Membres de la Communauté* (Paris, LGDJ, 1994); Vlad Constantinesco, "L'Article 5 CEE, de la Bonne Foi à la Loyauté Communautaire", in Francesco Capotorti *et al.* (eds.), *Du*

since the entry into force of the Treaty of Maastricht, the EU has the explicit "task ... to organise, in a manner demonstrating consistency and *solidarity*, relations between the Member States and between their peoples".[45]

Community solidarity has always been closely linked to the idea of reciprocity. When referring to Article 5, the European Court of Justice has on several occasions spoken about "the rule imposing *reciprocal* obligations of *bona fide* co-operation".[46] By providing assistance or making concessions to a partner that finds itself in difficulty, the other Member States and the EU institutions expect a similar treatment whenever they would appeal to the solidarity principle. While the Court has explicitly recognised that the Member States accepted the Community legal system "on a basis of reciprocity",[47] it has strongly rejected Member State attempts to use the reciprocity or counter-measure argument to excuse their non-observance of Community obligations, underlining that the Community is a legal order where Member States "shall not take the law into their own hands".[48]

Solidarity is not merely a legal concept, but something real in the EU's political practice. Firstly, solidarity plays an important role during the EU decision-making process. Even where Council decisions can be adopted by qualified majority voting, the drafting process of Community directives and regulations is characterised by a constant attempt to avoid the minorisation of particular Member States. In the words of seasoned European Parliament official Dietmar Nickel, even in those areas where the Council is able to vote by majority, political proposals

---

Droit International au Droit de l'Intégration. Liber Amicorum Pierre Pescatore (Baden-Baden, Nomos, 1987), 97; Claire-Françoise Durand, "Les Principes", in *Commentaire Mégret. Le Droit de la CEE. Vol. 1: Préamule, Principes, Libre Circulation des Marchandises* (Brussels, Ed. de l'Université de Bruxelles, 1992, 2nd ed.), 25; Laurence W. Gormley, "The Development of General Principles of Law Within Article 10 (ex Article 5) EC", in Bernitz and Nergelius (eds.), *General Principles of European Community Law*, 113; John Temple Lang, "Community Constitutional Law: Article 5 EEC Treaty", *Common Market Law Review*, 27 (1990) 645; John Temple Lang, "The Core of Constitutional Law of the Community – Article 5 EC", in Lawrence W. Gormley (ed.), *Current and Future Perspectives on EC Competition Law* (The Hague, Kluwer Law International, 1997), 41.

[45] Consolidated TEU, art. 1.

[46] See, for instance, Case 358/85, France v. European Parliament, E.C.R. 1988, 4821, para. 21.

[47] Costa v. ENEL, E.C.R. 1964, 594.

[48] See, for instance, Cases 90 and 91/63, Commission v. Belgium and Luxembourg, E.C.R. 1964, 625 at 631. For more details see the Geert Wils, "The Concept of Reciprocity in EEC Law: An Exploration into these Realms", *Common Market Law Review*, 28 (1991) 245.

certainly cannot be promoted against a group of Member States, or even one Member State if it were seen as a concerted attempt to overturn the vital interests of this Member State. The solidarity between the Member States in the Council would never admit such a result. Nobody, and certainly not the Commission would seriously try. Everybody would know that this would overstretch the rules of the game.[49]

Instead, the EU's legislation is often accompanied by assurances in the form of transition periods and – less frequently – specific derogations for Member States facing particular problems.[50] It is not surprising therefore that, upon leaving his post as Minister of Foreign Affairs of Luxembourg in 1999, Jacques Poos explicitly thanked his colleagues for their "unfailing support to the smallest of the Member States" and for their "spirit of solidarity which characterises the General Affairs Council".[51]

Secondly, EU solidarity takes a financial form. International trade agreements concluded by the EU often go hand in hand with internal compensatory adjustment in the form of financial aid or intervention promises in such fields as agriculture or textiles. The purpose is to provide assistance to Member States that might suffer specific negative consequences from the application of the international agreements in question.[52] The best known example of financial solidarity in the EU is its extensive economic and social cohesion effort.[53] Since the Single European Act of 1986, the EC aims explicitly "at reducing disparities between the levels of development of the various regions and the backwardness of the least favoured regions or islands, including rural areas".[54] This objective is pursued through the transfer of financial means from the rich to the needy regions via the Community's budget allocations from the Structural Funds (the European Agricultural Guidance and Guarantee Fund, the European Social Fund, the European Regional Development Fund, the Financial Instrument for Fisheries Guidance) and the Cohesion Fund. While less than 5% of the budget in

---

49   Dietmar Nickel, "The Amsterdam Treaty: a Shift in the Balance between the Institutions?", Harvard Jean Monnet Chair Working Paper Series (1998/14) available in <http://www.law.harvard.edu/Programs/JeanMonnet/papers/98/ 980701.html>.

50   For examples of transition periods and derogations during the EC's legislative process, see de Schoutheete, *Une Europe pour Tous*, 103.

51   *Agence Europe*, June 23, 1999, 8.

52   For examples related to the EU's conclusion of the Uruguay Round see Youri Devuyst, "The European Community and the Conclusion of the Uruguay Round", in Rhodes and Mazey (eds.), *The State of the European Union. Vol. III*, 456.

53   On the EU's cohesion policy see Liesbet Hooghe (ed.), *Cohesion Policy and European Integration: Building Multilevel Governance* (Oxford, Oxford University Press, 1996); Liesbet Hooghe, "EU Cohesion Policy and Competing Models of European Capitalism", *Journal of Common Market Studies*, 36 (1998) 457.

54   Consolidated TEC, art. 158.

1975, cohesion spending increased to 35% in 2002. Although an expression of solidarity, the cohesion effort is also very much the result of reciprocity during the Maastricht negotiations.[55] The Cohesion Fund was established due to the insistence of Spain and the other poorer Member States. In view of their important investment needs in basic infrastructure, the poorer Member States agreed to go along with the strict budgetary criteria in the EMU framework only on the condition that they would receive additional cohesion assistance from the Community. And reciprocity went both ways since the actual use of the Cohesion Fund was made conditional on the respect of the Maastricht Treaty's deficit reduction objectives.[56] Although economic disparities between the Member States persist, the EU's cohesion efforts have contributed to diminishing the gap. Ireland is the clearest example, with per capita GDP rising from 64% of the EU average in 1988 to 119% in 2000. The extent to which Greece, Portugal and Spain lag behind the EU average has shrunk by almost one third between 1988 and 2000, i.e. from 68 to 79%.[57]

With the Agenda 2000 debate regarding the EU's financial per-spectives for the period between 2000 and 2006, the solidarity theme became a hot issue on the European political agenda in 1998 and 1999.[58] Germany, backed by the Netherlands, Sweden and Austria, called for a mechanism to correct budgetary imbalances. Their purpose was to obtain a cut in their net contribution to the EU budget.[59] At the start of the debate, German Chancellor Gerhard Schröder declared that it had become necessary to change traditional German policy. "In the past", he said, "many of the necessary compromises could be achieved because the Germans have paid for them. This policy has come to an end".[60] Schröder and several of his colleagues from the richer countries tackled the debate on the basis of Commission figures calculating for each Mem-

---

[55] David Allen, "Cohesion and Structural Adjustment", in Wallace and Wallace (eds.), *Policy-Making in the European Union* (1996, 3rd ed.), 209.

[56] Gary Marks, "Structural Policy and Multilevel Governance", in Alan W. Cafruny and Glenda G. Rosenthal (eds.), *The State of the European Union. Vol. II: The Maastricht Debates and Beyond* (Boulder, Lynne Rienner, 1993), 391.

[57] Commission of the European Communities, "First Progress Report on Economic and Social Cohesion", COM(2002) 46 final, January 30, 2002, 8.

[58] Commission of the European Communities, "Agenda 2000. For a Stronger and Wider Union", COM(97) 2000 final, 1997.

[59] For a critical comment see Laureano Lazaro Araujo, "La Unión Europea, Entre la Cohesión y la Desintegración", *Politica Exterior*, (1999/68) 81.

[60] "Spiegel-Gespräch mit Gerhard Schröder. Uns die Last erleichtern", *Der Spiegel*, January 4, 1999, 44 (Translation by the author).

ber State the balance between budgetary contributions and receipts.[61]
The view that budget contributions should be equivalent to the budget
returns – the so-called "*juste retour*" theory – was strongly condemned in
the European Parliament. Jutta Haug, Parliament's *rapporteur* on the
issue, underlined that the "*juste retour*" attitude was "contrary to the
indivisible nature of the financial and non-financial rights, benefits and
obligations deriving from Union membership and from the principle of
solidarity between the Member States".[62] As budgetary calculations do
not include the benefits that are derived from the Internal Market or the
Euro, Haug emphasised that the net-contributor concept was methodo-
logically extremely imprecise. While recognising that the full benefits of
EU membership cannot be measured solely in budgetary terms, the
agreement on the EU's financial perspectives reached at the Berlin European Council of March 1999 did lead to a correction of the "politically
unacceptable anomalies in burden-sharing", thus allowing for a moderate
reduction in the financial contributions of Austria, Germany, the Netherlands and Sweden.[63] The UK abatement was maintained. More significant was the overall reduction in EU funding that resulted from the
Berlin European Council.[64] As a result of the Member States' eagerness
to cut their contributions to the EU budget, the Berlin financial perspectives include a general decrease in the transfer of budgetary means from
the Member States to the EU. In 1999, the ceiling for total appropriations
for payments for the EU stood at 1.24% of the EU's combined GDP.[65]
The Berlin financial perspectives aim at reducing this level from 1.13%
in 2000 to 0.97% in 2006. This caused sharp criticism by the European
Parliament which regretted that – at times when more action is expected
from the EU in a host of areas – the financial perspectives made no
provision for realistic levels of funding, unless activities would be

---

[61] Commission of the European Communities, "Financing the European Union.
      Commission Report on the Operation of the Own Resources System", COM(1998)
      560 final, October 7, 1998.

[62] Jutta Haug, "Report on the Need to Modify and Reform the European Union's Own
      Resources System", European Parliament Session Documents, March 8, 1999, 17.

[63] David Galloway, "Agenda 2000 – Packaging the Deal", *Journal of Common Market
      Studies (European Union Annual Review 1998/1999)*, 37 (1999) 9; Brigid Laffan,
      "The Agenda 2000 Negotiations: la Présidence Coûte Cher?", *German Politics*, 9
      (2000/3) 1. See also Berlin European Council, "Presidency Conclusions", March 24-
      25, 1999, para. 4.

[64] On the Berlin's budgetary results, see Brigid Laffan, "The Berlin Summit: Process
      and Outcome of the Agenda 2000 Budgetary Proposals", 12 *ECSA Review* (Fall
      1999) 6

[65] Commission of the European Communities, "The Community Budget: The Facts in
      Figures", SEC (99) 1100, 1999, table 16.

significantly reduced.[66] Parliamentarians feared that EU solidarity risked ending up as mere rhetoric in view of the Member States' tendency to retreat behind their own budget walls.

The debate on solidarity reappeared on the agenda in the framework of the enlargement negotiations. The Member States agreed that the ceiling for enlargement-related expenditure set out for the years 2004-2006 by the European Council in Berlin had to be respected.[67] One of the more controversial issues concerned expenditure in the agricultural area. The new Member States will receive a rural development package that is specifically adapted to their requirements and has more favourable conditions than those applied to the present EU Member States. However, direct agricultural aids for the new Member States will be phased in only gradually over a period of ten years, starting at a level of 25% of the full EU rate in 2004 and climbing to 100% in 2013.[68] For the Commission and the current Member States, this gradual approach was justified by the need to push agricultural restructuring in the new Member States. Applying the full direct payments to the farmers in the new Member States would increase their income well above the level of other workers, thus discouraging rationalisation in the agricultural sector.

Some of the current net contributing Member States had indicated their concern over the generosity of this approach. However, in the end, Germany proved ready to pay for "its" enlargement. Candidate countries like Poland, Hungary and the Czech Republic nevertheless expressed disappointment with the EU's approach to direct farm aid. For them, the decisions on direct aid "do not guarantee respect of the principle many times underlined by the European Union that all member countries must be treated on equal footing".[69]

That the current Member States are nervous about the financial consequences of enlargement was also visible during the negotiations of the Treaty of Nice. At Nice, Spain, Greece and Portugal initially objected to the proposal to move from unanimity to qualified majority voting regarding the definition of the Structural Fund rules, objectives and organisation. They feared that the redistribution of the funds after the accession of the Central and Eastern European countries would be to the detriment of the Southern European Member States. In the end, it was agreed that the Council is able to act by qualified majority with respect to

---

[66] European Parliament, "Resolution on the Results of the Extraordinary European Council in Berlin on 24/25 March 1999", O.J. C 219, 1999, 191, paras. 4 and 5.

[67] Brussels European Council, "Presidency Conclusions", October 24-25, 2002, para. 10.

[68] Copenhagen European Council, "Presidency Conclusions", December 12-13, 2002, Annex I.

[69] *Agence Europe*, February 1, 2002, 13.

the Structural Funds from January 2007, but only if by that date the EU's multi-annual financial perspectives for the subsequent years have been adopted.[70] Each Member State thus maintains the right to block any "unfavourable" distribution of the Structural Funds from 2007 till 2013, which is the expected duration of the multi-annual financial perspectives after 2006.[71] This outcome is characteristic for the negotiations at Nice. The Member States avoided discussions on long-term solidarity, but focused on a self-centred approach by maintaining short-term veto rights.

III. Between Philosophical Openness and a "Christian Europe"

The EU has never identified itself with particular religious or philosophical values. Among the founders of the European integration process, one finds religiously inspired politicians like Robert Schuman as well as humanist freethinkers like Paul-Henri Spaak. There is only one reference to religion in the Treaties. As stipulated in the Treaty of Amsterdam, the Community has as one of its tasks to combat discrimination based on "religion or belief".[72] Like the Council of Europe, the EU has thus opted for a formula protecting the various religious and non-religious philosophical beliefs on an equal footing.[73]

During the negotiations of the Treaty of Amsterdam, German Chancellor Helmut Kohl had suggested to also insert a Treaty paragraph emphasising Europe's Christian values and the role of the churches in the European construction. The attempt was resisted, in particular by Belgian Minister of Foreign Affairs Eric Derycke. He notably underlined the constitutional problems that would arise in Belgium should the Treaty of Amsterdam include a discrimination against the non-religious community. The Belgian Constitution, indeed, provides for explicit equal treatment between the recognised religions and the non-confessional

---

[70] Treaty of Nice, art. 2(14) amending Consolidated TEC, art. 161.

[71] Greece, Spain and Portugal agreed to move to qualified majority on the basis that the word "multi-annual" means that the financial perspectives applicable from January 2007 and the Inter-Institutional agreement relating thereto will have the same duration as the current financial perspective. See the Nice Declaration by Greece, Spain and Portugal on Article 161 of the Treaty establishing the European Community. This Declaration was countered by the Nice Declaration by Denmark, Germany, the Netherlands and Austria on Article 161 of the Treaty establishing the European Community. These Member States stated that the Declaration by Greece, Spain and Portugal is without prejudice to actions of the European Commission, in particular with respect to its right of initiative.

[72] Consolidated TEC, art. 13.

[73] European Convention on the Protection of Human Rights and Fundamental Freedoms, art. 9.

community.[74] In the end, a Declaration was adopted on the status of churches and non-confessional organisations.[75] It simply underlined that the EU respects and does not prejudice the status under national law of churches and equally respects the status of philosophical and non-confessional organisations.

In the context of the Convention that created the EU's Charter of Fundamental Rights, proclaimed in December 2000, a new series of proposals were formulated to include a reference to God and to recognise the EU's Christian origins.[76] The draft Charter referred explicitly to the EU's religious (and humanist) heritage.[77] However, in the end, all references to the EU's religious roots were deleted from the Charter on the insistence of French Premier Lionel Jospin.[78] He warned that references of a religious nature would be incompatible with France's status as a lay or secular State and would therefore pose a major legal and political obstacle to the Charter's acceptance.

The absence of a reference to Europe's religious heritage in the Charter on Fundamental Rights immediately resulted in expressions of disappointment by the Conference of European Churches.[79] The churches therefore approached the European Convention on the Constitutional Treaty to nevertheless obtain their objective.[80] They received political support, notably by Ingo Friedrich, Vice-President of the European Parliament and Joachim Wuermeling, one of the European Parliament's alternate representatives in the Convention on the EU's future. The two Bavarian Christian Social Union-politicians announced their intention to push for an explicit reference to God and to Europe's religious heritage in the Constitutional Treaty.[81] Their efforts resulted in a contribution that

---

[74] Belgian Constitution, arts. 11, 19, 20, 21, 131.

[75] Amsterdam Declaration 11 on the status of churches and non-confessional organisations.

[76] See the following documents of the Convention on Fundamental Rights, CHARTE 4128/00 ADD1, March 7, 2000; CHARTE 4233/00, April 18, 2000; CHARTE 4323/00, May 24, 2000; CHARTE 4365/00, June 14, 2000; CHARTE 4468/00, September 18, 2000; CHARTE 4490/00, September 29, 2000.

[77] Convention on Fundamental Rights, "Draft Charter of Fundamental Rights of the European Union", CHARTE 4470/1/00 REV. 1, September 21, 2000, preamble.

[78] "Charter of Fundamental Rights of the European Union", O.J. C 364, 2000, 1.

[79] Jonathan Luxmoore, "European Union Charter Omits Church History", *Christianity Today*, November 13, 2000.

[80] Conference of European Churches, "First Submission to the Convention on the Future of Europe", May 2002; Conference of European Churches, "Churches and Communities in a Constitutional Treaty of the European Union", September 2002.

[81] Joachim Wuermeling, "EU-Reform : Werte-Osterweiterung-Gottesbezug", November 14, 2002; Elmar Brok and Joachim Wuermeling, "Konvents-Telegramm Nr. 11", September 9, 2002. See also Henri Tincq, "Le Débat sur l'Identité Religieuse de l'Europe entre à la Convention", *Le Monde*, November 7, 2002

was signed by 21 members and alternate members of the Convention.[82] Furthermore, the draft for a Constitution of the European Union that was presented in November 2002 by the European People's Party (EPP) – the largest group in the European Parliament – explicitly referred to "what Europe owes to its religious heritage".[83] Following the Polish Constitution, the EPP draft also stated that the EU's values "include the values of those who believe in God as the source of truth, justice, good and beauty as well as those who do not share such a belief but respect these universal values arising from other sources".[84]

Not surprisingly, the European Humanist Federation strongly disagreed with such references. According to the Federation, to grant religion a particular status in the EU's Constitutional Treaty "would be tantamount to creating a discrimination between beliefs of those citizens who believe in heaven and those who do not".[85] Moreover, the Federation underlined that a Union that, like the kings of the Middle Ages, is seeking its legitimacy by appealing to religion can no longer pretend to represent the entire population and endangers the separation between religion and public authority. The Union's task is to defend Europe's the general interest, not its religious heritage or values, the Humanist Federation argued. As was stated by Keith Porteus Wood, the executive director of Britain's National Secular Society: "The only way to ensure that all of Europe's citizens feel equally valued [in the EU] is to leave religion out of its pronouncements and to secularise its structure and workings".[86]

During the drafting of the Constitutional Treaty, the issue of religious heritage interacted with the question of a possible Turkish accession. In November 2002, the President of the European Convention, Valéry Giscard d'Estaing, declared that Turkey was not a European country and that it was characterised by another culture and another way of life.[87] These comments immediately provoked a reaction from the Turkish side. Giscard is "the equivalent of a Muslim integrationist", said Ali Tekin, a Member of the Turkish Parliament who also served as a representative to

---

[82] The European Convention, "Contribution by Mr Joachim Wuermeling: Religious Reference in the Constitutional Treaty", CONV 480/03, January 10, 2003.

[83] EPP, "The Constitution of the European Union. Discussion Paper", November 10, 2002, preamble.

[84] EPP, "The Constitution of the European Union. Discussion Paper", November 10, 2002, art. 57.

[85] European Humanist Federation, "Contribution to the Convention : The Future of Europe", June 2, 2002, 6.

[86] William J. Cole, "Is Europe a Christian Continent ?", *The Washington Post*, June 22, 2002.

[87] Arnaud Leparmentier and Laurent Zecchini, "Pour ou Contre l'Adhésion de la Turquie à l'Union européenne", *Le Monde*, November 9, 2002.

the European Convention. "He is a Christian integrationist who thinks the Union is a Christian club".[88]

While pleading for an EU that would continue to be characterised by philosophical openness, Belgian Prime Minister Guy Verhofstadt reacted as follows to both Giscard's comments and the attempts to include references to religion in the Constitutional Treaty:

> Some dream of a mono-cultural Europe, the Europe of Christian values, as if Europe were not also founded on the Jewish heritage as well as on a strong humanist tradition … This reasoning [in favour of a Christian Europe] is absurd. It runs counter to the achievement of the Enlightenment, that of separation of Church and State, which put an end to age-old religious conflicts … [89]

---

[88] "Turquie: Surprise et Colère après les Propos de M. Giscard d'Estaing", *Le Monde*, November 10, 2002.

[89] Guy Verhofstadt, "Montesquieu and the European Union", Speech at the College of Europe, Bruges, November 18, 2002, 1.

Conclusion

While adopting the Euro as the single currency and entering into new policy areas such as security and defence as well as police and judicial co-operation, the EU is simultaneously pursuing the most challenging enlargement in its history. Still, in institutional terms, the EU's future is unclear. After the Treaties of Maastricht, Amsterdam and Nice, the EU's constitutional order is hanging somewhere between what remains of the supranational components of the Treaty of Rome's Community method and a series of compromise solutions that tend to steer the EU in a more intergovernmental direction. In contrast with the policy domains that work under the Community method, the EU's intergovernmental fields of action have been characterised by the famous "capability-expectations gap".

After the disruptive debate at Maastricht on the EU's "federal" vocation, the Member States have tried for a decade to avoid discussions on the EU's institutional future. Instead of striving for long-term efficiency and coherence in the perspective of enlargement, the Heads of State or Government have tended to focus on the short-term. The Nice European Council was the culmination of this approach. For some, the process towards the Treaty of Nice was a clear indication that the Member States have opted for the EU's widening at the expense of the deepening of European integration. Portuguese State Secretary for European Affairs Francisco Seixas da Costa expressed this position as follows:

> To make possible the enlargement of Europe to the Eastern European countries and offer them political stability and economic development, the Fifteen have made an implicit choice, opting for a Union that differs from the one that has existed to date. The challenge of enlargement has changed the quality of the Union and reduced the ambition of the European undertaking. This may be regrettable but could not be avoided.[1]

However, precisely because enlargement without a profound institutional adaptation would undermine the EU's efficiency, the accession process can also be seen as the key to a new "institutional spillover". As Robert O. Keohane and Stanley Hoffmann have described in another context, enlargement, first appearing as an antithesis to effective decision-making, could in a dialectic manner become the decisive element that provokes institutional reform aiming at greater decision-making efficiency.[2] The higher the number of new Member States, the greater the

---

[1] *Agence Europe*, January 14, 2000, 3.

[2] Robert O. Keohane and Stanley Hoffmann, "Institutional Change in Europe in the 1980s", in Robert O. Keohane and Stanley Hoffmann (eds.), *The New European*

centrifugal effects of enlargement and the more pressing the need for the strengthening of the EU's decision-making capability and of those institutions defending the Community's common interest as opposed to the individual Member State interests. Already, the Heads of State and Government's failure at Nice to produce a forward-looking reform made them realise that a new method for Treaty change would be necessary to avoid the Union's paralysis after the enlargement. In this context, the creation of the Convention of the future of Europe, involving not only the governments of the Member States, but also representatives from the European and national parliaments and observers from Europe's regions and social partners, could be regarded as a first concrete step towards an institutional spillover fostered by the prospect of enlargement. At least some candidate countries have already signalled that they are demanding such an institutional jump too. The Hungarian government formulated this most clearly in its submission for the Nice IGC:

> Hungary feels deeply interested in ensuring the efficient and smooth functioning of the Union. With this basic objective in mind we are in favour of widening the scope of qualified majority voting. Extending the range of decisions taken by qualified majority voting is an incremental process reflecting the strengthening of the integration and the degree of resolve and determination of the Member States to move forward. It would be erroneous to presume that such resolve would by nature decrease due to the accession.[3]

An important hurdle that must be overcome in the attempt to make an institutional jump in preparation for enlargement is the legal requirement that new Treaty provisions can enter into force only after having been ratified by all Member States.[4] In the past, this unanimity requirement has torpedoed several attempts to generate institutional change beyond the lowest common denominator. If the current reform process would again fail to produce a forward-looking constitutional document that improves the EU's decision-making capacity, proposals for a "two-circle Europe" along the lines suggested by former Commission President Jacques Delors and German Minister of Foreign Affairs Joschka Fischer could regain in significance.[5] Under their schemes, the EU would

---

Community. *Decision-making and Institutional Change* (Boulder, Westview Press, 1991), 22.

[3]   Conference of the Representatives of the Governments of the Member States, IGC 2000: Contribution from the government of Hungary, CONFER/VAR 3952/00, February 24, 2000, 3.

[4]   See, for instance, Alain Lamassoure, "De la nécessité d'un manifeste fédéral", *Le Figaro*, February 28, 2002.

[5]   Jacques Delors, "Reuniting Europe: Our Historic Mission", *Agence Europe*, January 3-4, 2000, 2; Joschka Fischer, "From Confederacy to Federation – Thoughts on the Finality of European Integration", Speech at the Humbold University, Berlin, May 12, 2000.

become the home of the greater Europe, including those countries prefer-ring a lesser degree of political integration. A more ambitious *avant-garde*, open to all European countries having the necessary political determination to leave ancient notions of sovereignty behind, would form a new European Federation (of Nation States).

Not everywhere has the idea for a two-circle Europe, along the models proposed by Fischer and Delors, been received with so much enthusiasm. Former Polish Minister of Foreign Affairs Bronislaw Geremek, for instance, has emphasised that the idea of developing a two-circle Europe with a Federation at its core is "contrary to the way of thinking of the candidate countries which have just regained their inde-pendence and sovereignty".[6] Jan Zielonka has reached the conclusion that "enlargement and Fischer's vision are basically incompatible ... a political federation within an enlarged Union is no longer possible".[7] This, however, is precisely one of the main arguments behind the proposals of Fischer and Delors. They fear that an enlarged EU, with a multitude of old and new Member States defending an even greater variety of viewpoints than today, will not be able to pursue the ambitious goal of political union. In that context, an *avant-garde* looks essential to continue the deepening of the integration process. In Fischer's wording: "[p]recisely in an enlarged and thus necessarily more heterogeneous Union, further differentiation will be inevitable".[8]

Whether the accession process will lead to a direct institutional spillover following the European Convention or might provoke the creation of a "two-circle Europe" along the lines proposed by Delors and Fischer remains to be seen. The alternative would be a further erosion of the EU to the level of an uninspiring League of Nations. Such an erosion would have important consequences, for Member States and third countries alike. While the Community method has proved an exception-ally efficient instrument for reconciliation among large and small States, Europe's history provides no credible alternatives for an equally effective and peaceful collective decision-making system.[9]

---

[6]   *Agence Europe*, May 19, 2000, 4.

[7]   Jan Zielonka, "Enlargement and the Finality of European Integration", in Joerges, Mény and Weiler (eds.), *What Kind of Constitution for What Kind of Polity?*, 152.

[8]   Fischer, "From Confederacy to Federation", 8.

[9]   See John J. Mearsheimer, "Back to the Future. Instability in Europe After the Cold War", *International Security*, 15 (1990) 5; Gregory F. Treverton, "Europe's Past, Europe's Future. Finding an Analogy for Tomorrow", *Orbis*, 10 (1993) 1.

Bibliography[*]

Speeches and Writings by Political Leaders

Barshefsky Charlene, "Reflections at a Moment of Transition: The Transatlantic Relationship and its Future", Speech at the European-American Business Council, Washington, D.C., January 17, 2001

Blair Tony, "A Clear Course for Europe", Cardiff, November 28, 2002

Blair Tony, "The Challenge of Reform in Europe", Birmingham, November 23, 2001

Blair Tony, "Prime Minister's Speech to the Polish Stock Exchange", Warsaw, October 6, 2000

Chirac Jacques, "Notre Europe", Speech at the Bundestag, Berlin, June 27, 2000

Couve de Murville Maurice, *Une Politique Etrangère 1958-1969* (Paris, Plon, 1971)

De Gaulle Charles, *Mémoires d'Espoir. Le Renouveau, 1958-1962* (Paris, Plon, 1970)

Delors Jacques, "Reuniting Europe: Our Historic Mission", *Agence Europe*, January 3-4, 2000

Derycke Erik, "The Present Challenges of the European Union", Address before the Symposium Austria: A New Partner in the European Union, April 3, 1995

Fischer Joschka, "From Confederacy to Federation – Thoughts on the Finality of European Integration", Speech at the Humbold University, Berlin, May 12, 2000

Giscard d'Estaing Valéry, "Introductory Speech to the Convention on the Future of Europe", February 28, 2002

Giscard d'Estaing Valéry and Helmut Schmidt, "Europe's Lessons", *Agence Europe*, April 17, 2000

Hallstein Walter, *Europe in the Making* (London, Allan & Unwin, 1972)

Hallstein Walter, "Primauté du Droit Communautaire", Address before the European Parliament, Strasbourg, June 17, 1965

Hallstein Walter, *United Europe. Challenge and Opportunity* (Cambridge, MA, Harvard University Press, 1962)

Jospin Lionel, "L'Avenir de l'Europe Elargie", Paris, May 28, 2001

Kohl Helmut with Kai Diekmann and Ralf-Georg Reuth, *Ich Wollte Deutschlands Einheit* (Berlin, Ullstein Buchverlag/Propyläen Verlag, 1996)

Lamassoure Alain, "De la nécessité d'un manifeste fédéral", *Le Figaro*, February 28, 2002

Lipponen Paavo, "Address at the College of Europe", Bruges, November 10, 2000

Lipponen Paavo, "Speech at the College of Europe", Bruges, November 10, 2000

Major John, "Statement on the Working Time Directive", November 12, 1996

---

[*]   The bibliography contains the list of books, academic articles, speeches and European Parliament reports that have been referred to in this book. It does not include official reports that do not identify individual authors.

Major John, "Europe: A Future that Works", William and Mary Lecture at the Universiteit Leiden, September 7, 1994

Marjolin Robert, *Architect of European Unity: Memoirs, 1911-1986* (London, Weidenfeld and Nicolson, 1989)

Mitterrand François, *De l'Allemagne, de la France* (Paris, Odile Jacob, 1997)

Monnet Jean, *Mémoires* (Paris, Fayard, 1976)

Patten Christopher, "External Relations: Demands, Constraints and Priorities", *Agence Europe*, June 10, 2000

Prodi Romano, "An Enlarged and More United Europe, A Global Player", Speech at the College of Europe, Bruges, November 12, 2001

Prodi Romano, "A Wider Europe : A Proximity Policy as the Key to Stability", Speech at the Sixth ECSA-World Conference, Brussels, December 6, 2002

Prodi Romano, "Europe and the Mediterranean : Time for Action", Speech at the Université Catholique de Louvain-la-Neuve, November 26, 2002

Prodi Romano, "For a Strong Europe, with a Grand Design and the Means of Action", Speech at the Institut d'Etudes Politiques, Paris, May 29, 2001

Prodi Romano, "On the Road to Laeken", Speech at the European Parliament, Strasbourg, July 4, 2001

Prodi Romano, "Pour une Europe Forte, Dotée d'un Grand Projet et de Moyens d'Action", Speech at the Institut d'Etudes Politiques, Paris, May 29, 2001

Prodi Romano, "The European Union's New Institutional Structure", Speech at the Institut d'Etudes Politiques, Paris, May 29, 2001

Prodi Romano, "The New Europe in the Transatlantic Partnership", Speech before the European Parliament, Strasbourg, December 5, 2002

Prodi Romano, "The State of the Union in 2001", Speech before the European Parliament, Strasbourg, February 13, 2001

Prodi Romano, "The time has come for a properly structured debate on the future of Europe", Speech before the European Parliament, Strasbourg, January 17, 2001

Rau Johannes, "Plea for a European Constitution", Speech to the European Parliament, Strasbourg, April 4, 2001

Schröder Gerhard and Tony Blair, "Reform of the European Council. Joint Letter to Prime Minister Aznar", February 25, 2002

Schröder Gerhard, "Nach der Reform: Zukunftsstrategien für Gesamteuropa", Speech at the International Bertelsmann-Forum 2001, January 19, 2001

Schuman Robert, "Declaration of 9 May 1950", in Peter M. R. Stirk and David Weigall (eds.), *The Origins and Development of European Integration: A Reader and Commentary* (London, Pinter, 1999), 76

Solana Javier, "Lecture at the Inauguration of the Diplomatic Academy of the Ministry of Foreign Affairs of the Republic of Poland", Warsaw, October 16, 2002

Spaak Paul-Henri, *Combats Inachevés. Vol. II: De l'Espoir aux Déceptions* (Paris, Fayart, 1969)

Straw Jack, "Reforming Europe: New Era, New Questions", The Hague, February 21, 2002

Tugendhat Christopher, *Making Sense of Europe* (Harmondsworth, Viking, 1986)

Talbott Strobe, "Transatlantic Ties", *Newsweek*, October 18, 1999, 34

Védrine Hubert, *Les Mondes de François Mitterrand* (Paris, Fayard, 1996)

Verhofstadt Guy, "A Vision of Europe", Speech at the European Policy Center, Brussels, September 21, 2000

Verhofstadt Guy, "Montesquieu and the European Union", Speech at the College of Europe, Bruges, November 18, 2002

European Parliament Reports

Böge Reimer, "Report on the European Commission's Follow-Up of the Recommendations made by the Committee of Inquiry into BSE", European Parliament Session Document, November 14, 1997

Brok Elmar and Dimitrios Tsatsos, "Overview of the Results of the Intergovernmental Conference", European Parliament, December 19, 2000

Carnero Gonzalez Carlos, "Report on the Legal Personality of the European Union", European Parliament Session Document, November 21, 2001

Dimitrakopoulos Giorgios and Jo Leinen, "Report on the Preparation of the Reform of the Treaties and the Next Intergovernmental Conference", European Parliament Session Document, November 10, 1999

Duhamel Olivier, "Report on the Constitutionalisation of the Treaties", European Parliament Session Document, October 12, 2000

Fontaine Nicole, Renzo Imbeni, Joseph Verdi i Aldea, "Codecision Procedure under Article 189b of the Treaty of Maastricht. Activity Report of the Delegations to the Conciliation Committee, November 1, 1993 – April 30, 1999. From Entry into Force of the Treaty of Maastricht to Entry into Force of the Treaty of Amsterdam", European Parliament, Delegations to the Conciliation Committee, 1999

Gil-Robles Gil-Delgado José Maria, "Report on Reinforced Cooperation", European Parliament, Committee on Constitutional Affairs, October 12, 2000

Haug Jutta, "Report on the Need to Modify and Reform the European Union's Own Resources System", European Parliament Session Document, March 8, 1999

Lalumière Catherine, "Report on the Establishment of a Common European Security and Defence Policy of the European Union after Cologne and Helsinki", European Parliament Session Document, November 21, 2000

Lamassoure Alain, "Working Document on the Division of Powers between the Union and the Member States", European Parliament Committee on Constitutional Affairs, March 15, 2001

Napolitano Giorgio, "Report on Relations between the European Parliament and the National Parliaments in European Integration", European Parliament Session Document, January 23, 2002

Poos Jacques, "Report on Reform of the Council", European Parliament Session Document, September 17, 2001

Books and Articles

Albors-Llorens Albertina, "Changes in the Jurisdiction of the European Court of Justice under the Treaty of Amsterdam", *Common Market Law Review*, 35 (1998) 1273

Allcott Philip, "The Crisis of European Constitutionalism: Reflections on the Revolution in Europe", *Common Market Law Review*, 34 (1997) 439

Allen David, "Cohesion and Structural Adjustment", in Wallace and Wallace (eds.), *Policy-Making in the European Union* (1996, 3rd ed.), 209

Allen David, Reinhardt Rummel and Wolfgang Wessels (ed.), *European Political Cooperation. Towards a Foreign Policy for Western Europe* (London, Butterworth, 1982)

Alter Karen, *Establishing the Supremacy of European Law. The Making of an International Rule of Law in Europe* (Oxford, Oxford University Press, 2001)

Andenas Mads and Alexander Türk (eds.), *Delegated Legislation and the Role of Committees in the EC* (The Hague, Kluwer Law International, 2000)

Andenas Mads and John Usher (eds.), *The Treaty of Nice. Enlargement and Constitutional Reform* (Oxford, Hart, 2002)

Arnull Anthony and Daniel Wincott (eds.), *Accountability and Legitimacy in the European Union* (Oxford, Oxford University Press, 2002)

Arnull Anthony, Alan Dashwood, Malcolm Ross and Derrick Wyatt, *European Union Law* (London, Sweet & Maxwell, 2000)

Arnull Anthony, "Taming the Beast? The Treaty of Amsterdam and the Court of Justice", in O'Keeffe and Twomey (eds.), *Legal Issues of the Amsterdam Treaty*, 109

Arnull Anthony, *The European Union and its Court of Justice* (Oxford, Oxford University Press, 1999)

Aron Raymond and Daniel Lerner (eds.), *France Defeats EDC* (New York, Praeger, 1957)

Baldwin Richard, Erik Berglöf, Francesco Giavazzi and Mika Widgrén, *Nice Try: Should the Treaty of Nice be Ratified?* (London, Centre for Economic Policy Research, 2001)

Banchoff Thomas, "History and Memory: German Policy Towards the European Union", *German Politics*, 6 (1997) 60

Barents René, "The Community and the Unity of the Common Market: Some Reflections on the Economic Constitution of the Community", *German Yearbook of International Law*, 33 (1990) 9

Barnard Catherine, "Article 13: Through the Looking Glass of Union Citizenship", in O'Keeffe and Twomey (eds.), *Legal Issues of the Amsterdam Treaty*, 375

Baun Michael J., *A Wider Europe. Process and Politics of European Union Enlargement* (Lanham, Rowman & Littlefield, 2000)

Baun Michael J., *An Imperfect Union. The Maastricht Treaty and the New Politics of European Integration* (Boulder, Westview Press, 1996)

Baun Michael J., "The Länder and German European Policy: The 1996 IGC and Amsterdam Treaty", *German Studies Review*, 21 (1998) 329

Bavasso Antonio F., "Gencor: A Judicial Review of the Commission's Policy and Practice. Many Lights and Some Shadows", *World Competition*, 22 (1999/4) 45

Begg Iain and Nigel Grimwade, *Paying for Europe* (Sheffield, Sheffield Academic Press, 1998)

Bell David S. and Christopher Lord (eds.), *Transnational Parties in the European Union* (Aldershot, Ashgate, 1998)

Bell Mark, "The New Article 13 EC Treaty: A Sound Basis for European Anti-Discrimination Law?", *Maastricht Journal of European and Comparative Law*, 6 (1999) 5

Bellamy Christopher and Graham Child with Peter M. Roth (ed.), *European Community Law of Competition* (London, Sweet & Maxwell, 2001)

Bermann George A., "Taking Subsidiarity Seriously: Federalism in the European Community and the United States", *Columbia Law Review*, 94 (1994) 331

Bermann George A., "The Single European Act: A New Constitution for the Community? ", *Columbia Journal of Transnational Law*, 27 (1989) 529

Bernitz Ulf and Joakim Nergelius (eds.), *General Principles of European Community Law* (The Hague, Kluwer Law International, 2000)

Best Edward, Mark Gray and Alexander Stubb (eds.), *Rethinking the European Union. IGC 2000 and Beyond* (Maastricht, European Institute of Public Administration, 2000)

Bieber Roland and Jörg Monar (eds.), *Justice and Home Affairs in the European Union: Development of the Third Pillar* (Brussels, European Interuniversity Press [P.I.E.-E.I.P.], 1995)

Bieber Roland, Karel de Gucht, Koen Lenaerts and Joseph Weiler (eds.), *In the Name of the Peoples of Europe: A Catalogue of Fundamental Rights* (Baden-Baden, Nomos, 1996)

Blanquet Marc, *L'Article 5 du Traité CEE: Recherche sur les Obligations de Fidélité des Etats Membres de la Communauté* (Paris, LGDJ, 1994)

Bloes Robert, *Le Plan Fouchet et le Problème de l'Europe Politique* (Bruges, College of Europe, 1970)

Blumann Claude, "Le Pouvoir Exécutif de la Commission à la lumière de l'Acte Unique Européen", *Revue Trimestrielle de Droit Européen*, 1 (1988) 23

Boeder Thomas L., "The Boeing-McDonnell Douglas Merger", in Evenett, Lehmann and Steil (eds.), *Antitrust Goes Global,* 139

Bond Martin and Kim Feus (eds.), *The Treaty of Nice Explained* (London, Federal Trust, 2001)

Bossuat Gérard, "Le Choix de la Petite Europe par la France (1957-1963): Une Ambition pour la France et pour l'Europe", *Relations Internationales* (1995/82) 213

Bossuat Gérard, "The French Administrative Elite and the Unification of Western Europe, 1947-58", in Deighton (ed.), *Building Postwar Europe*, 21

Bourgeois Jacques H. J., Jean-Louis Dewost and Marie-Ange Gaiffe (eds.), *La Communauté Européenne et les accords Mixtes: Quelles Perspectives?* (Brussels, European Interuniversity Press [P.I.E.-E.I.P.], 1997)

Bourgeois Jacques H. J., "The Common Commercial Policy – Scope and Nature of the Powers", in Völker (ed.), *Protectionism*, 3

Bourgeois Jacques H. J., "The EC in the WTO and Advisory Opinion 1/94: an Echternach Procession", *Common Market Law Review*, 32 (1995) 763

Bourrinet Jacques (ed.), *Le Comité des Régions de l'Union Européenne* (Paris, Economica, 1997)

Bradley Kieran, "Comitology and the Law: Through a Glass, Darkly", *Common Market Law Review*, 29 (1992) 693

Bribosia Emmanuelle, Emmanuelle Dardenne, Paul Magnette and Anne Weyembergh (eds.), *Union Européenne et Nationalités: le Principe de Non-Discrimination et ses Limites* (Brussels, Bruylant, 1999)

Brown L. Neville and Tom Kennedy, *The Court of Justice of the European Communities* (London, Sweet & Maxwell, 2000)

Bulmer Simon and William E. Paterson, "Germany in the European Union: Gentle Giant or Emergent Leader", *International Affairs*, 72 (1996) 9

Bulmer Simon and Wolfgang Wessels, *The European Council. Decision-Making in European Politics* (Basingstoke, Macmillan, 1987)

Bulmer Simon, "The Governance of the European Union: A New Institutionalist Approach", *Journal of Public Policy*, 13 (1994) 351

Bulmer Simon, Charlie Jeffery and William E. Patterson, *Germany's European Diplomacy. Shaping the Regional Milieu* (Manchester, Manchester University Press, 2000)

Bungenberg Marc, "Dynamische Integration, Art. 308 und die Forderung nach dem Kompetenzkatalog", *Europarecht*, 35 (2000) 879

Burrows Noreen, "Question of Community Accession to the European Convention Determined", *European Law Review*, 22 (1997) 58

Cafruny Alan W. and Glenda G. Rosenthal (eds.), *The State of the European Union. Vol. II: The Maastricht Debates and Beyond* (Boulder, Lynne Rienner, 1993)

Calliess Christian, *Subsidiaritäts- und Solidaritätsprinzip in der Europäischen Union: Vorgaben für die Anwendung von Art. 5 (ex-Art. 3b) EGV Nach dem Vertrag von Amsterdam* (Baden-Baden, Nomos, 1999)

Cameron David R., "The 1992 Initiatives: Causes and Consequences", in Sbragia (ed.), *Euro-Politics*, 23

Camps Miriam, *European Unification in the Sixties: From the Veto to the Crisis* (New York, McGraw-Hill, 1966)

Capotorti Francesco *et al.* (eds.), *Du Droit International au Droit de l'Intégration. Liber Amicorum Pierre Pescatore* (Baden-Baden, Nomos, 1987)

Chaltiel Florence, "L'Union Européenne doit-elle Adhérer à la Convention Européenne des Droits de l'Homme?", *Revue du Marché Commun et de L'Union Européenne*, (1997) 34

Chiti Eduardo, "The Emergence of a Community Administration: The Case of European Agencies", *Common Market Law Review*, 37 (2000) 309

Christiansen Thomas and Emil J. Kirchner (eds.), *Committee Governance in the European Union* (Manchester, Manchester University Press, 2000)

Clemens Clay and William E. Paterson (eds.), *The Kohl Chancellorship* (London, Frank Cass, 1998)

Clergerie Jean-Louis, "L'Improbable Censure de la Commission Européenne", *Revue du Droit Public et de la Science Politique*, 111 (1995) 201

Cloos Jim, Gaston Reinesch, Daniel Vignes and Joseph Weyland, *Le Traité de Maastricht: Génèse, Analyse, Commentaires* (Brussels, Bruylant, 1994)

Cogan Charles G., *The Third Option: The Emancipation of European Defence, 1989-2000* (Westport, Praeger, 2001)

Cohen-Jonathan Gérard, "La Protection des Droits Fondamentaux par la Cour de Justice des Communautés européennes", in Bieber, De Gucht, Lenaerts and Weiler (eds.), *In the Name of the Peoples of Europe*, 44

Constantinesco Vlad, "L'Article 5 CEE, de la Bonne Foi à la Loyauté Communautaire", in Capotorti *et al.* (eds.), *Du Droit International au Droit de l'Intégration*, 97

Constantinesco Vlad, Yves Gautier and Denys Simon (eds.), *Le Traité de Nice. Premières Analyses* (Strasbourg, Presses Universitaires de Strasbourg, 2001)

Corbett Richard, "Academic Modelling of the Codecision Procedure: A Practitioner's Puzzled Reaction", *European Union Politics*, 1 (2000) 373

Corbett Richard, Francis Jacobs and Michael Shackleton (eds.), *The European Parliament* (London, John Harper, 2000)

Corbett Richard, *The European Parliament's Role in Closer EU Integration* (Basingstoke, Macmillan, 1998)

Corbett Richard, *The Treaty of Maastricht* (London, Cartermill, 1993)

Cosgrove-Sacks Carol (ed.), *Europe, Diplomacy and Development. New Issues in EU Relations with Developing Countries* (Basingstoke, Palgrave, 2001)

Costa Olivier, *Le Parlement Européen, Assemblée Délibérante* (Brussels, Ed. de l'Université de Bruxelles, 2000)

Cowles Maria Green and Michael Smith (eds.), *The State of the European Union. Vol. 5: Risks, Reforms, Resistance or Revival?* (Oxford, Oxford University Press, 2001)

Cowles Maria Green, "Setting the Agenda for a New Europe: The ERT and EC 1992", *Journal of Common Market Studies*, 33 (1995) 501

Craig Paul and Grainne de Burca (eds.), *The Evolution of EU Law* (Oxford, Oxford University Press, 1999)

Craig Paul and Grainne de Burca, *EU Law: Texts, Cases and Materials* (Oxford, Oxford University Press, 2002)

Craig Paul, "The Fall and Renewal of the Commission: Accountability, Contract and Administrative Organisation", *European Law Journal*, 6 (2000) 98

Cram Laura, Desmond Dinan and Neill Nugent (eds.), *Developments in the European Union* (Basingstoke, Macmillan, 1999)

Cram Laura, "The Commission", in Cram, Dinan and Nugent (eds.), *Developments in the European Union*, 44

Cremona Marise, "EC External Commercial Policy after Amsterdam: Authority and Interpretation within Interconnected Legal Orders", in Weiler (ed.), *The EU, the WTO, and the NAFTA*, 5

Cremona Marise, "External Relations and External Competence: The Emergence of an Integrated Policy", in Craig and de Burca (eds.), *The Evolution of EU Law*, 137

Cremona Marise (ed.), *The Enlargement of the European Union* (Oxford, Oxford University Press, 2003)

Curtin Deirdre and Ige Dekker, "The EU as a 'Layered' International Organization: Institutional Unity in Disguise", in Craig and de Burca (eds.), *The Evolution of EU Law*, 83

Curtin Deirdre, "The Constitutional Structure of the Union: A Europe of Bits and Pieces", *Common Market Law Review*, 30 (1993) 17

Daalder Ivo H. and James M. Goldgeier, "Putting Europe First", *Survival*, 43 (2001) 71

Daalder Ivo H., "Are the United States and Europe Heading for Divorce?", *International Affairs*, 3 (2001) 553

Damro Chad, "Building an International Identity: The EU and Extraterritorial Competition Policy", *Journal of European Public Policy*, 8 (2001) 208

Dashwood Alan and Christophe Hillion (eds.), *The General Law of E.C. External Relations* (London, Sweet & Maxwell, 2000)

Dashwood Alan and Joni Heliskoski, "The Classic Authorities Revisited", in Dashwood and Hillion (eds.), *The General Law of E.C. External Relations*, 3

Dashwood Alan, "External Relations Provisions of the Amsterdam Treaty", *Common Market Law Review*, 35 (1998) 1019

de Bassompierre Guy, *Changing the Guard in Brussels: An Insider's View of the EC Presidency* (New York, Praeger, 1988)

de Burca Grainne and J. H. H. Weiler (eds.), *The European Court of Justice* (Oxford, Oxford University Press, 2001) de Burca Grainne, "The Drafting of the EU Charter of Fundamental Rights", *European Law Review*, 26 (2001) 126

de Burca Grainne, "Proportionality and Subsidiarity as General Principles of Law", in Bernitz and Nergelius (eds.), *General Principles*, 95

de Burca Grainne, "Reappraising Subsidiarity's Significance after Amsterdam", *Harvard Jean Monnet Chair Working Paper Series* (1999/07)

de Burca Grainne, "The Institutional Development of the EU: A Constitutional Analysis", in Craig and de Burca (eds.), *The Evolution of EU Law*, 55

de Burca Grainne, "The Principle of Subsidiarity and the Court of Justice as an Institutional Actor", *Journal of Common Market Studies*, 36 (1998) 217

Deeg Richard E., "Germany's Länder and the Federalization of the European Union", in Rhodes and Mazey (eds.), *The State of the European Union. Vol. 3*, 197

Deighton Anne and Eric Remacle (eds.), "The Western European Union, 1948-1998", *Studia Diplomatica*, 51 (1998/1-2)

Deighton Anne (ed.), *Building Postwar Europe. National Decision-Makers and European Institutions, 1948-63* (Basingstoke, Macmillan, 1995)

Deighton Anne (ed.), *Western European Union 1954-1997. Defence, Security, Integration* (Oxford, St Antony's College, 1997)

Deighton Anne, "Britain and the Creation of Western European Union, 1954", in Deighton (ed.), *Western European Union 1954-1997*, 11

Deighton Anne, "The Military Security Pool: Towards a New Security Regime for Europe?", *International Spectator*, 35 (2000-4) 41

de la Mare Thomas, "Article 177 in Social and Political Context", in Craig and de Burca (eds.), *The Evolution of EU Law*, 215

Deloche-Gaudez Florence, *La Convention pour l'Elaboration de la Charte des Droits Fondamentaux: Une Méthode d'Avenir?* (Paris, Notre Europe, Etudes et Recherches No. 15, November 2001)

den Boer Monica, "Not Merely a Matter of Moving House: Police Co-operation from Schengen to the TEU", *Maastricht Journal of European and Comparative Law*, 7 (2000) 336

de Ruyt Jean, *L'Acte Unique Européen* (Brussels, Ed. de l'Université de Bruxelles, 1989)

de Schoutheete Philippe, "The European Council", in Peterson and Shackleton (eds.), *The Institutions of the European Union*, 21

de Schoutheete Philippe, "The European Community and its Sub-Systems", in Wallace (ed.), *The Dynamics of European Integration*, 113

de Schoutheete Philippe, *Une Europe pour Tous. Dix Essais sur la Construction Européenne* (Paris, Odile Jacob, 1997)

De Schutter Olivier and Yves Lejeune, "L'Adhésion de la Communauté à la Convention des Droits de l'Homme. A Propos de l'Avis 2/94 de la Cour de Justice des Communautés", *Cahiers de Droit Européen*, 32 (1996) 555

Devuyst Youri, "The Community Method after Amsterdam", *Journal of Common Market Studies*, 37 (1999) 109

Devuyst Youri, "The European Community and the Conclusion of the Uruguay Round", in Rhodes and Mazey (eds.), *The State of the European Union. Vol. 3*, 449

Devuyst Youri, "Transatlantic Competition Relations", in Pollack and Shaffer (eds.), *Transatlantic Governance*, 127

Devuyst Youri, "European Unity in Transatlantic Commercial Diplomacy", in Philippart and Winand (eds.), *Ever Closer Partnership*, 283

Devuyst Youri, "The EC's Common Commercial Policy and the Treaty of European Union: An Overview of the Negotiations", *World Competition*, 16 (1992) 67

Devuyst Youri, "The European Union's Constitutional Order? Between Community Method and *Ad Hoc* Compromise", *Berkeley Journal of International Law*, 18 (2000) 1

Devuyst Youri, "Treaty Reform in the European Union: the Amsterdam Process", *Journal of European Public Policy*, 5 (1998) 615

de Witte Bruno, "Direct Effect, Supremacy, and the Nature of the Legal Order", in Craig and de Burca (eds.), *The Evolution of EU Law*, 179

de Witte Bruno, "Sovereignty and European Integration: The Weight of Legal Tradition", *Maastricht Journal of European and Comparative Law*, 2 (1995) 145

de Witte Bruno, "The Pillar Structure and the Nature of the European Union: Greek Temple or French Gothic Cathedral?", in Heukels, Blokker and Brus (eds.), *The European Union after Amsterdam*, 51

de Zwaan Jaap W., "Opting In and Opting Out of Rules concerning the Free Movement of Persons. Problems and Practical Arrangements", *Cambridge Yearbook of European Legal Studies 1998*, 1 (1999) 107

Di Nolfo Ennio (ed.), *Power in Europe? II: Great Britain, France, Germany and Italy and the Origins of the EEC, 1952-1957* (Berlin, Walter de Gruyter, 1992)

Diebold William, *The Schuman Plan* (New York, Praeger, 1959)

Dinan Desmond, *Ever Closer Union: An Introduction to European Integration* (Basingstoke, Macmillan, 1999)

Dittert Daniel, *Die ausschliesslichen Kompetenzen der europäischen Gemeinschaften im System des EG-Vertrags* (Bern, Peter Lang, 2001)

Dony Marianne and Emmanuelle Bribosia (eds.), *L'Avenir du Système Juridictionnel de l'Union Européenne* (Bruxelles, Ed. de l'Université de Bruxelles, 2002)

Dony Marianne (ed.), *L'Union Européenne et le Monde après Amsterdam* (Brussels, Ed. de l'Université de Bruxelles, 1999)

Dony Marianne (ed.), *Mélanges en Hommage à Michel Waelbroeck* (Brussels, Bruylant, 1999)

Duchêne François, *Jean Monnet. The First Statesman of Interdependence* (New York, Norton, 1994)

Due Ole, "The Impact of the Amsterdam Treaty upon the Court of Justice", *Fordham International Law Journal*, 22 (1999) 548

Duff Andrew, *The Treaty of Amsterdam. Text and Commentary* (London, Sweet & Maxwell, 1997)

Duke Simon (ed.), *Between Vision and Reality. CFSP's Progress on the Path to Maturity* (Maastricht, European Institute of Public Administration, 2000)

Duke Simon, "CESDP: Nice's Overtrumped Success?", *European Foreign Affairs Review*, 6 (2001), 155

Duke Simon, *The Elusive Quest for European Security. From EDC to CFSP* (Basingstoke, Macmillan, 2000)

Dumoulin André and Eric Remacle, *L'Union de l'Europe Occidentale, Phénix de la Défense Européenne* (Brussels, Bruylant, 1998)

Dumoulin Michel, *Spaak* (Brussels, Ed. Racine, 1999)

Durand Claire-Françoise, "Les Principes", in *Commentaire Mégret. Le Droit de la CEE. Vol. 1: Préambule, Principes, Libre Circulation des Marchandises* (Brussels, Ed. de l'Université de Bruxelles, 1992, 2nd ed.), 25

Dutheil de la Rochère Jacqueline, "EMU: Constitutional Aspects and External Representation", *Yearbook of European Law*, 19 (1999/2000) 427

Dutzler Barbara, "EMU and the Representation of the Community in International Organisations", in Stefan Griller and Birgit Weidel (eds.), *External Economic Relations and Foreign Policy in the European Union* (Wien, Springer Verlag, 2002), 445

Duvigneau Johan Ludwig, "From Advisory Opinion 2/94 to the Amsterdam Treaty: Human Rights Protection in the European Union", *Legal Issues of European Integration*, 25 (1998) 61

Dyson Kenneth and Kevin Featherstone, *The Road to Maastricht. Negotiating Economic and Monetary Union* (Oxford, Oxford University Press, 1999)

Earnshaw David and David Judge, "The Life and Times of the European Union's Co-operation Procedure", *Journal of Common Market Studies*, 35 (1997), 543

Eder Klaus and Bernhard Giesen (eds.), *European Citizenship between National Legacies and Postnational Projects* (Oxford, Oxford University Press, 2001)

Edwards Geoffrey and David Spence (eds.), *The European Commission* (Harlow, Cartermill, 1997)

Eeckhout Piet, "The EU Charter of Fundamental Rights and the Federal Question", *Common Market Law Review*, 39 (2002) 945

Egan Michelle and Dieter Wolf, "Regulation and Comitology: The EC Committee System in Regulatory Perspective", *Columbia Journal of European Law*, 4 (1998) 499

Egan Michelle, *Constructing a European Market. Standards, Regulation, and Governance* (Oxford, Oxford University Press, 2001)

Ehlermann Claus D., "The Scope of Article 113 of the EEC Treaty", in *Etudes de Droit des Communautés Européennes: Mélanges offerts à Pierre-Henri Teitgen* (Paris, Pedone, 1984), 147

Ehlermann Claus-Dieter, "Retrospective: Differentiation, Flexibility, Closer Co-operation: The New Provisions of the Amsterdam Treaty", *European Law Journal*, 4 (1998) 246

Eichengreen Barry and Jeffry Frieden (eds.), *The Political Economy of European Monetary Unification* (Boulder, Westview Press, 1994)

Eleftheriadis Pavlos, "The Direct Effect of Community Laws: Conceptual Issues", *Yearbook of European Law*, 16 (1996) 205

Eliassen Kjell A. (ed.), *Foreign and Security Policy in the European Union* (London, Sage, 1998)

Ellis Evelyn, "The Recent Jurisprudence of the Court of Justice in the Field of Sex Equality", *Common Market Law Review*, 37 (2000) 1403

Evenett Simon, Alexander Lehmann and Benn Steil (eds.), *Antitrust Goes Global. What Future for Transatlantic Cooperation?* (Washington, D.C., Brookings Institution, 2000)

Everling Ulrich, "The Maastricht Judgment of the German Federal Constitutional Court and its Significance for the Development of the European Union", *Yearbook of European Law*, 14 (1994) 1

Ezrachi Ariel, "Limitations on the Extraterritorial Reach of the European Merger Regulation", *European Competition Law Review*, 22 (2001) 137

Faull Jonathan and Ali Nikpay (eds.), *The EC Law of Competition* (Oxford, Oxford University Press, 1999)

Featherstone Kevin, "Jean Monnet and the "Democratic Deficit" in the European Union", *Journal of Common Market Studies*, 32 (1994) 149

Fernandez Esteban Maria Luisa, *The Rule of Law in the European Constitution* (The Hague, Kluwer Law International, 1999)

Feus Kim (ed.), *A Simplified Treaty for the European Union?* (London, Federal Trust, Constitution for Europe Series 2, 2001)

Feus Kim (ed.), *The EU Charter of Fundamental Rights – Text and Commentaries* (London, Federal Trust, Constitution for Europe Series 1, 2000)

Flynn Leo, "The Implications of Article 13 EC – After Amsterdam, Will Some Forms of Discrimination be More Equal than Others?", *Common Market Law Review*, 36 (1999) 1127

Fontaine Pascal, *A New Idea for Europe. The Schuman Declaration 1950-2000* (Luxembourg: EC, 2000)

Forster Anthony and William Wallace, "Common Foreign and Security Policy. From Shadow to Substance?", in Wallace and Wallace (eds.), *Policy-Making in the European Union* (2000, 4th ed.), 461

Fox Eleanor, "The Merger Regulation and its Territorial Reach: Gencor Ltd. v. Commission", *European Competition Law Review*, 20 (1999) 334

Frey Silvain, "Aspects de l'Organisation de la Défense Collective en Europe Occidentale", *Travaux et Conférences de la Faculté de Droit de l'Université Libre de Bruxelles*, (1962) 110

Frid Rachel, "The European Community – A Member of a Specialized Agency of the United Nations", *European Journal of International Law*, 4 (1993) 239

Friedrich Axel, Matthias Tappe and Rudiger K. W. Wurzel, "A New Approach to EU Environmental Policy-Making? The Auto-Oil I Programme", *Journal of European Public Policy*, 7 (2000) 593

Fursdon Edward, *The European Defence Community: a History* (London, Macmillan, 1980)

Gaja Giorgio, "How Flexible is Flexibility Under the Amsterdam Treaty?", *Common Market Law Review*, 35 (1998) 855

Gaja Giorgio, "Identifying the Status of General Principles in European Community Law", in *Scritti in Onore di Giuseppe Federico Manchini. Vol. II*, 450

Galloway David, "Agenda 2000 – Packaging the Deal", *Journal of Common Market Studies (European Union Annual Review 1998/1999)*, 37 (1999) 9

Galloway David, *The Treaty of Nice and Beyond. Realities and Illusions of Power in the EU* (Sheffield, Sheffield Academic Press, 2001)

Garot Marie José, *La Citoyenneté de l'Union Européenne* (Paris, L'Harmattan, 1999)

Gegout Catherine, "The Quint", *Journal of Common Market Studies*, 40 (2002) 331

George Stephen and Ian Bache, *Politics in the European Union* (Oxford, Oxford University Press, 2001)

Gerbet Pierre, "Les Origines du Plan Schuman: Le Choix de la Méthode Communautaire par le Gouvernement Français", in Poidevin (ed.), *Histoire des Débuts de la Construction Européenne,* 199

Gerkrath Jörg, *L'Emergence d'un Droit Constitutionnel pour l'Europe: Modes de Formation et Sources d'Inspiration de la Constitution des Communautés et de l'Union Européenne* (Brussels, Ed. de l'Université de Bruxelles, 1997)

Gillingham John, *Coal, Steel and the Rebirth of Europe, 1945-1955: The Germans and French from Ruhr Conflict to Economic Community* (Cambridge, Cambridge University Press, 1991)

Giotakos Dimitri et al., "General Electric/Honeywell – An Insight into the Commission's Investigation and Decision", *Competition Policy Newsletter*, 2001/3) 5

Gonzalez-Diaz Francisco Enrique, "Recent Developments in EC Merger Control Law. The Gencor Judgment", *World Competition*, 22 (1999/3), 3

Gormley Laurence W., "Reflections on the Architecture of the European Union after the Treaty of Amsterdam", in O'Keeffe and Twomey (eds.), *Legal Issues of the Amsterdam Treaty*, 57

Gormley Laurence W., "The Development of General Principles of Law Within Article 10 (ex Article 5) EC", in Bernitz and Nergelius (eds.), *General Principles*, 113

Gormley Lawrence W. (ed.), *Current and Future Perspectives on EC Competition Law* (The Hague, Kluwer Law International, 1997)

Gosalbo Bono Ricardo, "Co-Decision: An Appraisal of Experience of the European Parliament as Co-Legislator", *Yearbook of European Law*, 14 (1994) 21

Gray Margaret, "A Recalcitrant Partner: The UK Reaction to the Working Time Directive", *Yearbook of European Law*, 17, 1997, 323

Griffiths Richard T. (ed.), *Explorations in OEEC History* (Paris, OECD, 1997)

Griller Stefan and Birgit Weidel (eds.), *External Economic Relations and Foreign Policy in the European Union* (Wien, Springer Verlag, 2002)

Grilli Enzo R., *The European Community and the Developing Countries* (Cambridge, Cambridge University Press, 1993)

Grosser Alfred, *The Western Alliance. Euro-American Relations since 1945* (Basingstoke, Macmillan, 1980)

Groux Jean, "Le Parallélisme des Compétences Internes et Externes de la Communauté Economique Européenne", *Cahiers de Droit Européen*, 14 (1978) 3

Haines C. Grove (ed.), *European Integration* (Baltimore, Johns Hopkins University Press, 1957)

Ham Allard D., "International Cooperation in the Anti-Trust Field and in Particular the Agreement between the United States of America and the Commission of the European Communities", *Common Market Law Review*, 30 (1993) 571

Harck Sten and Henrik Palmer Olsen, "Decision concerning the Maastricht Treaty, Supreme Court of Denmark, April 6, 1998", *American Journal of International Law*, 93 (1999) 209

Harlow Carol, *Accountability in the European Union* (Oxford, Oxford University Press, 2002)

Harrison Michael M., *The Reluctant Ally. France and Atlantic Security* (Baltimore, Johns Hopkins University Press, 1981)

Hawk Barry E. (ed.), *2000 Annual Proceedings of the Fordham Corporate Law Institute Conference on International Antitrust Law and Policy* (New York, Fordham Corporate Law Institute, 2001)

Hawk Barry E. (ed.), *1989 Annual Proceedings of the Fordham Corporate Law Institute International Antitrust Law and Policy Conference* (New York, Fordham Corporate Law Institute, 1990)

Hayes-Renshaw Fiona and Helen Wallace, *The Council of Ministers* (Basingstoke, Macmillan, 1997)

Heregen Matthias, "Maastricht and the German Constitutional Court: Constitutional Restraints for an 'Ever Closer Union'", *Common Market Law Review*, 31 (1994) 235

Herrmann Christoph W., "Common Commercial Policy after Nice: Sisyphus Would Have Done a Better Job", *Common Market Law Review*, 39 (2002) 7

Heukels Ton, Niels Blokker and Marcel Brus (eds.), *The European Union after Amsterdam. A Legal Analysis* (The Hague, Kluwer Law International, 1998)

Hilf Meinhard, Francis G. Jacobs and Ernst-Ulrich Petersmann, *The European Community and GATT* (Deventer, Kluwer, 1986)

Hilf Meinhard, "The ECJ's Opinion 1/94 on the WTO – No Surprize, but Wise?", *European Journal of International Law*, 6 (1995) 245

Hiljemark Linda, "A Voyage around Article 8: An Historical and Comparative Evaluation of the Fate of European Citizenship", *Yearbook of European Law*, 17 (1997) 135

Hill Christopher, "The EU's Capacity for Conflict Prevention", *European Foreign Affairs Review*, 6 (2001) 315

Hill Christopher, "Closing the Capabilities-Expectations Gap?", in Peterson and Sjursen (eds.), *A Common Foreign Policy for Europe?*, 18

Hill Christopher, "The Capability-Expectations Gap, or Conceptualizing Europe's International Role", *Journal of Common Market Studies*, 31 (1993) 305

Hitchcock William I., *France Restored: Cold War Diplomacy & the Quest for Leadership in Europe, 1944-1954* (Chapel Hill, University of North Carolina Press, 1998)

Hitchcock William I., "France, the Western Alliance, and the Origins of the Schuman Plan, 1948-1950", *Diplomatic History*, 21, 1997, 633

Hix Simon and Christopher Lord, *Political Parties in the European Union* (Basingstoke, Macmillan, 1997)

Hobe Stephan, "The Long and Difficult Road Towards Integration: The Legal Debate on the Maastricht Treaty in Germany and the Judgment of the German Constitutional Court of October 12, 1993", *Leiden Journal of International Law*, 7 (1994) 23

Hodson Dermot and Imelda Maher, "The Open Method as a New Mode of Governance: The Case of Soft Economic Policy Co-ordination", *Journal of Common Market Studies*, 39 (2001) 726

Holland Martin, *The European Union and the Third World* (Basingstoke, Palgrave, 2002)

Hooghe Liesbet (ed.), *Cohesion Policy and European Integration: Building Multilevel Governance* (Oxford, Oxford University Press, 1996)

Hooghe Liesbet, "EU Cohesion Policy and Competing Models of European Capitalism", *Journal of Common Market Studies*, 36 (1998) 457

Hourquebie Fabrice, *Les Organes Spécialisés dans les Affaires Communautaires des Parlements Nationaux: les Cas Français et Allemands* (Paris, L'Harmattan, 1999)

Howorth Jolyon, "CESDP after 11 September: From Short-term Confusion to Long-term Cohesion?", in *EUSA Review*, 15 (2002/1) 1

Howorth Jolyon, "Britain, France and the European Defence Initiative", *Survival*, 42 (2000/2) 33

Howorth Jolyon, *European Integration and Defence: The Ultimate Challenge?* (Paris, Institute for Security Studies of WEU, Chaillot Paper 43, 2000)

Howorth Jolyon, "Franco-British Defence Cooperation and the Compatibility of ESDP with NATO", in Duke (ed.), *Between Vision and Reality*, 35

Hrbek Rudolf, "The German Länder and EC Integration", *Journal of European Integration*, 15 (1992) 180

Janow Merit E., "Transatlantic Cooperation on Competition Policy", in Evenett, Lehmann and Steil (eds.), *Antitrust Goes Global*, 253

Jansen Thomas, *The European People's Party: Origins and Development* (Basingstoke, Macmillan, 1998)

Jeffery Charlie (ed.), *The Regional Dimension of the European Union. Towards a Third Level in Europe?* (London, Frank Cass, 1997)

Joerges Christian and Ellen Vos (eds.), *EU Committees. Social Regulation, Law & Politics* (Oxford, Hart, 1999)

Joerges Christian, Yves Mény and J. H. H. Weiler (eds.), *What Kind of Constitution for What Kind of Polity?* (Florence, European University Institute, 2000)

Johnson Michael, *European Community Trade Policy and the Article 113 Committee* (London, Royal Institute of International Affairs, 1998).

Johnston Angus, "Judicial Reform and the Treaty of Nice", *Common Market Law Review*, 38 (2001) 499

Johnston Mary Troy, *The European Council: Gatekeeper of the European Community* (Boulder, Westview Press, 1994)

Jones Tim, "France's Bid to Fast-Track Currency Deals Shot Down", *European Voice*, November 23-29, 2000, 1

Jouve Edmond, *Le Général de Gaulle et la Construction de l'Europe (1940-1966)* (Paris, Librairie Général de Droit et de Jurisprudence, 1967)

Jyränki Antero (ed.), *National Constitutions in the Era of Integration* (The Hague, Kluwer Law International, 1999)

Kaila Heidi, "Qualified Majority Voting: The Key to Efficient Decision-Making in an Enlarged Union", in Best, Gray and Stubb (eds.), *Rethinking the European Union*, 131

Karen E. Smith, *The Making of EU Foreign Policy. The Case of Eastern Europe 1988-95* (Basingstoke, Macmillan, 1998)

Keeling David T., "In Praise of Judicial Activism. But What Does it Mean? And Has the European Court of Justice ever Practiced it?", in *Scritti in Onore di Guiseppe Federico Manchini. Vol. II*, 505

Keohane Robert O. and Stanley Hoffmann (eds.), *The New European Community. Decision-making and Institutional Change* (Boulder, Westview Press, 1991)

Keohane Robert O. and Stanley Hoffmann, "Institutional Change in Europe in the 1980s", in Keohane and Hoffmann (eds.), *The New European Community*, 22

Kersten Albert, "A Welcome Surprise? The Netherlands and the Schuman Plan Negotiations", in Schwabe, *The Beginnings of the Schuman Plan*, 285

Kirchner Emil J., *Decision-Making in the European Community. The Council Presidency and European Integration* (Manchester, Manchester University Press, 1992)

Kokott Juliane, "Federal States in Federal Europe: German Länder and Problems of European Integration", in Jyränki (ed.), *National Constitutions in the Era of Integration*, 175

Korah Valentine, *Introductory Guide to EC Competition Law and Practice* (Oxford, Hart, 2000)

Kortenberg Helmut, "Closer Cooperation in the Treaty of Amsterdam", *Common Market Law Review*, 35 (1998) 833

Koskenniemi Martti (ed.), *International Law Aspects of the European Union* (The Hague, Kluwer Law International, 1998)

Kottmann Jan, "Europe and the Regions: Sub-National Entity Representation at Community Level", *European Law Review*, 26 (2001) 159

Krenzler Horst Günter and Christian Pitschas, "Progress or Stagnation?: The Common Commercial Policy after Nice", *European Foreign Affairs Review*, 6 (2001) 291

Kreppel Amie, *The European Parliament and Supranational Party System. A Study in Institutional Development* (Cambridge, Cambridge University Press, 2002)

Kuijper P. J., "Some Legal Problems associated with the Communautarization of Policy on Visas, Asylum and Immigration under the Amsterdam Treaty and Incorporation of the Schengen Acquis", *Common Market Law Review*, 37 (2000) 345

Kumm Mattias, "Who is the Final Arbiter of Constitutionality in Europe?: Three Conceptions of the Relationship between the German Federal Constitutional Court and the European Court of Justice", *Common Market Law Review*, 36 (1999) 315

Kusters Hanns Jürgen, "Die Verhandlungen über das institutionelle System zur Gründung der Europäischen Gemeinschaft für Kohle und Stahl", in Schwabe, *The Beginnings of the Schuman Plan*, 73

Küsters Hanns Jürgen, *Fondements de la Communauté Economique Européenne* (Luxembourg, EC, 1990)

Küsters Hanns Jürgen, "The Federal Republic of Germany and the EEC Treaty", in Serra (ed.), *The Relaunching*, 495

La Malfa Ugo, "The Case for European Integration: Economic Considerations", in Haines (ed.), *European Integration*, 64

Lacouture Jean, *Mitterrand: Une Histoire de Français, Vol. 2: Les Vertiges du Sommet* (Paris, Seuil, 1998)

Ladrech Robert, *Social Democracy and the Challenge of European Union* (Boulder, Lynne Rienner, 2000)

Laffan Brigid and Michael Shackleton, "The Budget", in Wallace and Wallace (eds.), *Policy-Making in the European Union* (2000, 4th ed.), 211

Laffan Brigid, "The Agenda 2000 Negotiations: La Présidence Coûte Cher?", *German Politics*, 9 (2000/3) 1

Laffan Brigid, "The Berlin Summit: Process and Outcome of the Agenda 2000 Budgetary Proposals", 12 ECSA Review (Fall 1999) 6

Laffan Brigid, *The Finances of the European Union* (Basingstoke, Macmillan, 1997)

Lafflan Birgit (ed.), *Constitution-Building in the European Union* (Dublin, Institute of European Affairs, 1996)

Lambert John, "The Constitutional Crisis, 1965-66", *Journal of Common Market Studies*, 4 (1966) 205.

Lange Dieter G. F. and John Byron Sandage, "The Wood Pulp Decision and its Implications for the Scope of EC Competition Law", *Common Market Law Review*, 26 (1989) 137

Lasok K. P. E., *Law & Institutions of the European Union* (London, Butterworths, 2001)

Laursen Finn and Sophie Vanhoonacker (eds.), *The Intergovernmental Conference on Political Union* (Maastricht, European Institute of Public Administration, 1992)

Laursen Finn (ed.), *The Amsterdam Treaty. National Preference Formation, Interstate Bargaining and Outcome* (Odense, Odense University Press, 2002)

Lazaro Araujo Laureano, "La Union Europea, Entre la Cohesion y la Desintegracion", *Politica Exterior*, (1999/68) 81

Lebullenger Joël, "La Projection Externe de la Zone Euro", *Revue Trimestrielle de Droit Européen*, 34 (1998) 459

Lee Sabine, "German Decision-Making Elites and European Integration: German 'Europolitik' during the Years of the EEC and Free Trade Area Negotiations", in Deighton (ed.), *Building Postwar Europe*, 38

Lenaerts Koen and Amaryllis Verhoeven, "Towards a Legal Framework for Executive Rule-Making in the EU? The Contribution of the New Comitology Decision", *Common Market Law Review*, 37 (2000) 645

Lenaerts Koen and Eddy De Smijter, "A 'Bill of Rights' for the European Union", *Common Market Law Review*, 38 (2001) 273

Lenaerts Koen and Eddy De Smijter, "The EU as an Actor in International Law", *Yearbook of European Law*, 19 (1999/2000) 95

Lenaerts Koen and Eddy De Smijter, "The European Community's Treaty-Making Competence", *Yearbook of European Law*, 16 (1996) 1

Lenaerts Koen and Patrick van Ypersele, "Le Principe de Subsidiarité et son Contexte: Etude de l'Article 3b du Traité CE", *Cahiers de Droit Européen*, 30 (1994) 3

Lenaerts Koen et al., "Le Livre Blanc de la Commission sur la Modernisation des Règles de Concurrence", *Cahiers de Droit Européen*, 35 (2001) 133

Lenaerts Koen, "Fundamental Rights in the European Union", *European Law Review*, 25 (2000) 575

Lenaerts Koen, "Le Respect des Droits Fondamentaux en tant que Principe Constitutionnel de l'Union Européenne", in Dony (ed.), *Mélanges en Hommage à Michel Waelbroeck*, 423

Lequesne Christian, "La Commission Européenne entre Autonomie et Dépendance", *Revue Française de Science Politique*, 46 (1996) 389

Lewis Jeffrey, "National Interests: Coreper", in Peterson and Shackleton (eds.), *The Institutions of the European Union*, 277

Ludlow Peter, *The Laeken Council* (Brussels, EuroComment, 2002)

MacDonagh Bobby, *Original Sin in a Brave New World: An Account of the Negotiation of the Treaty of Amsterdam* (Dublin, Institute of European Affairs, 1998)

Maduro Miguel Poiares, *We the Court. The European Court of Justice and the European Economic Constitution. A Critical Reading of Article 30 of the EC Treaty* (Oxford, Hart, 1998)

Magnette Paul (ed.), *La Constitution de l'Europe* (Brussels, Ed. de l'Université de Bruxelles, 2000)

Magnette Paul and Eric Remacle (eds.), *Le Nouveau Modèle Européen* (Brussels, Ed. de l'Université de Bruxelles, 2000)

Magnette Paul and Eric Remacle, "La grande transformation de l'Europe", in Magnette and Remacle (eds.), *Le Nouveau Modèle Européen*, 7

Magnette Paul, *La Citoyenneté Européenne* (Brussels, Ed. de l'Université de Bruxelles, 1999)

Majone Giandomenico, "Functional Interests: European Agencies", in Peterson and Shackleton (eds.), *The Institutions of the European Union*, 299

Marenco Guiliano, "Les Conditions d'Application de l'Article 235 du Traité CEE", *Revue du Marché Commun*, 12 (1970) 147

Maresceau Marc (ed.), *The Community's Commercial Policy after 1992: The Legal Dimension* (Dordrecht, Martinus Nijhoff, 1993)

Maresceau Marc, "The Concept 'Common Commercial Policy' and the Difficult Road to Maastricht", in Maresceau (ed.), *The Community's Commercial Policy*, 3

Marks Gary, "Structural Policy and Multilevel Governance", in Cafruny and Rosenthal (eds.), *The State of the European Union. Vol. 2*, 391

Mathiopoulos Margarita and Istvan Gyarmati, "Saint Malo and Beyond: Toward European Defense, *Washington Quarterly*, 22 (1999-4) 65

Mathieu Sandrine, "L'Adhésion de la Communauté à la CEDH: Un Problème de Compétence ou un Problème de Soumission?", *Revue du Marché Commun et de l'Union Européenne*, (1998) 31

Mattli Walter and Anne-Marie Slaughter, "Revisiting the European Court of Justice", *International Organization*, 52 (1998) 177

Maurer Andreas, "(Co-)Governing after Maastricht. The European Parliament's Institutional Performance 1994-1998. Lessons for the Implementation of the Treaty of Amsterdam", European Parliament Directorate-General for Research, 1999

Maull Hanns W., "German Foreign Policy, Post-Kosovo: Still a 'Civilian Power'?", *German Politics*, 9 (2000) 1

Maull Hanns W., "Germany and the Use of Force: Still a 'Civilian Power'?", *Survival*, 42 (2000) 56

Mayhew Alan, *Recreating Europe. The European Union's Policy towards Central and Eastern Europe* (Cambridge, Cambridge University Press, 1998)

McCarthy Rosarie E., "The Committee of the Regions: An Advisory Body's Tortuous Path to Influence", *Journal of European Public Policy*, 4 (1997) 439

Mearsheimer John J., "Back to the Future. Instability in Europe After the Cold War", *International Security*, 15 (1990) 5

Merlinger Michael, Cas Mudde and Ulrich Sedelmeier, "European Norms, Domestic Politics and Sanctions Against Austria", *Journal of Common Market Studies*, 39 (2001) 59

Meunier Sophie and Kalypso Nicolaïdes, "EU Trade Policy: The "Exclusive" vs. Shared Competence Debate", in Cowles and Smith (eds.), *The State of the European Union. Vol. 5,* 325

Meunier Sophie and Kalypso Nicolaïdes, "Trade Competence in the Nice Treaty", *ECSA Review*, 14:2 (2001) 7

Meunier Sophie and Kalypso Nicolaïdes, "Who Speaks for Europe? The Delegation of Trade Authority in the European Union", *Journal of Common Market Studies*, 37 (1999) 477

Meunier Sophie, "Divided but United: European Trade Policy Integration and EC-US Agricultural Negotiations in the Uruguay Round", in Rhodes (ed.), *The European Union in the World Community*, 193

Millar David, John Peterson and Andrew Scott, "Subsidiarity: A 'Europe of the Regions' v. the British Constitution", 32 *Journal of Common Market Studies*, 32 (1994) 47

Milward Alan S., *The European Rescue of the Nation-State* (London, Routledge, 1992)

Milward Alan S., *The Reconstruction of Western Europe 1945-51* (London, Methuen, 1984)

Mishalani Philip, Annette Robert, Christopher Stevens and Ann Weston, "The Pyramid of Privilege", in Stevens (ed.), *EEC and the Third World*, 60

Moberg Axel, "The Nice Treaty and Voting Rules in the Council", *Journal of Common Market Studies*, 40 (2002) 259

Moens Alexander, "Developing a European Intervention Force", *International Journal*, 50 (2000) 247

Monar Jörg and Roger Morgan (eds.), *The Third Pillar of the European Union: Cooperation in the fields of Justice and Home Affairs* (Brussels, European Interuniversity Press [P.I.E.-E.I.P.], 1994)

Monar Jörg and Wolfgang Wessels (eds.), *The European Union after the Treaty of Amsterdam* (London, Continuum, 2001)

Monar Jörg, "Justice and Home Affairs after Amsterdam: the Treaty Reforms and the Challenge of their Implementation", in Monar and Wessels (eds.), *The European Union after the Treaty of Amsterdam*, 267

Monar Jörg, "The Justice and Home Affairs Dimension of EU Enlargement", *International Spectator*, 36 (2001/3) 37

Monar Jörg, "The European Union's Foreign Affairs System after the Treaty of Amsterdam: A 'Strengthened Capacity for External Action'?", *European Foreign Affairs Review*, 2 (1997) 423

Monar Jörg, Werner Ungerer and Wolfgang Wessels (eds.), *The Maastricht Treaty on European Union. Legal Complexity and Political Dynamic* (Brussels, European Interuniversity Press [P.I.E.-E.I.P.], 1993)

Moravcsik Andrew and Kalypso Nicolaïdes, "Explaining the Treaty of Amsterdam: Interests, Influence, Institutions, *Journal of Common Market Studies*, 37 (1999) 59

Moravcsik Andrew and Kalypso Nicolaïdes, "Federal Ideals and Constitutional Realities in the Treaty of Amsterdam", *Journal of Common Market Studies*, (European Union Annual Review 1997) 13

Moravcsik Andrew, "Negotiating the Single European Act", in Robert O. Keohane and Stanley Hoffmann (eds.), *The New European Community. Decisionmaking and Institutional Change* (Boulder, Westview Press, 1991) 41

Moravcsik Andrew, *The Choice for Europe. Social Purpose & State Power from Messina to Maastricht* (London, University College London Press, 1999)

Neframi Eleftheria, "Quelques Réflexions sur la Réforme de la Politique Commerciale par le Traité d'Amsterdam: le Maintien du Status Quo et l'Unité de la Représentation Internationale de la Communauté", *Cahiers de Droit Européen*, 34 (1998) 137

Neunreither Karlheinz, "The European Union in Nice: A Minimalist Approach to a Historic Challenge", *Government and Opposition*, 36 (2001) 184

Nicholas Emiliou and David O'Keeffe (eds.), *The European Union and World Trade Law* (Chichester, John Wiley & Sons, 1996)

Nickel Dietmar, "The Amsterdam Treaty: A Shift in the Balance between the Institutions?", *Harvard Jean Monnet Chair Working Paper Series* (1998/14)

Nugent Neill (ed.), *At the Heart of the Union: Studies of the European Commission* (Basingstoke, Macmillan, 1997)

Nugent Neill, *The European Commission* (Basingstoke, Palgrave, 2001)

Nugent Neill, *The Government and Politics of the European Union* (Basingstoke, Macmillan, 2003)

Nuttall Simon J., *European Foreign Policy* (Oxford, Oxford University Press, 2000)

Nuttall Simon J., *European Political Cooperation* (Oxford, Oxford University Press, 1992)

O'Keeffe David (ed.), *Judicial Review in European Union Law. Liber Amicorum in Honour of Lord Slyn of Hadley* (The Hague, Kluwer Law International, 2000), Volume 1

O'Keeffe David and Henry G. Schermers (eds.), *Mixed Agreements* (Dordrecht, Kluwer, 1983)

O'Keeffe David and Patrick Twomey (eds.), *Legal Issues of the Amsterdam Treaty* (Oxford, Hart, 1999)

O'Keeffe David, "Community and Member State Competence in External Relations Agreements of the EU", *European Foreign Affairs Review*, 4 (1999) 7

O'Leary Siofra, *The Evolving Concept of Community Citizenship: From Free Movement of Persons to Union Citizenship* (The Hague, Kluwer Law International, 1996)

O'Neill Michael (ed.), *The Politics of European Integration. A Reader* (London, Routledge, 1996)

O'Sullivan David, "La Réforme de la Commission Européenne", *Revue du Droit de l'Union Européenne* (2000/4) 723

Paasivirta Esa, "The European Union: From an Aggregate of States to a Legal Person?", *Hofstra Law & Policy Symposium*, 2 (1997) 37

Paemen Hugo and Alexandra Bensch, *From the GATT to the WTO. The European Community in the Uruguay Round* (Leuven, Leuven University Press, 1995)

Pallemaerts Marc, "The Decline of Law as an Instrument of Community Environmental Policy", *Law and European Affairs*, 9 (1999) 338

Papadopoulou Triantafyllia, *Politische Parteien auf Europäischer Ebene: Auslegung und Ausgestaltung von Art. 191 (ex 138a) EGV* (Baden-Baden, Nomos, 1999).

Paterson William E., "Helmut Kohl, 'The Vision Thing' and Escaping the Semi-Sovereignty Trap", in Clemens and Paterson (eds.), *The Kohl Chancellorship*, 28

Pedler Robin H. and Günter F. Schaefer (eds.), *Shaping European Law and Policy: The Role of Committees and Comitology in the Political Process* (Maastricht, European Institute of Public Administration, 1996)

Peers Steve, "*Caveat Emptor?* Integrating the Schengen *Acquis* into the European Union Legal Order", *Cambridge Yearbook of European Legal Studies 1999*, 2 (2000) 87

Peers Steve, *EU Justice and Home Affairs Law* (London, Longman, 2000)

Pernice Ingolf, "Multilevel Constitutionalism and the Treaty of Amsterdam: European Constitution-Making Revisited?", *Common Market Law Review*, 36 (1999) 703

Pescatore Pierre, "External Relations in the Case-Law of the Court of Justice of the European Communities", *Common Market Law Review*, 16 (1979) 615

Pescatore Pierre, "Les Travaux du Groupe Juridique dans la Négotiation des Traités de Rome", *Studia Diplomatica*, 34 (1981) 168.

Pescatore Pierre, "L'Exécutif Communautaire: Justification du Quadripartisme Institué par les Traités de Paris et de Rome", *Cahiers de Droit Européen*, 4 (1978) 387

Pescatore Pierre, "Opinion 1/94 on "Conclusion" of the WTO Agreement: Is there an Escape from a Programmed Disaster", *Common Market Law Review*, 36 (1999) 387

Petersmann Ernst-Ulrich, "Participation of the European Communities in the GATT: International Law and Community Law aspects", in O'Keeffe and Schermers (eds.), *Mixed Agreements*, 167

Petersmann Ernst-Ulrich, "The EEC as a GATT Member – Legal Conflicts between GATT Law and European Community Law", in Hilf, Jacobs and Petersmann, *The European Community and GATT*, 23

Peterson John and Helene Sjursen (eds.) *A Common Foreign Policy for Europe?* (London, Routledge, 1998)

Peterson John and Michael Shackleton (eds.), *The Institutions of the European Union* (Oxford, Oxford University Press, 2001)

Peterson John and Michael Shackleton, "The EU's Institutions: An Overview", in Peterson and Shackleton (eds.), *The Institutions of the European Union*, 6

Peterson John, "Subsidiarity: A Definition to Suit Any Vision?", *Parliamentary Affairs*, 47 (1994) 116

Peterson John, "The College of Commissioners", in Peterson and Shackleton (eds.), *The Institutions of the European Union*, 71

Peterson John, "The Santer Era: The European Commission in Normative, Historical and Theoretical Perspective", *Journal of European Public Policy*, 6 (1999) 46

Peterson John, "Decision-Making in the European Union: Towards a Framework of Analysis", *Journal of European Public Policy*, 2 (1995) 69

Petite Michel, "Avis de Temps Calme sur l'Art. 189 A Paragraphe 1: Point d'Equilibre entre le Droit d'Initiative de la Commission et le Pouvoir Décisionnel du Conseil", *Revue du Droit de l'Union Européenne* (1998/3), 197

Petite Michel, "Le Traité d'Amsterdam: Ambition et Réalisme", *Revue du Marché Unique Européen* (1997) 17

Petite Michel, "Nice, Traité Existentiel, Non Essentiel", *Revue du Droit de l'Union Européenne* (2000/4) 887

Philippart Eric and Geoffrey Edwards, "The Provisions on Closer Co-operation in the Treaty of Amsterdam", *Journal of Common Market Studies*, 37 (1999) 87

Philippart Eric and Pascaline Winand (eds.), *Ever Closer Partnership. Policy-Making in US-EU Relations* (Brussels, P.I.E.-Peter Lang, 2001)

Piening Christopher, *Global Europe. The European Union in World Affairs* (Boulder, Lynne Rienner, 1997)

Pierson Paul, "The Path to European Integration: a Historical Institutionalist Analysis", *Comparative Political Studies*, 29 (1996) 123

Pijpers Alfred, Elfriede Regelsberger and Wolfgang Wessels (eds.), *European Political Cooperation in the 1980s. A Common Foreign Policy for Western Europe?* (Dordrecht, Nijhoff, 1988)

Piris Jean-Claude, "Does the European Union Have a Constitution? Does it Need One?", *European Law Review*, 24 (1999) 557

Poidevin Raymond (ed.), *Histoire des Débuts de la Construction Européenne (mars 1948-mai 1950)* (Brussels, Bruylant, 1986)

Poidevin Raymond, *Robert Schuman, Homme d'Etat, 1886-1963* (Paris, Imprimerie Nationale, 1986)

Pollack Mark A. and Gregory C. Shaffer (eds.), *Transatlantic Governance in the Global Economy* (Lanham, Rowman & Littlefield, 2001)

Pollack Mark A., "Creeping Competence: The Expanding Agenda of the European Community", *Journal of Public Policy*, 14 (1994) 95

Pollack Mark A., "Neoliberalism and Regulated Capitalism in the Treaty of Amsterdam", *University of Wisconsin Working Paper on European Studies* No. 2 (1998) 5

Pollack Mark, "The End of Creeping Competence? EU Policy-Making since Maastricht", *Journal of Common Market Studies*, 38 (2000) 519

Ponzano Paolo, "Le Processus de Décision dans l'Union Européenne", *Revue du Droit de l'Union Européenne* (2002/1) 35

Pratt Timothy, "The Role of National Parliaments in the Making of European Law", *Cambridge Yearbook of European Legal Studies,* 1 (1999) 217

Prechal Sacha, *Directives in European Community Law. A Study of Directives and their Enforcement in National Courts* (Oxford, Clarendon Press, 1995)

Prechal Sacha, "Does Direct Effect Still Matter?", *Common Market Law Review*, 37 (2000) 1047

Preeg Ernest H., *Traders in a Brave New World: The Uruguay Round and the Future of the International Trading System* (Chicago, Chicago University Press, 1995)

Raunio Tapio, "Political Interests: The EP's Party Groups", in Peterson and Shackleton (eds.), *The Institutions of the European Union*, 258

Regan Eugene (ed.), *The New Third Pillar. Cooperation against Crime in the European Union* (Dublin, Institute of European Affairs, 2000)

Regelsberger Elfriede, Philippe de Schoutheete and Wolfgang Wessels (eds.), *Foreign Policy of the European Union: Form EPC to CFSP and Beyond* (Boulder, Lynne Rienner, 1997)

Reichenbach Horst, Thea Emmerling, Dirk Staudenmayer and Sönke Schmidt, *Integration: Wanderung über Europäische Gipfel* (Baden-Baden, Nomos, 1999)

Renaudière Philippe, "Phénomènes et Instruments "Consensuels" ou Non-Contraignants en Droit Communautaire de l'Environnement", *Aménagement-Environnement* (Special Issue, 1997) 3

Reuter Paul, *La Communauté du Charbon et de l'Acier* (Paris, LGDJ, 1953)

Rhodes Carolyn (ed.), *The European Union in the World Community* (Boulder, Lynne Rienner, 1998)

Rhodes Carolyn and Sonia Mazey (eds.), *The State of the European Union. Vol. 3: Building a European Polity?* (Boulder, Lynne Rienner, 1995)

Riechenberg Kurt, "Local Administration and the Binding Nature of Community Directives: A Lesser Known Side of European Legal Integration", *Fordham International Law Journal*, 22 (1999) 696

Rivas José and Margot Horspool (eds.), *Modernisation and Decentralisation of EC Competition Law* (The Hague, Kluwer Law International, 2000)

Robertson A. H., *The Council of Europe* (London, Stevens, 1956)

Rodriguez Iglesias Gil Carlos, "The Protection of Fundamental Rights in the Case Law of the Court of Justice of the European Communities", *Columbia Journal of European Law*, 1 (1994-5) 169

Rosas Allan, "Mixed Union – Mixed Agreements", in Koskenniemi (ed.), *International Law Aspects of the European Union*, 125

Rudolf Beate, "Commission of the European Communities v. Council of the European Union. Case C-25/94", *American Journal of International Law*, 91 (1997) 349

Rutten Maartje (ed.), *From St. Malo to Nice. European Defence: Core Documents* (Paris, Institute of Security Studies of WEU, Chaillot Paper 47, 2001)

Sandholz Wayne and Alec Stone Sweet (eds.), *European Integration and Supranational Governance* (Oxford, Oxford University Press, 1998)

Sandholtz Wayne and John Zysman, "1992: Recasting the European Bargain", *World Politics*, 42 (1989) 95

Sauter Wolf, "The Economic Constitution of the European Union", *Columbia Journal of European Law*, 4 (1998) 27

Sbragia Alberta (ed.), *Euro-Politics: Institutions and Policymaking in the 'New' European Community* (Washington, D.C., Brookings Institution, 1992)

Sbragia Alberta, "The European Community: A Balancing Act", *Publius*, 23 (1993) 23

Scharpf Fritz, *Governing Europe: Effective and Democratic?* (Oxford, Oxford University Press, 1999)

Schermers Henry G. and Denis F. Waelbroeck, *Judicial Protection in the European Union* (The Hague, Kluwer Law International, 2001)

Schermers Henry G., Christiaan W. A. Timmermans, Alfred E. Kellermann and J. Steward Watson (eds.), *Article 177 EEC: Experiences and Problems* (Amsterdam, North-Holland, 1987)

Schwabe Klaus (ed.), *The Beginnings of the Schuman Plan 1950/51* (Brussels, Bruylant, 1988)

Schwarze Jürgen (ed.), *National Constitutional Law vis-à-vis European Integration. FIDE Kongress, Vol. I*, (Baden-Baden, Nomos, 1996)

Schwarze Jürgen and Henry G. Schermers (eds.), *Structure and Dimensions of European Community Policy* (Baden-Baden, Nomos, 1988)

Schwob Jacques, "L'Amendement de l'Acte Constitutif de la FAO visant à Permettre l'Admission en Qualité de Membres d'Organisations d'Intégration Economique Régionale et la Communauté Economique Européenne", *Revue Trimestrielle de Droit Européen*, 29 (1993) 1

Sciarra Silvana, "The Employment Title in the Amsterdam Treaty: A Multi-Language Legal Discourse", in O'Keeffe and Twomey (eds.), *Legal Issues of the Amsterdam Treaty*, 157

Serra Enrico (ed.), *The Relaunching of Europe and the Treaties of Rome* (Brussels, Bruylant, 1989)

Shackleton Michael, "The European Parliament's New Committees of Inquiry: Tiger or Paper Tiger?", *Journal of Common Market Studies*, 36 (1998) 115

Shackleton Michael, "The Politics of Codecision", *Journal of Common Market Studies*, 38 (2000) 336

Shaw Jo, "Postnational Constitutionalism in the European Union", *Journal of European Public Policy*, 6 (1999) 579

Shaw Jo, "The Treaty of Amsterdam: Challenges of Flexibility and Legitimacy", *European Law Journal*, 4 (1998) 63

Sherrington Philippa, *The Council of Ministers: Political Authority in the European Union* (London, Pinter, 2000)

Simon Denys, *La Directive Européenne* (Paris, Dalloz, 1997)

Smets Paul-F. (ed.), *La Pensée Européenne et Atlantique de Paul-Henri Spaak* (Brussels, Goemaere, 1980)

Smith Brendan and William Wallace, "Constitutional Deficits of EU Justice and Home Affairs: Transparency, Accountability and Judicial Control", in Monar and Wessels (eds.), *The European Union after the Treaty of Amsterdam*, 125

Smith Brendan P. G., *Constitution Building in the European Union. The Process of Treaty Reform* (The Hague, Kluwer Law International, 2002)

Smith Hazel, *European Union Foreign Policy. What it Is and What it Does* (London, Pluto Press, 2002)

Smith Julie, *Europe's Elected Parliament* (Sheffield, Sheffield Academic Press, 1999)

Smith Karen E. and Margot Light (eds.), *Ethics and Foreign Policy* (Cambridge, Cambridge University Press, 2001)

Smith Karen E., "The EU, Human Rights and Relations with Third Countries: 'Foreign Policy' with an Ethical Dimension?", in Smith and Light (eds.), *Ethics and Foreign Policy*, 185

Smith Karen E., "The End of Civilian Power EU: A Welcome Demise or Cause for Concern?", *International Spectator*, 35 (2000-2) 11

Smith Karen E., *The Making of EU Foreign Policy. The Case of Eastern Europe 1988-95* (Basingstoke, Macmillan, 1998)

Snyder Francis (ed.), *Constitutional Dimensions of European Economic Integration* (The Hague, Kluwer Law International, 1996)

Spence David, "Plus ça Change, Plus c'est la Même Chose? Attempting to Reform the European Commission", *Journal of European Public Policy*, 7 (2000) 1

Spierenburg Dirk and Raymond Poidevin, *The History of the High Authority of the European Coal and Steel Community: Supranationality in Operation* (London, Weidenfeld and Nicholson, 1994)

Stein Eric, "Lawyers, Judges, and the Making of a Transnational Constitution", *American Journal of International Law*, 75 (1981) 1

Stelandre Yves, "Les Pays du Benelux, l'Europe Politique et les Négotiations Fouchet (26 juin 1959-17 avril 1962)", *Journal of European Integration History*, 2 (1997) 21

Stevens Anne and Handley Stevens, *Brussels Bureaucrats? The Administration of the European Union* (Basingstoke, Palgrave, 2001)

Stevens Christopher (ed.), *EEC and the Third World: A Survey 1* (London, Hodder and Stoughton, 1981)

Stirk Peter M. R. and David Weigall (eds.), *The Origins and Development of European Integration: A Reader and Commentary* (London, Pinter, 1999)

Stirk Peter M. R., *A History of European Integration since 1914* (London, Pinter, 1996)

Stone Sweet Alec and James A. Caporaso, "From Free Trade to Supranational Polity: The European Court and Integration", in Sandholz and Stone Sweet (eds.), *European Integration and Supranational Governance*, 92

Stone Sweet Alec and Thomas L. Brunell, "The European Court and the National Courts: a Statistical Analysis of Preliminary References, 1961-95", *Journal of European Public Policy*, 5 (1998) 66

Streit Manfred E. and Werner Mussler, "The Economic Constitution of the European Community – From Rome to Maastricht", in Snyder (ed.), *Constitutional Dimensions of European Economic Integration*, 109

Stubb Alexander C-G., "A Categorization of Differentiated Integration", *Journal of Common Market Studies*, 34 (1996) 283

Stubb Alexander, *Negotiating Flexibility in the European Union. Amsterdam, Nice and Beyond* (Basingstoke, Palgrave, 2002)

Tavares de Pinho Antonio, "L'Admission de la Communauté Economique Européenne comme Membre de l'Organisation des Nations Unies pour l'Alimentation et l'Agriculture (FAO)", *Revue du Marché Commun et de l'Union Européenne*, 370 (1993) 656

Temple Lang John, "Community Constitutional Law: Article 5 EEC Treaty", *Common Market Law Review*, 27 (1990) 645

Temple Lang John, "The Core of Constitutional Law of the Community – Article 5 EC", in Gormley (ed.), *Current and Future Perspectives on EC Competition Law*, 41

Thielemann Eiko R., "Institutional Limits of a Europe with Regions: EC State Aid Control Meets German Federalism", *Journal of European Public Policy*, 6 (1999), 399

Timmermans C. W. A., "The Uneasy Relationship between the Communities and the Second Pillar: Back to the 'Plan Fouchet'?", *Legal Issues of European Integration* (1996) 61

Timmermans Christiaan, "Community Directives Revisited", *Yearbook of European Law*, 17 (1999) 1

Toner Helen, "Judicial Interpretation of European Union Citizenship: Transformation or Consolidation?", *Maastricht Journal of European and Comparative Law*, 7 (2000) 158

Toth A. G., "Is Subsidiarity Justiciable?", *European Law Review*, 19 (1994) 268

Trachtenberg Marc, *A Constructed Peace. The Making of the European Settlement 1945-1963* (Princeton, Princeton University Press, 1999), 242

Trausch Gilbert (ed.), *The European Integration from the Schuman Plan to the Treaties of Rome* (Brussels, Bruylant, 1993)

Treverton Gregory F., "Europe's Past, Europe's Future. Finding an Analogy for Tomorrow", *Orbis*, 10 (1993) 1

Tridimas Takis and Piet Eeckhout, "The External Competence of the Community in the Case-Law of the Court of Justice: Principle versus Pragmatism", *Yearbook of European Law*, 14 (1994) 143

Tridimas Takis, "The Court of Justice and Judicial Activism", *European Law Review*, 21 (1996) 199

Tsebelis George and Xenophon Yataganas, "Veto Players and Decision-Making in the EU After Nice", *Journal of Common Market Studies*, 40 (2002) 283

Urwin Derek W., *The Community of Europe: A History of European Integration since 1945* (London, Longman, 1995)

Usher John A., "The Gradual Widening of European Community Policy on the Basis of Article 100 and 235 of the EEC Treaty", in Schwarze and Schermers (eds.), *Structure and Dimensions of European Community Policy*, 30

Van Eekelen Willem, *Debating European Security 1948-1998* (Brussels, Centre for European Policy Studies, 1998)

Van Gerven Walter, "EC Jurisdiction in Antitrust Matters: The Wood Pulp Judgement", in Hawk (ed.), *Annual Proceedings*, 451

van Gerven Yves and Lorelien Hoet, "Gencor: Some Notes on Transnational Competition Law Issues", *Legal Issues of Economic Integration*, 28 (2001) 195

Vaïse Maurice, *La Grandeur. Politique Etrangère du Général de Gaulle 1958-1969* (Paris, Fayard, 1998)

Van Oudenaren John, *Uniting Europe: European Integration and the Post-Cold War World* (Lanham, Rowman & Littlefield, 2000)

Vandersanden Georges, "Le Tribunal de Première Instance des Communautés Européennes: Dix Ans d'Existence", in Magnette and Remacle (eds.), *Le Nouveau Modèle Européen*, 105

Venturini Patrick, "Social Policy and Employment Aspects of the Treaty of Amsterdam", *Fordham International Law Journal*, 22 (1999) 549

Völker E. L. M. (ed.), *Protectionism and the European Community* (Deventer, Kluwer, 1987)

von der Groeben Hans, *The European Community. The Formative Years. The Struggle to Establish the Common Market and the Political Union 1958-66* (Luxembourg, EC, 1987)

Vos Ellen, "Reforming the European Commission: What Role to Play for EU Agencies?", *Common Market Law Review*, 37 (2000) 1113

Wachtsmann Patrick, "L'Avis 2/94 de la Cour de Justice Relatif à l'Adhésion de la Communauté Européenne à la Convention de Sauvegarde des Droits de l'Homme et des Libertés Fondamentales", *Revue Trimestrielle de Droit Européen*, 32 (1996) 467

Wallace Helen and William Wallace (eds.), *Policy-Making in the European Union* (Oxford, Oxford University Press, 2000, 4th ed.)

Wallace Helen, "The Institutional Setting: Five Variations on a Theme", in Wallace and Wallace (eds.), *Policy-Making in the European Union* (2000, 4th ed.), 33

Wallace William (ed.), *The Dynamics of European Integration* (London, Pinter, 1990)

Wallace William, "European Defence Co-operation: The Reopening Debate", *Survival*, 26 (1984) 251

Warleigh Alex, *Flexible Integration: What Model for the European Union?* (London, Continuum, 2002)

Webber Douglas (ed.), "New Europe, New Germany, Old Foreign Policy? German Foreign Policy Since Unification", *German Politics* (Special Issue), 10 (2001) 1

Weiler J. H. H. (ed.), *The EU, the WTO, and the NAFTA. Towards a Common Law of International Trade?* (Oxford, Oxford University Press, 2000)

Weiler J. H. H. and Nicolas J. S. Lockhart, "'Taking Rights Seriously' Seriously: The European Court of Justice and its Fundamental Rights Jurisprudence", *Common Market Law Review*, 32 (1995) 51 and 579

Weiler J. H. H., "Journey to an Unknown Destination: A Retrospective and Prospective of the European Court of Justice in the Area of Political Integration", *Journal of Common Market Studies*, 31 (1993) 418

Weiler J. H. H., *The Constitution of Europe. 'Do the New Clothes have an Emperor?'* (Cambridge, Cambridge University Press, 1999)

Weiler J. H. H., "The Transformation of Europe", *Yale Law Journal*, 100 (1991) 2403

Weiler Joseph H. H., "Neither Unity nor Three Pillars – The Trinity Structure of the Treaty on European Union", in Monar, Ungerer and Wessels (eds.), *The Maastricht Treaty on European Union*, 49

Werts Jan, *The European Council* (Amsterdam, North-Holland, 1992)

Wessel Ramses A., *The European Union's Foreign and Security Policy. A Legal Institutional Perspective* (The Hague, Kluwer Law International, 1999)

Wessels Bernhard and Richard S. Katz (eds.), *The European Parliament, National Parliaments and European Integration* (Oxford, Oxford University Press, 1999)

Wessels Wolfgang, "Nice Results: The Millennium IGC in the EU's Evolution", *Journal of Common Market Studies*, 39 (2001) 197

Westlake Martin, *The Council of the European Union* (London, Cartermill, 1999)

Westlake Martin, "The European Parliament's Powers of Appointment", *Journal of Common Market Studies*, 36 (1998) 431

Whish Richard, *Competition Law* (London, Butterworths, 2001)

Wilks Stephen and Lee McGowan, "Disarming the Commission: The Debate over a European Cartel Office", *Journal of Common Market Studies*, 33 (1995) 259

Wils Geert, "The Concept of Reciprocity in EEC Law: An Exploration into these Realms", *Common Market Law Review*, 28 (1991) 245

Wils Wouter P. J., "The Modernisation of the Enforcement of Articles 81 and 82 EC: a Legal and Economic Analysis of the Community's Proposal for a new Council Regulation replacing Regulation No. 17", in Hawk (ed.), *2000 Annual Proceedings*, 313

Winand Pascaline, *Eisenhower, Kennedy and the United States of Europe* (New York, St. Martin's Press, 1993)

Winand Pascaline, "Le Comité d'Action pour les Etats-Unis d'Europe de Jean Monnet", in *20 Ans d'Action du Comité Jean Monnet (1955-1975)* (Paris, Notre Europe, Problématiques Européennes No. 8, May 2001)

Woolcock Stephen and Michael Hodges, "EU Policy in the Uruguay Round", in Wallace and Wallace (eds.), *Policy-Making in the European Union* (1996, 3rd ed.), 317

Woolcock Stephen, "European Trade Policy", in Wallace and Wallace (eds.), *Policy-Making in the European Union* (2000, 4th ed.), 373

Wooley John T., "Linking Political and Monetary Union: The Maastricht Agenda and German Domestic Politics", in Eichengreen and Frieden (eds.), *The Political Economy of European Monetary Unification*, 67

Zelikow Philip and Condoleeza Rice, *Germany Unified and Europe Transformed. A Study in Statecraft* (Cambridge, Mass.: Harvard University Press, 1995)

Zielonka Jan, "Enlargement and the Finality of European Integration", in Joerges, Mény and Weiler (eds.), *What Kind of Constitution for What Kind of Polity?*, 152

Zilioli Chiara and Martin Selmayr, "The External Relations of the Euro Area: Legal Aspects", *Common Market Law Review*, 36 (1999) 273

Index

The Author

Professor Youri Devuyst teaches Politics and Institutions of the European Union at the Vrije Universiteit Brussel (Free University of Brussels). He has served in the Cabinet of three successive Belgian Ministers of Foreign Affairs as well as in the Cabinet of European Commissioner for competition policy Karel Van Miert.

Professor Devuyst received a doctorate in political science, an LL.M. in international and comparative law and a postgraduate degree in international and European law at the Vrije Universiteit Brussel. He also holds an M.A. in international relations from the Johns Hopkins University's School of Advanced International Studies (Bologna and Washington, D.C.).

His work has appeared in journals such as the *Journal of Common Market Studies, the Journal of European Public Policy,* the *European Foreign Affairs Review,* the *Journal of European Integration, Global Governance,* the *Journal of World Trade, World Competition* and in several edited volumes.

The views expressed in this book are purely those of the writer and may not in any circumstances be regarded as stating an official position of the institutions for which the author is or has been working.

"European Policy"

"European Policy" is an interdisciplinary series devoted to the study of European integration in a broad sense. Although mostly focusing on the European Union, it also encourages the publication of books addressing the wider, pan-European context, as well as comparative work, including on other forms of regional integration on the world scene. The core disciplines are politics, economics, law, and history. While being committed to high academic standards, "European Policy" seeks to be accessible to a wide readership, including policy-makers and practitioners, and to stimulate a debate on European issues. The collection publishes both in English and in French.

Series Editor: **Pascaline WINAND**,
Professor at the Université libre de Bruxelles and Research Associate at the Fonds National de la Recherche Scientifique (Belgium)

Published Books

No.27: *The European Union at the Crossroads. The EU's Institutional Evolution from the Schuman Plan to the European Convention*, Youri DEVUYST, 2nd edition, 2003, 199 p., ISBN 90-5201-183-4

No.26: *The Atlantic Alliance for the 21ˢᵗ Century*, Alfred CAHEN, Atlantic Treaty Association, 2001, 139 p., ISBN 90-5201-946-0

N° 25: *L'Alliance Atlantique pour le XXIᵉ siècle*, Alfred CAHEN, Association du Traité Atlantique, 2001, 139 p., ISBN 90-5201-945-2

No.24: *Ever Closer Partnership. Policy-Making in US-EU Relations*, Eric PHILIPPART & Pascaline WINAND (eds.), 2001, 477 p., ISBN 90-5201-938-X

N°23: *Le pouvoir renforcé du Parlement européen après Amsterdam*, Andreas MAURER, Groupe d'Études Politiques Européennes, 2000, 126 p., ISBN 90-5201-928-2

N°22: *L'Europe et ses citoyens*, Louis le HARDŸ de BEAULIEU (ed.), Groupe d'Études Politiques Européennes, 2000, 238 p., ISBN 90-5201-929-0

N°21: *The Euro and European Integration / L'Euro et l'intégration européenne*, EURO INSTITUTE / INSTITUT DE L'EURO, Jean-Victor LOUIS & Hajo BRONKHORST (eds.), 1999, 366 p., ISBN 90-5201-912-6

N°20: *L'idée fédéraliste dans les États-nations. Regards croisés entre la Wallonie et le monde*, Philippe DESTATTE (dir.), Institut Jules Destrée, 1999, 464 p., ISBN 90-5201-902-9

N°19: *L'identité européenne de sécurité et de défense. Des coopérations militaires croisées au Livre blanc européen*, André DUMOULIN, 1999, 294 p., ISBN 90-5201-901-0

N°18: *Union européenne: quels défis pour l'an 2000 ? Emploi, union monétaire, élargissement*, Franklin DEHOUSSE, Jacques VANHAMME & Louis le HARDŸ de BEAULIEU (dir.), Groupe d'Études Politiques Européennes, 1998, 250 p., ISBN 90-5201-810-3

N°17: *L'Union européenne au-delà d'Amsterdam. Nouveaux concepts d'intégration européenne*, Martin WESTLAKE (dir.), Préface de J. Delors, 1998, 250 p., ISBN 90-5201-809-X

N°16: *Lobbyisme, pluralisme et intégration européenne – Lobbying, Pluralism and European Integration*, Paul-H. CLAEYS, Corinne GOBIN, Isabelle SMETS & Pascaline WINAND (eds.), Groupe d'étude du Lobbyisme Européen, 1998, 456 p., ISBN 90-5201-803-0

N° 15: *La dimension sociale de l'Union européenne. L'impact de l'élargissement et de l'approfondissement*, Johannes PAKASLAHTI, 1999, 132 p., ISBN 90-5201-701-8

N° 14: *Europe and Nuclear Disarmament. Debates and Political Attitudes in 16 European Countries*, Harald MÜLLER (ed.), Peace Research Institute Frankfurt, 1998, 311 p., ISBN 90-5201-702-6

N° 13: *Quadrillage du futur – 2005, des réponses*, SCEPS-EPM, 1997, 117 p., ISBN 90-5201-707-7

N° 12: *Regionalism and Multilateralism after the Uruguay Round. Convergence, Divergence and Interaction*, Paul DEMARET, Jean-François BELLIS & Gonzalo GARCIA JIMENEZ (eds.), Institut d'Études Juridiques Européennes, 1997, 862 p., ISBN 90-5201-706-9

N° 11: *From Europe Agreements to Accession. The Integration of the Central and Eastern European Countries into the European Union*, Paul VAN DEN BEMPT & Greet THEELEN, Trans European Policy Studies Association, 1996, 168 p., ISBN 90-5201-614-3

N° 10: *European Non-Proliferation Policy 1993-1995*, Harald MÜLLER (ed.), Peace Research Institute Frankfurt, 1996, 315 p., ISBN 90-5201-513-5

N° 9: *L'Union européenne et l'avenir de ses institutions*, Jean-Victor LOUIS, Groupe d'Études Politiques Européennes, 1996, 192 p., ISBN 90-5201-612-7